POCKET WORLD IN FIGURES
2005 EDITION

Pocket Asia
Pocket Europe in Figures

Guide to Analysing Companies
Guide to Business Modelling
Guide to Business Planning
Guide to Economic Indicators
Guide to European Union
Guide to Financial Markets
Guide to Management Ideas
Numbers Guide
Style Guide

Dictionary of Business
Dictionary of Economics
International Dictionary of Finance

Business Ethics
Business Strategy
China's Stockmarket
Dealing with Financial Risk
Emerging Markets
Globalisation
Successful Innovation
Successful Mergers
The City
Wall Street

Essential Director
Essential Economics
Essential Finance
Essential Internet
Essential Investment
Essential Negotiation

Pocket
World in
Figures

2005 Edition

THE ECONOMIST IN ASSOCIATION WITH
PROFILE BOOKS LTD

Published by Profile Books Ltd,
58A Hatton Garden, London EC1N 8LX

This special paperback edition produced in association with and
exclusively for The Economist

Material researched and compiled by
Andrea Burgess, Marianne Comparet, Ulrika Davies, Mark Doyle,
Andrew Gilbert, Conrad Heine, Carol Howard, Stella Jones,
David McKelvey, Keith Potter, Simon Wright

Typeset in Officina by MacGuru Ltd
info@macguru.org.uk

Printed in the United States

A CIP catalogue record for this book is available
from the British Library

ISBN 1 86197 799 9

Contents

CONTENTS

CONTENTS

107 Part II   Country Profiles

Notes

This 2005 edition of *The Economist Pocket World in Figures*
includes new rankings on young and old populations,
contraceptives, office rents, teenagers' behaviour and several
environmental measures and killer diseases. The country
profiles cover 67 major countries. The world rankings consider
182; all those with a population of at least 1m or a GDP of at
least $1bn; they are listed on page 248. Also included are a
profile of the euro area and the world. The extent and quality
of the statistics available varies from country to country. Every
care has been taken to specify the broad definitions on which
the data are based and to indicate cases where data quality or
technical difficulties are such that interpretation of the
figures is likely to be seriously affected. Nevertheless, figures
from individual countries may differ from standard
international statistical definitions. The term "country" can
also refer to territories or economic entities.

Some country definitions

Macedonia is officially known as the Former Yugoslav Republic
of Macedonia. Data for Cyprus normally refer to Greek Cyprus
only. Data for China do not include Hong Kong or Macau. For
countries such as Morocco they exclude disputed areas. Congo
refers to the Democratic Republic of Congo, formerly known as
Zaire. Congo-Brazzaville refers to the other Congo. Data for
the EU refer to the 15 members as at January 1 2004: Austria,
Belgium, Denmark, Finland, France, Germany, Greece,
Ireland, Italy, Luxembourg, Netherlands, Portugal, Spain,
Sweden and the United Kingdom. The euro area includes all of
the 15 except Denmark, Sweden and the United Kingdom.

Statistical basis

The all-important factor in a book of this kind is to be able to
make reliable comparisons between countries. Although this
is never quite possible for the reasons stated above, the best
route, which this book takes, is to compare data for the same
year or period and to use actual, not estimated, figures
wherever possible. Where a country's data is excessively out of
date, it is excluded, which is the reason there is no country
profile of Iraq in this edition. The research for this edition of
The Economist Pocket World in Figures was carried out in 2004
using the latest available sources that present data on an
internationally comparable basis. Data, therefore, unless

otherwise indicated, refer to the year ending December 31 2002.

In the country profiles, life expectancy, crude birth, death and fertility rates are based on 2000–05 averages; human development indices and energy data are for 2001; marriage and divorce data refer to the latest year with available figures. Employment, health and education data are for the latest year between 1998 and 2002.

Other definitions

Data shown on country profiles may not always be consistent with those shown on the world rankings because the definitions or years covered can differ. Data may also differ between two different rankings.

Most countries' national accounts are now compiled on a GDP basis so, for simplicity, the term GDP has been used interchangeably with GNP or GNI.

Statistics for principal exports and principal imports are normally based on customs statistics. These are generally compiled on different definitions to the visible exports and imports figures shown in the balance of payments section.

Definitions of the statistics shown are given on the relevant page or in the glossary on page 246. Figures may not add exactly to totals, or percentages to 100, because of rounding or, in the case of GDP, statistical adjustment. Sums of money have generally been converted to US dollars at the official exchange rate ruling at the time to which the figures refer.

Energy consumption data are not always reliable, particularly for the major oil producing countries; consumption per head data may therefore be higher than in reality. Energy exports can exceed production and imports can exceed consumption if transit operations distort trade data or oil is imported for refining and re-exported.

Abbreviations

bn	billion (one thousand million)	GNP	Gross national product
CIS	Commonwealth of Independent States	GRT	Gross tonnage
		ha	Hectare
EU	European Union	m	million
kg	kilogram	PPP	Purchasing power parity
km	kilometre	trn	trillion (one thousand billion)
GDP	Gross domestic product	...	not available
GNI	Gross national income		

World
rankings

Countries: *natural facts*

Countries: *the largest[a]*

'000 sq km

1	Russia	17,075	31	Tanzania	945
2	Canada	9,971	32	Nigeria	924
3	China	9,561	33	Venezuela	912
4	United States	9,373	34	Namibia	824
5	Brazil	8,512	35	Pakistan	804
6	Australia	7,682	36	Mozambique	799
7	India	3,287	37	Turkey	779
8	Argentina	2,767	38	Chile	757
9	Kazakhstan	2,717	39	Zambia	753
10	Sudan	2,506	40	Myanmar	677
11	Algeria	2,382	41	Afghanistan	652
12	Congo	2,345	42	Somalia	638
13	Saudi Arabia	2,200	43	Central African Rep	622
14	Greenland	2,176	44	Ukraine	604
15	Mexico	1,973	45	Madagascar	587
16	Indonesia[b]	1,904	46	Kenya	583
17	Libya	1,760	47	Botswana	581
18	Iran	1,648	48	France	544
19	Mongolia	1,565	49	Yemen	528
20	Peru	1,285	50	Thailand	513
21	Chad	1,284	51	Spain	505
22	Niger	1,267	52	Turkmenistan	488
23	Angola	1,247	53	Cameroon	475
24	Mali	1,240	54	Papua New Guinea	463
25	South Africa	1,226	55	Sweden	450
26	Colombia	1,142	56	Morocco	447
27	Ethiopia	1,134		Uzbekistan	447
28	Bolivia	1,099	58	Iraq	438
29	Mauritania	1,031	59	Paraguay	407
30	Egypt	1,000	60	Zimbabwe	391

Mountains: *the highest[c]*

	Name	Location	Height (m)
1	Everest	Nepal-China	8,848
2	K2 (Godwin Austen)	Pakistan	8,611
3	Kangchenjunga	Nepal-Sikkim	8,586
4	Lhotse	Nepal-China	8,516
5	Makalu	Nepal-China	8,463
6	Cho Oyu	Nepal-China	8,201
7	Dhaulagiri	Nepal	8,167
8	Manaslu	Nepal	8,163
9	Nanga Parbat	Pakistan	8,125
10	Annapurna I	Nepal	8,091
11	Gasherbrum I	Pakistan-China	8,068
12	Broad Peak	Pakistan-China	8,047
13	Xixabangma (Gosainthan)	China	8,046
14	Gasherbrum II	Pakistan-China	8,035

a Includes freshwater.
b Excludes East Timor, 14,874 sq km.
c Includes separate peaks which are part of the same massif.

Rivers: *the longest*

	Name	Location	Length (km)
1	Nile	Africa	6,695
2	Amazon	South America	6,516
3	Yangtze	Asia	6,380
4	Mississippi-Missouri	North America	6,019
5	Ob'-Irtysh	Asia	5,570
6	Yenisey-Angara	Asia	5,550
7	Hwang He (Yellow)	Asia	5,464
8	Congo	Africa	4,667
9	Parana	South America	4,500
10	Mekong	Asia	4,425
11	Amur	Asia	4,416
12	Lena	Asia	4,400
13	Mackenzie	North America	4,250
14	Niger	Africa	4,030
15	Missouri	North America	3,969
16	Mississippi	North America	3,779
17	Murray-Darling	Australia	3,750

Deserts: *the largest*

	Name	Location	Area ('000 sq km)
1	Sahara	Northern Africa	8,600
2	Arabia	SW Asia	2,300
3	Gobi	Mongolia/China	1,166
4	Patagonian	Argentina	673
5	Great Victoria	W and S Australia	647
6	Great Basin	SW United States	492
7	Chihuahuan	N Mexico	450
8	Great Sandy	W Australia	400
9	Sonoran	Mexico/US	310
10	Kyzylkum	Central Asia	300

Lakes: *the largest*

	Name	Location	Area ('000 sq km)
1	Caspian Sea	Central Asia	371
2	Superior	Canada/US	82
3	Victoria	E Africa	69
4	Huron	Canada/US	60
5	Michigan	US	58
6	Aral Sea	Central Asia	34
7	Tanganyika	E Africa	33
8	Great Bear	Canada	31
9	Baikal	Russia	30
	Malawi	SE Africa	30

Notes: Estimates of the lengths of different rivers vary widely according to the rules adopted concerning the selection of tributaries to be followed, the path to take through a delta, where different hydrological systems begin and end etc. The Nile is normally taken as the world's longest river but some estimates put the Amazon as longer if a southerly path through its delta leading to the River Para is followed. The level of aridity commonly used to delimit desert areas is a mean annual precipitation value equal to 250ml or less.

Population: *size and growth*

Largest populations, 2002
Millions

1	China	1,294.4	31	Argentina	37.9
2	India	1,041.1	32	Tanzania	36.8
3	United States	288.5	33	Sudan	32.6
4	Indonesia	217.5	34	Kenya	31.9
5	Brazil	174.7	35	Algeria	31.4
6	Pakistan	148.7	36	Canada	31.3
7	Russia	143.8	37	Morocco	31.0
8	Bangladesh	143.4	38	Peru	26.5
9	Japan	127.5	39	Uzbekistan	25.6
10	Nigeria	120.0	40	Venezuela	25.1
11	Mexico	101.8	41	Uganda	24.8
12	Germany	82.0	42	Iraq	24.2
13	Vietnam	80.2		Nepal	24.2
14	Philippines	78.6	44	Afghanistan	23.3
15	Iran	72.4	45	Malaysia	23.0
16	Egypt	70.3	46	North Korea	22.6
17	Turkey	68.6	47	Taiwan	22.5
18	Ethiopia	66.0	48	Romania	22.3
19	Thailand	64.3	49	Saudi Arabia	21.7
20	France	59.7	50	Ghana	20.2
	United Kingdom	59.7	51	Yemen	19.9
22	Italy	57.4	52	Australia	19.5
23	Congo	54.3	53	Sri Lanka	19.3
24	Myanmar	49.0	54	Mozambique	19.0
25	Ukraine	48.7	55	Syria	17.0
26	South Korea	47.4	56	Madagascar	16.9
27	South Africa	44.2	57	Côte d'Ivoire	16.7
28	Colombia	43.5	58	Kazakhstan	16.0
29	Spain	39.9		Netherlands	16.0
30	Poland	38.5	60	Chile	15.6

Largest populations, 2025
Millions

1	China	1,445.1	18	Turkey	89.0
2	India	1,369.3	19	Germany	82.0
3	United States	358.0	20	Thailand	73.9
4	Indonesia	270.1	21	France	64.2
5	Pakistan	249.8	22	United Kingdom	63.3
6	Brazil	216.4	23	Myanmar	59.8
7	Bangladesh	208.3	24	Colombia	58.2
8	Nigeria	192.1	25	Uganda	54.9
9	Mexico	129.9	26	Tanzania	53.4
10	Russia	124.4	27	Italy	52.9
11	Japan	123.4	28	South Korea	50.2
12	Ethiopia	116.0	29	Sudan	47.5
13	Philippines	108.6	30	Argentina	47.0
14	Vietnam	104.6	31	Afghanistan	44.9
15	Egypt	103.2	32	Yemen	43.2
16	Congo	95.4	33	South Africa	43.0
17	Iran	90.9	34	Algeria	42.4

Fastest growing populations, 2020–25
Average annual growth, %

1	Niger	3.37	11	Liberia	2.50
2	Yemen	3.35	12	Congo-Brazzaville	2.49
3	Uganda	3.26	13	Congo	2.46
4	Somalia	3.14	14	Afghanistan	2.30
5	Mali	2.97	15	Madagascar	2.22
6	Burkina Faso	2.73	16	Burundi	2.15
	Guinea-Bissau	2.73	17	Mauritania	2.12
8	Angola	2.65	18	Ethiopia	2.03
9	West Bank and Gaza	2.59	19	Cayman Islands	1.96
10	Chad	2.54		Eritrea	1.96

Fastest growing populations, 1980–85
Average annual growth, %

1	Qatar	9.06	11	Iran	4.16
2	United Arab Emirates	8.49	12	Cambodia	4.10
3	Equatorial Guinea	7.15	13	Jordan	3.92
4	Saudi Arabia	5.92	14	Macau	3.89
5	Andorra	5.36	15	Zimbabwe	3.88
6	Oman	5.04	16	West Bank and Gaza	3.78
7	Kuwait	4.48	17	Kenya	3.77
8	Libya	4.37		Yemen	3.77
9	Côte d'Ivoire	4.32	19	Syria	3.68
10	Cayman Islands	4.18	20	Ghana	3.59

Slowest growing populations, 2020–25
Average annual growth, %

1	Estonia	-1.37	12	Italy	-0.49
2	Latvia	-1.10	13	Romania	-0.43
3	Ukraine	-0.88	14	Armenia	-0.42
4	Bulgaria	-0.81	15	Slovenia	-0.41
5	Russia	-0.73	16	Swaziland	-0.38
6	Georgia	-0.69	17	Japan	-0.35
7	Lesotho	-0.67	18	Bosnia	-0.33
8	Lithuania	-0.62		Moldova	-0.33
9	Botswana	-0.61		South Africa	-0.33
10	Belarus	-0.57		Switzerland	-0.33
11	Hungary	-0.51			

Slowest growing populations, 1980–85
Average annual growth, %

1	Afghanistan	-2.22	11	Luxembourg	0.15
2	Hungary	-0.24	12	United Kingdom	0.17
3	Germany	-0.16	13	Bulgaria	0.22
4	Denmark	-0.04	14	Barbados	0.30
5	Lebanon	-0.01	15	Norway	0.33
6	Belgium	0.00	16	Ukraine	0.36
7	Czech Republic	0.04	17	Macedonia	0.37
8	Italy	0.06	18	Croatia	0.43
9	Austria	0.08	19	Somalia	0.44
10	Sweden	0.10	20	Romania	0.47

Population: *matters of breeding*

Highest crude birth rates

Average no. of live births per 1,000 population, 2000–05

1	Niger	55.2	21	Zambia	42.2
2	Angola	52.3	22	Mauritania	41.8
3	Somalia	52.1	23	Madagascar	41.6
4	Uganda	50.7	24	Benin	41.5
5	Congo	50.2	25	Mozambique	41.2
6	Liberia	50.0	26	Eritrea	39.7
7	Guinea-Bissau	49.9	27	Tanzania	39.3
	Mali	49.9	28	Nigeria	39.1
9	Sierra Leone	49.6	29	West Bank and Gaza	38.8
10	Chad	48.4	30	Togo	38.5
11	Burkina Faso	47.8	31	Central African Rep	37.7
12	Afghanistan	47.4	32	Senegal	37.1
13	Yemen	45.0	33	Pakistan	35.9
14	Malawi	44.6	34	Gambia, The	35.8
15	Burundi	44.2	35	Laos	35.6
16	Congo-Brazzaville	44.2	36	Côte d'Ivoire	35.5
17	Rwanda	44.0	37	Cameroon	35.4
18	Equatorial Guinea	43.1	38	Iraq	35.1
19	Guinea	42.9	39	Bhutan	34.5
20	Ethiopia	42.5		Swaziland	34.5

Lowest crude birth rates

Average no. of live births per 1,000 population, 2000–05

1	Latvia	7.8		Sweden	10.3
2	Bulgaria	7.9	27	Georgia	10.4
3	Slovenia	8.3		Romania	10.4
4	Ukraine	8.4	29	Belgium	10.8
5	Hong Kong	8.5		Finland	10.8
6	Austria	8.6	31	Channel Islands	10.9
	Russia	8.6	32	Portugal	11.0
8	Estonia	8.7		United Kingdom	11.0
	Germany	8.7		Andorra	11.0
	Switzerland	8.7	35	Croatia	11.1
11	Belarus	8.8	36	Moldova	11.4
	Czech Republic	8.8	37	Cuba	11.6
	Hungary	8.8	38	Serbia & Montenegro	11.7
	Italy	8.8	39	Denmark	11.8
	Lithuania	8.8		Malta	11.8
16	Greece	9.1	41	South Korea	11.9
17	Japan	9.2	42	Norway	12.0
18	Spain	9.3	43	Netherlands	12.1
19	Poland	9.6	44	Barbados	12.2
20	Armenia	9.7	45	Australia	12.3
	Bosnia	9.7	46	Luxembourg	12.6
	Macau	9.7	47	France	12.8
23	Singapore	10.2	48	Aruba	13.0
	Slovakia	10.2		Bermuda	13.0
25	Canada	10.3		Taiwan	13.0

Highest fertility rates
Average no. of children per woman, 2000–05

1	Niger	8.00	24	Zambia	5.64
2	Somalia	7.25	25	Mozambique	5.63
3	Angola	7.20	26	West Bank and Gaza	5.57
4	Guinea-Bissau	7.10	27	Eritrea	5.43
	Uganda	7.10	28	Nigeria	5.42
6	Yemen	7.01	29	Togo	5.33
7	Mali	7.00	30	Tanzania	5.11
8	Afghanistan	6.80	31	Pakistan	5.08
	Burundi	6.80	32	Bhutan	5.02
	Liberia	6.80	33	Senegal	4.97
11	Congo	6.70	34	Oman	4.96
12	Burkina Faso	6.68	35	Central African Rep	4.92
13	Chad	6.65	36	Laos	4.78
14	Sierra Leone	6.50	37	Cambodia	4.77
15	Congo-Brazzaville	6.29		Iraq	4.77
16	Ethiopia	6.14	39	Côte d'Ivoire	4.73
17	Malawi	6.10	40	Gambia, The	4.70
18	Equatorial Guinea	5.89	41	Cameroon	4.61
19	Guinea	5.82	42	Namibia	4.56
20	Mauritania	5.79	43	Swaziland	4.54
21	Rwanda	5.74	44	Saudi Arabia	4.53
22	Madagascar	5.70	45	Guatemala	4.41
23	Benin	5.66	46	Sudan	4.39

Lowest fertility rates
Average no. of childre per woman, 2000–05

1	Hong Kong	1.00	25	Singapore	1.36
2	Bulgaria	1.10	26	Georgia	1.40
	Latvia	1.10		Moldova	1.40
	Macau	1.10	28	South Korea	1.41
5	Russia	1.14		Switzerland	1.41
	Slovenia	1.14	30	Portugal	1.45
7	Armenia	1.15	31	Canada	1.48
	Spain	1.15	32	Barbados	1.50
	Ukraine	1.15	33	Channel Islands	1.54
10	Czech Republic	1.16	34	Cuba	1.55
11	Belarus	1.20		Trinidad & Tobago	1.55
	Hungary	1.20	36	United Kingdom	1.60
	Andorra	1.20		Taiwan	1.60
14	Estonia	1.22	38	Sweden	1.64
15	Italy	1.23	39	Croatia	1.65
16	Lithuania	1.25		Serbia & Montenegro	1.65
17	Poland	1.26	41	Belgium	1.66
18	Greece	1.27	42	Australia	1.70
19	Austria	1.28	43	Netherlands	1.72
	Slovakia	1.28	44	Finland	1.73
21	Bosnia	1.30		Luxembourg	1.73
22	Japan	1.32	46	Denmark	1.77
	Romania	1.32		Malta	1.77
24	Germany	1.35			

Population: *age*

Highest median age[a]
Years, 2000

1	Japan	41.3
2	Italy	40.2
	Switzerland	40.2
4	Germany	39.9
5	Sweden	39.6
6	Finland	39.4
7	Belgium	39.1
	Bulgaria	39.1
	Greece	39.1
10	Croatia	38.9
11	Denmark	38.7
12	Channel Islands	38.6
13	Austria	38.3
14	Hungary	38.1
	Slovenia	38.1
16	Estonia	37.9
17	Latvia	37.8
18	United Kingdom	37.7
19	Czech Republic	37.6
	France	37.6
21	Netherlands	37.6
22	Spain	37.4
23	Ukraine	37.3

Lowest median age[a]
Years, 2000

1	Niger	15.1
	Uganda	15.1
3	Mali	15.4
	Yemen	15.4
5	Burkina Faso	15.5
6	Burundi	15.8
7	Somalia	16.0
8	Angola	16.3
9	Congo	16.5
10	Benin	16.6
	Guinea-Bissau	16.6
	Liberia	16.6
13	Chad	16.7
	Congo-Brazzaville	16.7
	Zambia	16.7
16	Tanzania	16.8
	West Bank and Gaza	16.8
18	Eritrea	16.9
	Ethiopia	16.9
20	Rwanda	17.0
21	Malawi	17.1
22	Nigeria	17.3
23	Swaziland	17.4

Highest median age[a]
Years, 2025

1	Italy	50.5
2	Japan	50.2
3	Switzerland	49.3
4	Andorra	49.0
5	Spain	48.4
6	Slovenia	48.2
7	Greece	48.1
8	Austria	47.6
9	Channel Islands	47.2
10	Czech Republic	46.9
	Germany	46.9
12	Singapore	46.8
13	Hong Kong	46.1
14	Bulgaria	46.0
15	Portugal	45.8
16	Hungary	45.6
17	Belgium	44.9
	Bosnia	44.9
19	Latvia	44.7
20	Finland	44.5
	Sweden	44.5

Lowest median age[a]
Years, 2025

1	Niger	16.1
2	Uganda	16.4
3	Angola	16.7
4	Mali	16.8
5	Somalia	16.9
6	Yemen	17.0
7	Burkina Faso	17.2
8	Guinea-Bissau	17.4
	Liberia	17.4
10	Burundi	17.6
	Congo	17.6
12	Chad	17.9
13	Congo-Brazzaville	18.0
14	Malawi	18.2
15	Zambia	18.4
16	Sierra Leone	18.9
17	Ethiopia	19.4
18	Afghanistan	19.6
19	Equatorial Guinea	19.8
20	Rwanda	20.0
21	Zimbabwe	20.1

a Age at which there are an equal number of people above and below.

Age structure

Highest pop. aged 0–14, %, 2000	
1 Uganda	49.9
2 Niger	49.8
3 Mali	49.1
Yemen	49.1
5 Burkina Faso	48.9
6 Burundi	48.0
7 Somalia	47.8
8 Angola	47.3
9 Congo	46.8
10 Guinea-Bissau	46.7
11 Liberia	46.6
12 Chad	46.5
13 Congo-Brazzaville	46.4
14 Zambia	46.3
15 Benin	46.2
16 Ethiopia	45.9
17 Eritrea	45.8
Tanzania	45.8
19 Malawi	45.6
20 Rwanda	45.4
21 Nigeria	45.0

Highest pop. aged 60 and over, %, 2000	
1 Italy	24.1
2 Greece	23.4
3 Japan	23.3
4 Germany	23.2
5 Sweden	22.3
6 Belgium	22.1
7 Bulgaria	21.7
8 Croatia	21.6
9 Switzerland	21.3
10 Estonia	21.2
Latvia	21.2
Spain	21.2
13 Portugal	20.8
14 Austria	20.7
United Kingdom	20.7
16 Ukraine	20.6
17 France	20.5
18 Denmark	20.0
19 Finland	19.9

Youngest populations

Aged 0–4, %, 2000	
1 Niger	21.1
2 Uganda	20.5
3 Somalia	20.1
4 Burkina Faso	19.8
5 Mali	19.7
6 Angola	19.6
7 Guinea-Bissau	19.4
8 Yemen	19.2
9 Malawi	19.1
10 Chad	19.0
11 Liberia	18.9
12 Congo	18.8
13 West Bank and Gaza	18.6
14 Congo-Brazzaville	18.5
15 Ethiopia	18.0
Sierra Leone	18.0
Zambia	18.0
18 Madagascar	17.9
Rwanda	17.9
20 Eritrea	17.8
Guinea	17.8
22 Benin	17.7
Burundi	17.7
24 Afghanistan	17.5
25 Equatorial Guinea	17.4
Tanzania	17.4

Oldest populations

Aged 80 and over, %, 2000	
1 Sweden	5.1
2 Norway	4.5
3 United Kingdom	4.1
4 Denmark	4.0
Switzerland	4.0
6 Italy	3.9
7 Japan	3.8
8 Belgium	3.7
France	3.7
10 Greece	3.6
Spain	3.6
12 Austria	3.5
Channel Islands	3.5
Faroe Islands	3.5
Germany	3.5
16 Finland	3.4
17 Netherlands	3.2
United States	3.2
19 Canada	3.0
Portugal	3.0
21 Andorra	2.9
Australia	2.9
Barbados	2.9
24 Martinique	2.8
New Zealand	2.8
Uruguay	2.8

City living

Biggest cities[a]
Population m, 2001

1	Tokyo, Japan	26.5	27	Bangkok, Thailand	7.5
2	Mexico City, Mexico	18.3	28	Chicago, USA	7.0
	São Paulo, Brazil	18.3		Hong Kong	7.0
4	New York, USA	16.8		Bogota, Colombia	7.0
5	Mumbai, India	16.5		Tehran, Iran	7.0
6	Kolkata, India	13.3	32	Chennai, India	6.5
	Los Angeles, USA	13.3		Essen, Germany	6.5
8	Dhaka, Bangladesh	13.2	34	Bangalore, India	5.8
9	Delhi, India	13.0	35	Hyderabad, India	5.6
10	Shanghai, China	12.8		Lahore, Pakistan	5.6
11	Buenos Aires, Arg.	12.1		Santiago, Chile	5.6
12	Jakarta, Indonesia	11.4	38	Kinshasa, Congo	5.3
13	Osaka, Japan	11.0		Wuhan, China	5.3
14	Beijing, China	10.8	40	Chongqing, China	5.1
	Rio de Janeiro, Brazil	10.8	41	Baghdad, Iraq	5.0
16	Karachi, Pakistan	10.4	42	Riyadh, Saudi Arabia	4.8
17	Manila, Philippines	10.1		Shenyang, China	4.8
18	Seoul, South Korea	9.9		Toronto, Canada	4.8
19	Paris, France	9.7	45	Ho Chi Minh City, Viet.	4.7
20	Cairo, Egypt	9.6	46	Ahmadabad, India	4.6
21	Istanbul, Turkey	9.2		St Petersburg, Russia	4.6
	Tianjin, China	9.2	48	Philadelphia, USA	4.5
23	Lagos, Nigeria	9.1		Yangon, Myanmar	4.5
24	Moscow, Russia	8.3	50	Belo Horizonte, Brazil	4.3
25	Lima, Peru	7.6			
	London, UK	7.6			

Fastest growing cities[b]
Average annual growth, 1975–2000, %

1	Sana'a, Yemen	33.3	19	Faridabad, India	13.5
2	Karaj, Iran	29.1	20	Douala, Cameroon	13.3
3	Ansan, South Korea	24.2	21	Lusaka, Zambia	13.2
4	Rajshahi, Bangladesh	23.5	22	Mogadishu, Somalia	13.1
5	Neijiang, China	22.1	23	Shenzhen, China	12.8
6	Riyadh, Saudi Arabia	21.6		Surat, India	12.8
7	Nanchong, China	20.9	25	Luanda, Angola	12.1
8	Dhaka, Bangladesh	19.0	26	Abidjan, Côte d' Ivoire	11.8
9	Yantai, China	18.8	27	Antananarivo, Madag.	11.7
10	Ulsan, South Korea	17.8	28	Porto, Portugal	11.5
11	Jedda, Saudi Arabia	17.5	29	Kabul, Afghanistan	11.4
12	Yaounde, Cameroon	16.6		Brazzaville, Congo-Braz.	11.4
13	Songnam, South Korea	16.2	31	Chittagong, Bang.	11.1
14	Nampho, North Korea	15.0	32	Asansol, India	10.7
15	Toluca, Mexico	14.8	33	Inch'on, South Korea	10.6
16	Lagos, Nigeria	14.3		Tijuana, Mexico	10.6
17	Santa Cruz, Bolivia	14.2		Valencia, Venezuela	10.6
18	Guatemala City, Guat.	14.1			

a Urban agglomerations. Estimates of cities' populations vary according to where geographical boundaries are defined.
b Urban agglomerations with a population of at least 1 million in 2000.

Proportion of a country's pop. residing in a single city[ab]

%, 2001

1	Hong Kong	100.0		16	Athens, Greece	29.4
	Singapore	100.0		17	Lima, Peru	29.1
3	Beirut, Lebanon	59.5		18	Guatemala City, Guat.	28.8
4	Brazzaville, Congo-Braz.	43.7		19	Tbilisi, Georgia	26.8
5	Panama City, Panama	41.5		20	Vienna, Austria	25.6
6	Montevideo, Uruguay	39.5		21	Copenhagen, Denmark	25.0
7	Lisbon, Portugal	39.3		22	Baku, Azerbaijan	24.3
8	Yerevan, Armenia	37.5		23	Abidjan, Côte d'Ivoire	24.2
9	Santiago, Chile	36.0		24	Amman, Jordan	23.4
10	San Juan, Puerto Rico	35.5		25	Zagreb, Croatia	23.2
11	Tel Aviv, Israel	32.8		26	Asuncion, Paraguay	23.1
	Tripoli, Libya	32.8		27	Riyadh, Saudi Arabia	22.6
13	Buenos Aires, Arg.	32.3		28	Dakar, Senegal	22.4
14	Santo Dom., Dom. Rep.	30.9		29	Port-au-Prince, Haiti	22.2
15	Auckland, New Zealand	29.7		30	San Salvador, El Sal.	21.6

Population living in urban areas

Highest, %, 2001 *Lowest, %, 2001*

1	Bermuda	100.0		1	Rwanda	6.3
	Cayman Islands	100.0		2	Bhutan	7.4
	Hong Kong	100.0		3	Burundi	9.3
	Singapore	100.0		4	Nepal	12.2
5	Guadeloupe	99.6		5	Uganda	14.5
6	Macau	98.9		6	Malawi	15.1
7	Belgium	97.4		7	Ethiopia	15.9
8	Kuwait	96.1		8	Burkina Faso	16.9
9	Martinique	95.2		9	Cambodia	17.5
10	Qatar	92.9		10	Papua New Guinea	17.6
11	Iceland	92.7		11	Eritrea	19.1
12	Bahrain	92.5		12	Laos	19.7
13	Andorra	92.2		13	Thailand	20.0
14	Uruguay	92.1		14	Niger	21.1
15	Luxembourg	91.9		15	Afghanistan	22.3

Quality of life index[c]

Highest, New York=100, Nov. 2003 *Lowest, New York=100, Nov. 2003*

1	Zurich, Switzerland	106.5		1	Baghdad, Iraq	14.5
	Geneva, Switzerland	106.5		2	Bangui, Cen. Afr. Rep.	28.5
3	Vancouver, Canada	106.0		3	Brazzaville, Congo-Braz.	29.5
	Vienna, Austria	106.0		4	Pointe Noire, Congo-Braz.	33.5
5	Auckland, NZ	105.0			Khartoum, Sudan	33.5
	Bern, Switzerland	105.0		6	Sana'a, Yemen	38.5
	Copenhagen, Denmark	105.0			Ouagadougou, Bur. Faso	38.5
	Frankfurt, Germany	105.0			Nouakchott, Mauritania	38.5
	Sydney, Australia	105.0			Ndjamena, Chad	38.5
10	Amsterdam, Neth.	104.5		10	Luanda, Angola	39.5
	Munich, Germany	104.5		11	Niamey, Niger	40.0
					Antananarivo, Madag.	40.0

c Based on 39 factors ranging from recreation to political stability.

Men and women

Most male populations
Number of males per 100 females

1	United Arab Emirates	189.7
2	Qatar	179.6
3	Kuwait	152.6
4	Oman	138.5
5	Bahrain	136.2
6	Saudi Arabia	117.5
7	Guam	110.0
8	Jordan	108.9
9	Brunei	108.7
10	Sri Lanka	107.8
11	Libya	107.3
12	French Polynesia	107.0
13	Papua New Guinea	106.9
14	Afghanistan	106.6
15	India	106.5
16	China	105.9
17	Bangladesh	105.4
18	New Caledonia	105.3
19	Pakistan	105.1
20	Albania	104.6
21	Nepal	104.4
22	Côte d'Ivoire	104.2
23	Taiwan	104.0
24	Costa Rica	103.5
	Fiji	103.5
26	West Bank and Gaza	103.4
27	Iran	103.2
	Malaysia	103.2
	Yemen	103.2

Most female populations
Number of males per 100 females

1	Latvia	85.0
2	Estonia	85.5
3	Ukraine	86.6
4	Lesotho	87.3
5	Lithuania	87.8
6	Russia	88.1
7	Belarus	88.4
8	Rwanda	89.8
9	Macau	90.8
10	Swaziland	91.0
11	Hungary	91.2
12	Georgia	91.3
	Virgin Islands	91.3
14	Martinique	91.5
15	Moldova	91.6
16	Mozambique	92.4
	Puerto Rico	92.4
18	Portugal	92.7
19	Croatia	92.8
20	Kazakhstan	92.9
21	Netherlands Antilles	93.0
22	Guadeloupe	93.7
23	Barbados	94.0
24	Cambodia	94.1
	Central African Rep	94.1
	Uruguay	94.1
27	Italy	94.2
28	Burundi	94.5

Use of contraceptives[a]

Highest, %

1	China	83.3
2	United Kingdom	82.0
3	Hong Kong	79.7
4	Switzerland	77.5
5	Netherlands	75.6
6	Finland	75.4
7	Belgium	74.3
8	Canada	73.3
9	Singapore	73.0
10	Australia	72.2
11	Sweden	72.0
	New Zealand	72.0
	Denmark	72.0
14	Germany	71.8
15	United States	70.5
16	Brazil	70.3

Lowest, %

1	Burundi	1.2
	Chad	1.2
	Mauritania	1.2
4	Afghanistan	1.6
5	Congo	2.0
6	Central African Rep	3.3
7	Benin	3.4
8	Eritrea	4.0
9	Guinea	4.2
10	Rwanda	4.3
11	Mali	4.5
12	Niger	4.6
13	Burkina Faso	4.8
14	Mozambique	5.1
15	Liberia	5.5
16	Ethiopia	6.3

a Married women aged 15–49 who use modern methods of contraception.

Refugees and asylum[a]

Largest refugee nationalities

'000, 2002

1	Afghanistan	2,480.9	11	Eritrea	315.6
2	Burundi	574.4	12	Liberia	274.5
3	Sudan	505.2	13	Croatia	269.7
4	Angola	432.8	14	Azerbaijan	254.7
5	Somalia	429.5	15	Serbia & Montenegro	161.3
6	West Bank and Gaza	428.7	16	Myanmar	148.5
7	Congo	415.5	17	Sierra Leone	139.2
8	Iraq	400.6	18	Sri Lanka	126.5
9	Bosnia	371.6	19	China	126.3
10	Vietnam	348.3	20	Bhutan	112.4

Countries with largest refugee populations

'000, 2002

1	Iran	1,306.6	11	Zambia	246.8
2	Pakistan	1,227.4	12	Saudi Arabia	245.3
3	Germany	903.0	13	Kenya	233.7
4	Tanzania	689.4	14	Uganda	217.3
5	United States	485.2	15	Guinea	182.2
6	Serbia & Montenegro	354.4	16	Algeria	169.2
7	Congo	333.0	17	India	168.9
8	Sudan	328.2	18	United Kingdom	159.2
9	China	297.3	19	Netherlands	148.4
10	Armenia	247.6	20	Sweden	142.2

Nationality of asylum applications in industrialised countries

'000, 2002

1	Iraq	51.0	11	Colombia	12.4
2	Serbia & Montenegro	33.1	12	Iran	11.6
3	Turkey	29.6	13	Mexico	10.7
4	China	26.3	14	Pakistan	10.4
5	Afghanistan	25.7	15	Sri Lanka	10.2
6	Russia	20.0	16	Algeria	9.8
7	India	14.9	17	Zimbabwe	8.6
8	Nigeria	13.6	18	Georgia	8.3
9	Congo	13.2	19	Armenia	8.1
10	Somalia	12.9	20	Bosnia	8.0

Asylum applications in industrialised countries

'000, 2002

1	United Kingdom	110.7	10	Netherlands	18.7
2	United States	81.1	11	Norway	17.5
3	Germany	71.1	12	Ireland	11.6
4	France	50.8	13	Slovakia	9.7
5	Austria	37.1	14	Czech Republic	8.5
6	Canada	33.4	15	Italy	7.2
7	Sweden	33.0	16	Hungary	6.4
8	Switzerland	26.2	17	Spain	6.2
9	Belgium	18.8	18	Australia	6.0

a As reported by UNHCR.

The world economy

Biggest economies
GDP, $bn

1	United States	10,383.1	26	Denmark	172.9
2	Japan	3,993.4		Indonesia	172.9
3	Germany	1,984.1	28	Hong Kong	161.5
4	United Kingdom	1,566.3	29	Greece	132.8
5	France[a]	1,431.3	30	Finland	131.5
6	China	1,266.1	31	Thailand	126.9
7	Italy	1,184.3	32	Portugal	121.6
8	Canada	714.3	33	Ireland	121.4
9	Spain	653.1	34	Iran	108.2
10	Mexico	637.2	35	South Africa	104.2
11	India	510.2	36	Israel	103.7
12	South Korea	476.7	37	Argentina	102.0
13	Brazil	452.4	38	Malaysia	94.9
14	Netherlands	417.9	39	Venezuela	94.3
15	Australia	409.4	40	Egypt	89.9
16	Russia	346.5	41	Singapore	87.0
17	Taiwan	281.6	42	Colombia	80.9
18	Switzerland	267.4	43	Philippines	78.0
19	Belgium	245.4	44	United Arab Emirates	71.0
20	Sweden	240.3	45	Czech Republic	69.5
21	Austria	204.1	46	Puerto Rico[b]	67.9
22	Norway	190.5	47	Hungary	65.8
23	Poland	189.0	48	Chile	64.2
24	Saudi Arabia	188.5	49	Pakistan	59.1
25	Turkey	183.7	50	New Zealand	58.6

Biggest economies by purchasing power
GDP PPP, $bn

1	United States	10,308	21	Thailand	432
2	China	5,861	22	Argentina	413
3	Japan	3,425	23	Poland	408
4	India	2,800	24	Taiwan	387
5	Germany	2,236	25	Philippines	333
6	France	1,601	26	Belgium	285
7	United Kingdom	1,549	27	Pakistan	281
8	Italy	1,525	28	Colombia	279
9	Brazil	1,355	29	Saudi Arabia	277
10	Russia	1,186	30	Egypt	253
11	Canada	925	31	Ukraine	237
12	Mexico	905	32	Austria	235
13	Spain	878	33	Sweden	232
14	South Korea	807	34	Bangladesh	230
15	Indonesia	683	35	Malaysia	222
16	Australia	556	36	Switzerland	219
17	Netherlands	470	37	Greece	199
18	South Africa	457	38	Portugal	186
19	Turkey	445	39	Vietnam	185
20	Iran	438	40	Hong Kong	183

a Includes overseas departments. b 2001
Note: For list of all countries with their GDP see pages 248–252.

Regional GDP

$bn, 2002		*% annual growth 1997–2002*	
World	32,300	World	3.3
Advanced economies	25,780	Advanced economies	2.6
G7	21,260	G7	2.3
EU15	8,630	EU15	2.5
Asia[a]	2,490	Asia[a]	5.8
Latin America	1,770	Latin America	1.4
Eastern Europe[b]	970	Eastern Europe[b]	3.7
Middle East[c]	860	Middle East[c]	4.1
Africa	430	Africa	3.2

Regional purchasing power

GDP, % of total		*$ per head*	
World	100.0	World	7,770
Advanced economies	55.7	Advanced economies	28,100
G7	44.0	G7	29,730
EU15	19.7	EU15	24,690
Asia[a]	22.9	Asia[a]	3,400
Latin America	7.9	Latin America	7,310
Eastern Europe[b]	6.3	Eastern Europe[b]	7,650
Middle East[c]	4.0	Middle East[c]	6,220
Africa	3.2	Africa	1,990

Regional population

% of total (6.2bn)		*No. of countries[d]*	
Advanced economies	15.4	Advanced economies	29
G7	11.5	G7	7
EU15	6.2	EU15	15
Asia[a]	52.3	Asia[a]	25
Latin America	8.4	Latin America	33
Eastern Europe[b]	6.4	Eastern Europe[b]	28
Middle East[c]	5.0	Middle East[c]	16
Africa	12.5	Africa	51

Regional international trade

Exports of goods and services, % of tot.		*Current account balances, $bn*	
Advanced economies	74.8	Advanced economies	-193.3
G7	45.4	G7	-304.8
EU15	38.8	EU15	66.8
Asia[a]	9.9	Asia[a]	68.1
Latin America	4.5	Latin America	-15.8
Eastern Europe[b]	4.8	Eastern Europe[b]	9.6
Middle East[c]	4.1	Middle East[c]	29
Africa	1.9	Africa	-7.4

a Excludes Hong Kong, Japan, Singapore, South Korea and Taiwan.
b Includes Russia and other CIS.
c Includes Malta and Turkey.
d IMF definition.

Living standards

Highest GDP per head

$

1	Luxembourg	46,930	36	Israel	16,460
2	Norway	42,330	37	Spain	16,370
3	Switzerland	37,150	38	Bahamas[d]	15,440
4	United States	35,990	39	New Zealand	15,420
5	Bermuda[a]	35,710	40	Macau	15,410
6	Denmark	32,630	41	French Polynesia[d]	14,310
7	Japan	31,320	42	Martinique[d]	14,230
8	Ireland	31,140	43	Cyprus	12,680
9	Cayman Islands[a]	30,240	44	Greece	12,530
10	Qatar	29,910	45	Taiwan	12,520
11	Iceland	29,850	46	Portugal	12,160
12	Sweden	27,310	47	Guadeloupe[d]	12,080
13	Aruba	26,790	48	New Caledonia[d]	11,970
14	United Arab Emirates	26,280	49	Bahrain	11,590
15	United Kingdom	26,240	50	Slovenia	10,980
16	Netherlands	26,120	51	Netherlands Antilles	10,960
17	Finland	25,290	52	Réunion[d]	10,460
18	Austria	25,190	53	South Korea	10,060
19	Germany	24,200	54	Malta	9,850
20	France	23,970	55	Barbados	9,420
21	Belgium	23,820	56	Saudi Arabia	8,690
22	Channel Islands[ab]	23,330	57	Oman	7,520
23	Hong Kong	23,080	58	Trinidad & Tobago	7,410
24	Canada	22,820	59	Czech Republic	6,750
25	Virgin Islands[a]	21,820	60	Hungary	6,650
26	Faroe Islands[ac]	21,740	61	Mexico	6,260
27	Australia	21,000	62	Poland	4,910
28	Singapore	20,710	63	Lebanon	4,800
29	Italy	20,630	64	Croatia	4,770
30	Guam[ac]	19,750	65	Estonia	4,650
31	Greenland[a]	19,300	66	Slovakia	4,390
32	Andorra[ad]	19,120	67	Equatorial Guinea	4,380
33	Brunei[a]	19,060	68	Panama	4,240
34	Kuwait	17,680	69	Malaysia	4,130
35	Puerto Rico	16,970	70	Chile	4,110

Lowest GDP per head

$

1	Ethiopia	90		Niger	190
2	Burundi	110	12	Tajikistan	200
	Congo	110	13	Rwanda	210
4	Myanmar[c]	120	14	Nepal	230
5	Eritrea	160		Uganda	230
	Guinea-Bissau	160	16	Chad	240
	Malawi	160	17	Tanzania	250
	Sierra Leone	160	18	Burkina Faso	260
9	Liberia	170		Gambia, The	260
10	Mozambique	190		Madagascar	260

a Estimate. b 1999 c 2001 d 2000

Highest purchasing power

GDP per head in PPP (USA = 100)

1	Luxembourg	147.6		Israel	52.6
2	Norway	101.6		Virgin Islands[ac]	52.6
3	United States	100.0	38	Greece	52.0
4	Bermuda[a]	97.5	39	Brunei[a]	51.5
5	Cayman Islands[a]	96.9	40	Cyprus	51.4
6	Switzerland	88.2	41	Slovenia	51.2
7	Denmark	84.7	42	Taiwan[a]	49.8
8	Ireland	81.9	43	Portugal	49.3
9	Iceland	81.0	44	Kuwait	49.2
10	Austria	80.1	45	Malta	49.0
	Canada	80.1	46	South Korea	47.0
12	Netherlands	78.5	47	Puerto Rico[c]	45.0
13	Belgium	77.9	48	Bahrain	44.8
14	French Polynesia[d]	77.6	49	Bahamas[d]	44.5
15	Aruba[a]	77.5	50	Czech Republic	41.3
16	Hong Kong	76.1	51	Barbados	40.6
17	Australia	76.0	52	Martinique[d]	38.9
18	Japan	75.8	53	New Caledonia[a]	38.8
19	France	74.9	54	Hungary	36.2
20	Germany	74.7	55	Oman	36.0
21	United Kingdom	73.6	56	Saudi Arabia	35.1
22	Italy	72.5	57	Slovakia	34.9
23	Finland	72.4	58	Guadeloupe[d]	33.2
24	Sweden	71.5	59	Estonia	32.2
25	United Arab Emirates	66.5	60	Netherlands Antilles[a]	31.6
26	Singapore	65.7	61	Mauritius	30.0
27	Channel Islands[ab]	64.5	62	Réunion[d]	29.1
28	Faroe Islands[ac]	60.9	63	Poland	28.9
29	Macau	60.7	64	Argentina	28.2
30	Spain	58.7		Lithuania	28.2
31	Guam[ad]	58.2	66	Croatia	27.7
32	New Zealand	56.9	67	South Africa	27.2
33	Qatar[a]	55.7	68	Chile	26.1
34	Greenland[ac]	55.4	69	Latvia	25.5
35	Andorra[ad]	52.6	70	Equatorial Guinea	25.2

Lowest purchasing power

GDP per head in PPP (USA = 100)

1	Sierra Leone	1.4		Niger	2.2
2	Malawi	1.6		Nigeria	2.2
	Tanzania	1.6		West Bank and Gaza[a]	2.2
4	Burundi	1.7		Yemen	2.2
	Congo	1.7		Zambia	2.2
	Somalia[a]	1.7	16	Afghanistan[a]	2.3
7	Guinea-Bissau	1.9	17	Mali	2.4
8	Congo-Brazzaville	2.0	18	Tajikistan	2.6
	Madagascar	2.0	19	Mozambique	2.7
10	Ethiopia	2.2			

Note: for definition of purchasing power parity see page 247.

The quality of life

Human development index[a]

Highest

1	Norway	94.4	31	Czech Republic	86.1
2	Iceland	94.2	32	Malta	85.6
3	Sweden	94.1	33	Argentina	84.9
4	Australia	93.9	34	Poland	84.1
5	Netherlands	93.8	35	Bahrain	83.9
6	Belgium	93.7	36	Hungary	83.7
	Canada	93.7	37	Slovakia	83.6
	United States	93.7	38	Uruguay	83.4
9	Japan	93.2	39	Estonia	83.3
	Switzerland	93.2	40	Costa Rica	83.2
11	Denmark	93.0	41	Chile	83.1
	Finland	93.0	42	Qatar	82.6
	Ireland	93.0	43	Lithuania	82.4
	Luxembourg	93.0	44	Kuwait	82.0
	United Kingdom	93.0	45	Croatia	81.8
16	Austria	92.9	46	United Arab Emirates	81.6
17	France	92.5	47	Bahamas	81.2
18	Germany	92.1	48	Latvia	81.1
19	Spain	91.8	49	Cuba	80.6
20	Italy	91.6	50	Belarus	80.4
21	Israel	90.5	51	Trinidad & Tobago	80.2
22	Portugal	89.6	52	Mexico	80.0
23	Greece	89.2	53	Bulgaria	79.5
24	Cyprus	89.1	54	Malaysia	79.0
25	Hong Kong	88.9	55	Panama	78.8
26	Barbados	88.8	56	Macedonia	78.4
27	Singapore	88.4	57	Libya	78.3
28	Slovenia	88.1	58	Colombia	77.9
29	South Korea	87.9		Mauritius	77.9
30	Brunei	87.2		Russia	77.9

Human development index[a]

Lowest

1	Sierra Leone	27.5	10	Guinea-Bissau	37.3
2	Niger	29.2	11	Chad	37.6
3	Burkina Faso	33.0	12	Angola	37.7
4	Burundi	33.7	13	Zambia	38.6
	Mali	33.7	14	Malawi	38.7
6	Mozambique	35.6	15	Côte d'Ivoire	39.6
7	Ethiopia	35.9	16	Tanzania	40.0
8	Central African Rep	36.3	17	Benin	41.1
	Congo	36.3	18	Rwanda	42.2

a GDP or GDP per head is often taken as a measure of how developed a country is, but its usefulness is limited as it refers only to economic welfare. In 1990 the UN Development Programme published its first estimate of a Human Development Index, which combined statistics on two other indicators – adult literacy and life expectancy – with income levels to give a better, though still far from perfect, indicator of human development. In 1991 average years of schooling was combined with adult literacy to give a knowledge variable. The HDI is shown here scaled from 0 to 100; countries scoring over 80 are considered to have high human development, those scoring from 50 to 79 medium and those under 50 low.

Economic freedom index[a]

1	Hong Kong	1.34		Bahrain	2.08
2	Singapore	1.61	22	Belgium	2.19
3	New Zealand	1.70		Lithuania	2.19
4	Luxembourg	1.71	24	El Salvador	2.24
5	Ireland	1.74	25	Bahamas	2.25
6	Estonia	1.76	26	Italy	2.26
7	United Kingdom	1.79	27	Spain	2.31
8	Denmark	1.80	28	Norway	2.35
9	Switzerland	1.84	29	Israel	2.36
10	United States	1.85		Latvia	2.36
11	Australia	1.88	31	Portugal	2.38
12	Sweden	1.90	32	Czech Republic	2.39
13	Chile	1.91	33	Barbados	2.41
14	Cyprus	1.95	34	Taiwan	2.43
	Finland	1.95	35	Slovakia	2.44
16	Canada	1.98	36	Trinidad & Tobago	2.45
17	Iceland	2.00	37	Malta	2.51
18	Germany	2.03	38	Japan	2.53
19	Netherlands	2.04	39	Botswana	2.55
20	Austria	2.08		Uruguay	2.55

Gender-related development index[b]

1	Norway	94.1	21	Italy	91.0
2	Iceland	94.0	22	Israel	90.0
	Sweden	94.0	23	Portugal	89.2
4	Australia	93.8	24	Cyprus	88.6
5	United States	93.5		Greece	88.6
6	Canada	93.4		Hong Kong	88.6
	Netherlands	93.4	27	Barbados	88.5
8	Belgium	93.1	28	Singapore	88.0
9	Denmark	92.8	29	Slovenia	87.9
	Finland	92.8	30	South Korea	87.3
	United Kingdom	92.8	31	Brunei	86.7
12	Switzerland	92.7	32	Czech Republic	85.7
13	Japan	92.6	33	Malta	84.4
14	Austria	92.4	34	Argentina	83.9
	Germany	92.4		Poland	83.9
16	France	92.3	36	Hungary	83.4
	Ireland	92.3		Slovakia	83.4
18	Luxembourg	92.0	38	Estonia	83.1
19	New Zealand	91.4	39	Uruguay	83.0
20	Spain	91.2	40	Bahrain	82.9

a Ranks countries on the basis of ten indicators of how government intervention can restrict the economic relations between individuals. The economic indicators, published by the Heritage Foundation, are trade policy, taxation, monetary policy, the banking system, foreign-investment rules, property rights, the amount of economic output consumed by the government, regulation policy, the size of the black market and the extent of wage and price controls. A country can score between 1 and 5 in each category, 1 being the most free and 5 being the least free.
b Combines similar data to the HDI (and also published by the UNDP) to give an indicator of the disparities in human development between men and women in individual countries. The lower the index, the greater the disparity.

Economic growth

Highest economic growth, 1992–2002

Average annual % increase in real GDP

1	Bosnia[a]	20.5		27	Bangladesh	4.9
2	Liberia	9.4			Benin	4.9
3	China	9.3			Cambodia	4.9
4	Mozambique	8.4		30	Mauritania	4.6
5	Myanmar[b]	8.1		31	Burkina Faso	4.5
6	Ireland	7.7			Kuwait	4.5
7	Vietnam	7.5		33	Costa Rica	4.4
8	Bhutan	7.0			Egypt	4.4
9	Uganda	6.7			Peru	4.4
10	Albania	6.3			Poland	4.4
	Laos	6.3			Puerto Rico[b]	4.4
12	Singapore	6.2			Sri Lanka	4.4
13	Eritrea	6.1		39	Bahrain	4.3
14	Ethiopia	6.0			Guinea	4.3
	Sudan	6.0			Nepal	4.3
16	India	5.9			Tunisia	4.3
17	Dominican Republic	5.7		43	Ghana	4.2
	Malaysia	5.7			Mali	4.2
19	South Korea	5.6			Namibia	4.2
20	Botswana	5.3			Oman	4.2
21	Mauritius	5.2			United Arab Emirates	4.2
22	Armenia	5.0		48	Senegal	4.1
	Chile	5.0		49	Jordan	4.0
	Luxembourg	5.0			Slovenia	4.0
	Taiwan	5.0		51	Australia	3.9
	Yemen	5.0			Malta	3.9

Lowest economic growth, 1992–2002

Average annual % change in real GDP

1	Ukraine	-5.0			Zimbabwe	0.5
2	Moldova	-3.8		21	Bulgaria	0.7
3	Congo	-3.6		22	Belarus	0.9
	Tajikistan	-3.6			Japan	0.9
5	West Bank and Gaza[a]	-1.7		24	Lithuania	1.1
6	Burundi	-1.6			Switzerland	1.1
	Sierra Leone	-1.6		26	Germany	1.3
8	Kirgizstan	-1.3		27	New Caledonia[c]	1.4
9	Russia	-1.1			Romania	1.4
10	Azerbaijan	-0.7			Rwanda	1.4
11	Georgia	-0.5		30	Turkmenistan	1.5
12	Venezuela	-0.2		31	Italy	1.6
13	Macedonia	0.0			Madagascar	1.6
14	Haiti	0.1			Paraguay	1.6
15	Kazakhstan	0.2			Saudi Arabia	1.6
16	Guinea-Bissau	0.4			Zambia	1.6
	Jamaica	0.4		36	Congo-Brazzaville	1.7
	Uruguay	0.4		37	France	1.9
19	Argentina	0.5			Uzbekistan	1.9

a 1994–2002   b 1992–2001   c 1992–2000

Highest economic growth, 1982–92

Average annual % increase in real GDP

1	China	10.2	12	Swaziland	6.6
2	Botswana	9.8	13	Malaysia	6.5
3	South Korea	8.7	14	Chile	6.4
4	Ecuador	8.5		Cyprus	6.4
	Taiwan	8.5		Hong Kong	6.4
6	Thailand	8.4	17	Chad	6.2
7	Macau	8.1	18	Pakistan	6.1
8	Oman	7.7	19	Mauritius	5.9
9	Indonesia	7.1		New Caledonia	5.9
10	Singapore	7.0	21	Luxembourg	5.5
11	Bhutan	6.7	22	India	5.4

Lowest economic growth, 1982–92

Average annual % increase in real GDP

1	Liberia	-15.7	12	Congo	-1.3
2	Georgia	-9.0		Peru	-1.3
3	Albania	-3.5	14	Hungary	-1.0
	Moldova	-3.5	15	Haiti	-0.8
5	Latvia	-2.7		Niger	-0.8
6	Estonia	-2.2	17	Russia	-0.6
7	Romania	-2.0	18	Central African Rep	-0.3
8	Nicaragua	-1.8	19	Bulgaria	0.0
9	Sierra Leone	-1.7		Mozambique	0.0
10	Slovakia[a]	-1.5	21	Ethiopia	0.1
11	Trinidad & Tobago	-1.4	22	Suriname	0.2

Highest services growth, 1992–2002

Average annual % increase in real terms

1	Bosnia[b]	35.9	10	Iran	7.5
2	Georgia[c]	17.9	11	Botswana	7.3
3	Albania	10.8	12	Bhutan	7.1
4	Equatorial Guinea	10.6	13	Laos[e]	6.9
5	China	8.6		Vietnam	6.9
6	Ethiopia	8.5	15	Mauritania	6.5
7	Myanmar[d]	8.1	16	Nicaragua	6.3
8	India	8.0		Singapore	6.3
9	Uganda	7.8			

Lowest services growth, 1992–2002

Average annual % increase in real terms

1	Congo	-9.6	7	Angola	-1.4
2	Ukraine	-6.8	8	Central African Rep	-1.3
3	Kirgizstan	-1.9	9	Burundi	-0.6
4	Azerbaijan	-1.8	10	Bulgaria	-0.5
5	Turkmenistan[e]	-1.7	11	Venezuela	-0.3
6	Sierra Leone	-1.5	12	Rwanda	-0.1

a 1984–92   b 1995–2000   c 1994–2002   d 1992–2000   e 1992–2001
Note: Rankings of highest industrial growth 1992–2002 can be found on page 44 and highest agricultural growth on page 47.

Trading places

Biggest exporters
% of total world exports (visible & invisible)

1	Euro area	17.16	23	Hong Kong	1.16
2	United States	13.59	24	Denmark	1.05
3	Germany	9.11	25	Australia	1.01
4	United Kingdom	6.63	26	Norway	0.98
5	Japan	6.11	27	Thailand	0.94
6	France	5.23	28	Saudi Arabia	0.90
7	China	4.13	29	India	0.88
8	Italy	3.95		Luxembourg	0.88
9	Canada	3.55	31	Brazil	0.81
10	Netherlands	3.35	32	Indonesia	0.74
11	Belgium	2.67	33	Finland	0.66
12	Spain	2.31	34	Poland	0.65
13	South Korea	2.18	35	Turkey	0.63
14	Mexico	1.96	36	Puerto Rico	0.62
15	Switzerland	1.89	37	United Arab Emirates	0.55
16	Taiwan	1.79	38	Czech Republic	0.53
17	Ireland	1.55	39	Philippines	0.50
18	Russia	1.40	40	Hungary	0.48
19	Austria	1.35	41	Portugal	0.47
	Sweden	1.35	42	Israel	0.46
21	Singapore	1.23	43	South Africa	0.41
22	Malaysia	1.22			

Most trade dependent
Trade as % of GDP[a]

1	Syria	118.2
2	Aruba	95.1
3	Malaysia	88.8
4	Swaziland	83.9
5	Liberia	79.7
6	Lesotho	76.3
7	Singapore	71.8
8	Bahrain	68.1
9	Belgium	67.0
10	Slovakia	65.2
11	Equatorial Guinea	64.2
12	Malta	63.5
13	Tajikistan	62.8
14	Estonia	62.5
15	United Arab Emirates	60.5
16	Belarus	58.9
17	Czech Republic	57.0
18	Ireland	56.3
19	Puerto Rico	56.1
20	Mongolia	53.8
21	Hungary	52.9

Least trade dependent
Trade as % of GDP[a]

1	Somalia	4.0
2	Barbados	5.0
3	North Korea	5.5
4	Cuba	7.4
5	Japan	8.7
	Rwanda	8.7
7	Guam	8.9
	United States	8.9
9	Burundi	9.4
10	Egypt	11.1
11	India	11.6
12	Brazil	11.9
13	Madagascar	12.4
14	Central African Rep	12.9
	Tanzania	12.9
16	Hong Kong	13.2
17	Peru	13.3
18	Uganda	13.7
19	Bangladesh	14.5
20	Euro area	14.7
21	Colombia	15.1

Notes: The figures are drawn from balance of payment statistics and, therefore, have differing technical definitions from trade statistics taken from customs or similar sources. The invisible trade figures do not show some countries due to unavailable data. For Hong Kong and Singapore, domestic exports and retained imports only are used.

Biggest visible traders
% of world visible exports

1	Euro area	15.19	24	Thailand	1.00
2	United States	14.97	25	India	0.95
3	Germany	8.96	26	Brazil	0.87
4	Japan	5.64	27	Denmark	0.83
5	United Kingdom	5.10		Saudi Arabia	0.83
6	China	4.91	29	Poland	0.81
7	France	4.87	30	Indonesia	0.77
8	Canada	3.97		Norway	0.77
	Italy	3.97	32	Turkey	0.72
10	Netherlands	3.19	33	United Arab Emirates	0.69
11	Mexico	2.67	34	Czech Republic	0.64
12	Belgium	2.66	35	Finland	0.62
13	South Korea	2.52		Puerto Rico	0.62
14	Spain	2.30	37	Hungary	0.56
15	Taiwan	1.90	38	Philippines	0.55
16	Switzerland	1.57	39	Portugal	0.54
17	Malaysia	1.36	40	Israel	0.48
	Russia	1.36	41	South Africa	0.47
19	Sweden	1.19	42	Iran	0.42
20	Austria	1.16	43	Syria	0.40
21	Ireland	1.11	44	Hong Kong	0.34
22	Australia	1.10	45	Greece	0.33
23	Singapore	1.01		Venezuela	0.33

Biggest invisible traders
% of world invisible exports

1	Euro area	19.32	24	India	0.95
2	United States	19.06	25	Australia	0.91
3	United Kingdom	11.21	26	Greece	0.76
4	Germany	7.33	27	Russia	0.67
5	France	5.87	28	Thailand	0.65
6	Japan	5.50	29	Malaysia	0.60
7	Italy	3.63		Turkey	0.60
8	Netherlands	3.36	31	Mexico	0.59
9	Hong Kong	3.03	32	Portugal	0.54
10	Spain	2.90	33	Finland	0.53
11	Belgium	2.57	34	Israel	0.48
12	Switzerland	2.48	35	Brazil	0.45
13	Luxembourg	2.46	36	Poland	0.42
14	Canada	2.01	37	Philippines	0.38
15	Ireland	1.91	38	Egypt	0.35
16	Austria	1.69	39	Czech Republic	0.32
17	China	1.68		Hungary	0.32
18	Singapore	1.54	41	Saudi Arabia	0.31
19	Sweden	1.43	42	Puerto Rico	0.30
20	Denmark	1.38	43	Indonesia	0.28
21	South Korea	1.22	44	New Zealand	0.22
22	Taiwan	1.11		South Africa	0.22
23	Norway	1.00			

a Average of imports and exports of goods as % of GDP.

Current account

Largest surpluses
$m

1	Japan	112,450		26	India	4,656
2	Euro area	64,390		27	Algeria	4,300
3	Germany	46,590		28	Philippines	4,197
4	China	35,422		29	Kuwait	4,192
5	Russia	29,520		30	Pakistan	3,871
6	Switzerland	26,011		31	Iran	3,731
7	France	25,740		32	Brunei[a]	3,492
8	Taiwan	25,730		33	Ukraine	3,174
9	Norway	25,148		34	Qatar	3,129
10	Singapore	18,704		35	Macau	2,565
11	Canada	14,909		36	Libya[b]	2,136
12	Hong Kong	13,725		37	Oman	1,948
13	Saudi Arabia	11,889		38	Luxembourg	1,636
14	Belgium	11,204		39	Morocco	1,472
15	Sweden	10,624		40	Syria[a]	1,062
16	Finland	10,205		41	Nigeria	1,001
17	Netherlands	10,116		42	Botswana[c]	817
18	Argentina	9,592		43	Côte d'Ivoire	767
19	United Arab Emirates	8,440		44	Bangladesh	742
20	Indonesia	7,823		45	Egypt	622
21	Thailand	7,650		46	Gabon	584
22	Venezuela	7,423		47	Austria	575
23	Malaysia	7,190		48	Yemen	538
24	South Korea	6,092		49	Cameroon[a]	510
25	Denmark	4,991		50	Jordan	468

Largest deficits
$m

1	United States	-480,860		21	Angola[c]	-1,431
2	United Kingdom	-26,710		22	Serbia & Montenegro	-1,384
3	Australia	-17,264		23	Israel	-1,226
4	Spain	-15,942		24	Ecuador	-1,222
5	Mexico	-14,020		25	Peru	-1,206
6	Greece	-10,405		26	Guatemala	-1,193
7	Portugal	-8,813		27	Jamaica	-1,119
8	Brazil	-7,696		28	Sudan	-960
9	Italy	-6,741		29	Costa Rica	-946
10	Poland	-5,007		30	Ireland	-925
11	Czech Republic	-4,485		31	Nicaragua	-888
12	Lebanon	-2,848		32	Dominican Republic	-875
13	Hungary	-2,644		33	Estonia	-800
14	New Zealand	-2,269		34	Azerbaijan	-768
15	Bosnia	-2,139		35	Tunisia	-746
16	Croatia	-1,908		36	Lithuania	-721
17	Slovakia	-1,900		37	Kazakhstan	-696
18	Colombia	-1,580		38	Bulgaria	-679
19	Romania	-1,525		39	Mozambique[c]	-657
20	Turkey	-1,521		40	Cuba[c]	-654

a 2000   b 1999   c 2001

Largest surpluses as % of GDP

%

1	Brunei[a]	53.7		26	Saudi Arabia	6.3
2	Macau	37.9		27	Thailand	6.0
3	Singapore	21.5		28	Mauritius	5.7
4	Qatar	17.9		29	Cameroon[a]	5.6
5	Botswana[c]	15.5		30	Philippines	5.4
6	Norway	13.2			Yemen	5.4
7	Kuwait	11.9		32	Paraguay	5.3
	United Arab Emirates	11.9		33	Syria[a]	5.1
9	Gabon	11.7		34	Jordan	5.0
10	Libya[b]	11.2		35	Belgium	4.6
11	Papua New Guinea[c]	10.0		36	Indonesia	4.5
12	Switzerland	9.7		37	Sweden	4.4
13	Oman	9.6		38	Trinidad & Tobago[c]	4.3
14	Argentina	9.4		39	Morocco	4.1
15	Taiwan	9.1		40	Iran	3.4
16	Hong Kong	8.5		41	Namibia	3.3
	Russia	8.5			Turkmenistan[c]	3.3
18	Venezuela	7.9		43	Bermuda	3.0
19	Finland	7.8			Uzbekistan	3.0
	Luxembourg	7.8		45	Denmark	2.9
21	Algeria	7.7		46	China	2.8
	Ukraine	7.7			Japan	2.8
23	Malaysia	7.6		48	Netherlands	2.4
24	Côte d'Ivoire	6.6		49	Germany	2.3
	Pakistan	6.6			Nigeria	2.3

Largest deficits as % of GDP

%

1	Bosnia	-38.2		21	Equatorial Guinea	-9.7
2	Chad[c]	-23.7		22	Senegal	-9.5
3	Nicaragua	-22.2		23	Liberia	-9.3
4	Bhutan[c]	-18.3		24	Mali[c]	-9.2
	Mozambique[c]	-18.3		25	Serbia & Montenegro	-8.8
6	Lesotho	-16.6		26	Macedonia	-8.6
7	Lebanon	-16.5		27	Croatia	-8.5
8	Zambia[a]	-15.8		28	Albania	-8.4
9	Sierra Leone[a]	-14.7		29	Slovakia	-8.0
10	Jamaica	-14.2		30	Greece	-7.8
11	Mongolia	-14.1		31	Latvia	-7.7
12	Suriname	-13.8		32	Georgia	-7.4
13	Eritrea	-13.2		33	Niger	-7.3
14	Aruba	-13.0			Rwanda	-7.3
15	Angola[c]	-12.7			Uganda	-7.3
16	Azerbaijan	-12.6		36	Bahamas[c]	-7.2
17	Estonia	-12.3			Portugal	-7.2
18	Togo	-11.2		38	Sudan	-7.1
19	Malawi	-10.6		39	Barbados	-6.8
20	Burkina Faso	-10.4			Madagascar	-6.8

a 2000   b 1999   c 2001

Inflation

Highest inflation, 2003
Consumer price inflation, %

1	Zimbabwe[a]	140.1		31	Botswana	9.2
2	Angola	98.2		32	Slovakia	8.6
3	Myanmar[a]	57.1		33	Mongolia[b]	8.0
4	Haiti	39.3		34	Ecuador	7.9
5	Congo[a]	32.0		35	Uganda	7.8
6	Venezuela	31.1		36	Honduras	7.7
7	Belarus	28.4		37	Sierra Leone	7.6
8	Turkey	25.3		38	Swaziland	7.3
9	Suriname	23.0		39	Namibia	7.2
10	Zambia[a]	22.2		40	Colombia	7.1
11	Uruguay	19.4		41	Rwanda	6.9
12	Ethiopia	17.8		42	Lesotho	6.7
13	Iran	16.5		43	Kazakhstan	6.4
14	Burundi	16.0			Sudan[c]	6.4
15	Laos	15.5		45	Sri Lanka	6.3
16	Romania	15.3		46	South Africa	6.0
17	Ghana[a]	14.8		47	Indonesia	5.8
18	Brazil	14.7		48	Nepal	5.7
	Papua New Guinea	14.7		49	Georgia[a]	5.6
20	Paraguay	14.2			Slovenia	5.6
21	Nigeria	14.0		51	Guatemala	5.5
22	Russia	13.7		52	Dominican Republic[a]	5.2
23	Argentina	13.4			Nicaragua	5.2
	Mozambique	13.4			Ukraine	5.2
25	Moldova	11.8		55	Gambia, The[a]	4.9
26	Yemen	10.8		56	Armenia	4.8
27	Jamaica	10.3			Bangladesh	4.6
28	Kenya	9.8			Hungary	4.6
29	Malawi	9.6			Mexico	4.6
30	Costa Rica	9.5		60	Tanzania	4.4

Highest inflation, 1998–2003
Average annual consumer price inflation, %

1	Congo[d]	246.1		17	Moldova	19.9
2	Angola	174.1		18	Haiti	16.6
4	Belarus	99.0		19	Iran	15.3
5	Zimbabwe[d]	79.9		20	Ukraine	13.3
6	Turkey	48.3		21	Papua New Guinea	13.2
7	Suriname	44.2		22	Kirgizstan	12.8
8	Ecuador	37.9		23	Nigeria	11.8
9	Romania	32.2		24	Mozambique	10.9
10	Laos	31.5		25	Indonesia	10.7
11	Russia	29.1		26	Costa Rica	10.2
12	Zambia[d]	24.1		27	Yemen	9.6
13	Malawi	23.7		28	Honduras	9.5
14	Myanmar[d]	22.5			Paraguay	9.5
15	Ghana[d]	21.1			Sudan[e]	9.5
16	Venezuela	21.0			Uruguay	9.5

Lowest inflation, 2003
Consumer price inflation, %

1	Hong Kong	-2.6	27	Qatar[a]	1.0
2	Chad	-1.9		Syria	1.0
3	Lithuania	-1.7	29	Germany	1.1
4	Niger	-1.6		Malaysia	1.1
5	Mali	-1.4	31	Bahrain[a]	1.2
6	Madagascar	-1.2		Cambodia	1.2
7	Togo	-1.0		Kuwait	1.2
8	Congo-Brazzaville	-0.9	34	Estonia	1.3
9	China[a]	-0.8	35	Austria	1.4
10	Israel	-0.6		Panama	1.4
11	Oman	-0.4	37	Benin	1.5
12	Japan	-0.3	38	Barbados	1.6
	Taiwan	-0.3		Belgium	1.6
14	Senegal	0.0	40	New Zealand	1.8
15	Croatia	0.1		Thailand	1.8
	Czech Republic	0.1	42	Sweden	1.9
	Macedonia	0.1	43	Burkina Faso	2.0
18	Albania	0.5		Netherlands Antilles	2.0
	Gabon[b]	0.5	45	Denmark	2.1
	Malta	0.5		El Salvador	2.1
	Singapore	0.5		Euro area	2.1
22	Finland	0.6		France	2.1
	Saudi Arabia	0.6		Iceland	2.1
	Switzerland	0.6		Luxembourg	2.1
25	Poland	0.7		Netherlands	2.1
26	Guinea-Bissau[a]	0.9			

Lowest inflation, 1998–2003
Average annual consumer price inflation, %

1	Hong Kong	-3.0	17	Switzerland	0.9
2	Syria[d]	-0.9	18	Niger	1.1
3	Azerbaijan[d]	-0.7		Panama	1.1
	Gabon[d]	-0.7	20	Thailand	1.2
5	Japan	-0.6	21	Cambodia	1.4
	Oman	-0.6		Jordan	1.4
	Saudi Arabia	-0.6		Mali	1.4
8	China[d]	-0.4		Senegal	1.4
9	Macedonia	-0.2	25	Burkina Faso	1.5
10	Bosnia	0.0		Germany	1.5
	Guinea	0.0		Morocco[d]	1.5
	Libya	0.0	28	Congo-Brazzaville	1.6
	Tajikistan	0.0		France	1.6
14	Taiwan	0.2		Qatar[d]	1.6
15	Lithuania	0.3		Sweden	1.6
16	Singapore	0.5			

a 2002 b 2000 c 2001 d 1998–2002 e 1998–2000
Notes: Inflation is measured as the % change in the consumer price index. The five-year figures shown are based on the changes in the average level of the index during the relevant years

Debt

Highest foreign debt[a]
$m, 2002

1	Brazil	227,932		25	Czech Republic	26,419
2	China	168,255		26	South Africa	25,041
3	Russia	147,541		27	Algeria	22,800
4	Mexico	141,264		28	Syria	21,504
5	Argentina	132,314		29	United Arab Emirates	19,697
6	Indonesia	132,208		30	Morocco	18,601
7	Turkey	131,556		31	Kazakhstan	17,538
8	South Korea	122,151		32	Lebanon	17,077
9	India	104,429		33	Bangladesh	17,037
10	Poland	69,521		34	Ecuador	16,452
11	Israel	66,104		35	Sudan	16,389
12	Philippines	59,343		36	Croatia	15,347
13	Thailand	59,211		37	Romania	14,683
14	Malaysia	48,557		38	Singapore	14,216
15	Hong Kong	47,996		39	Ukraine	13,555
16	Taiwan	45,078		40	Vietnam	13,349
17	Chile	41,945		41	Slovakia	13,013
18	Hungary	34,958		42	Serbia & Montenegro	12,688
19	Colombia	33,853		43	Tunisia	12,625
20	Pakistan	33,672		44	Côte d'Ivoire	11,816
21	Venezuela	32,563		45	Uruguay	10,736
22	Egypt	30,750		46	Bulgaria	10,462
23	Nigeria	30,476		47	Angola	10,134
24	Peru	28,167		48	Sri Lanka	9,611

Highest foreign debt
As % of exports of goods and services, average, 2000–02

1	Burundi	2,492		21	Guinea	391
2	Liberia	1,584		22	Uganda	378
3	Sierra Leone	1,181		23	Argentina	372
4	Guinea-Bissau	1,145		24	Eritrea	345
5	Rwanda	912		25	Lebanon	333
6	Congo	836		26	Cameroon	321
7	Central African Rep	831		27	Brazil	316
8	Sudan	620		28	Togo	314
9	Ethiopia	614		29	Ghana	291
10	Malawi	609		30	Benin	288
11	Mauritania	600		31	Kirgizstan	282
12	Zambia	566			Bolivia	282
13	Chad	542		33	Peru	280
14	Niger	527			Serbia & Montenegro	280
15	Laos	522		35	Mali	279
16	Nicaragua	501		36	Uruguay	274
17	Burkina Faso	493			Syria	274
18	Tanzania	483		38	Bhutan	265
19	Mozambique	444		39	Pakistan	256
20	Madagascar	417			Gambia, The	256

a Foreign debt is debt owed to non-residents and repayable in foreign currency; the figures shown include liabilities of government, public and private sectors. Developed countries have been excluded.

Highest foreign debt burden
Foreign debt as % of GDP, average, 2000–02

1	Liberia	526	23	Mali	109
2	Guinea-Bissau	354	24	Serbia & Montenegro	108
3	Mauritania	243	25	Madagascar	107
4	Congo-Brazzaville	241		Central African Rep	107
5	Sierra Leone	207	27	Ethiopia	103
6	Congo	178	28	Cameroon	102
7	Zambia	177	29	Mongolia	100
8	Burundi	176	30	Lebanon	96
9	Nicaragua	174	31	Niger	92
10	Malawi	168		Jordan	92
11	Laos	162	33	Indonesia	90
12	Gambia, The	150	34	Gabon	87
13	Mozambique	138		Ecuador	87
14	Sudan	137		Estonia	87
	Ghana	137	37	Honduras	86
16	Kirgizstan	126		Cambodia	86
17	Togo	125		Latvia	86
18	Angola	123		Moldova	86
19	Syria	116		Senegal	86
20	Côte d'Ivoire	114	42	Kazakhstan	85
21	Tajikistan	113		Papua New Guinea	85
22	Guinea	111	44	Rwanda	83

Highest debt service ratios[b]
%

1	Congo	89	22	Mexico	23
2	Brazil	72		Moldova	23
3	Burundi	48		Uzbekistan	23
	Turkey	48		Venezuela	23
5	Lebanon	43	26	Pakistan	22
6	Colombia	39		Romania	22
7	Hungary	37		Slovakia	22
	Kazakhstan	37	29	Algeria	20
9	Peru	33		Lithuania	20
	Uruguay	33		Philippines	20
11	Chile	32	32	Sierra Leone	19
12	Ecuador	30	33	Jamaica	18
13	Zambia	29		Panama	18
14	Bolivia	28	35	Bulgaria	17
	Croatia	28		Côte d'Ivoire	17
16	Kirgizstan	27		Latvia	17
17	Morocco	26		Mauritania	17
18	Poland	25	39	Argentina	16
19	Guinea-Bissau	24		Burkina Faso	16
	Indonesia	24		Guinea	16
	Thailand	24		India	16

b Debt service is the sum of interest and principal repayments (amortisation) due on outstanding foreign debt. The debt service ratio is debt service expressed as a percentage of the country's exports of goods and services.

Aid

Largest bilateral and multilateral donors[a]

$m

1	United States	13,140	13	Norway	1,517
2	Japan	9,731	14	Belgium	996
3	France	5,125	15	Australia	916
4	Germany	4,980	16	Switzerland	863
5	United Kingdom	4,581	17	Austria	488
6	Netherlands	3,068	18	Finland	434
7	Saudi Arabia	2,478	19	Ireland	360
8	Italy	2,157	20	Portugal	293
9	Canada	2,011	21	South Korea	279
10	Sweden	1,848	22	Greece	253
11	Spain	1,559	23	United Arab Emirates	156
12	Denmark	1,540	24	Luxembourg	139

Largest recipients of bilateral and multilateral aid

$m

1	Pakistan	2,144	34	Cambodia	487
2	Mozambique	2,058	35	Ukraine	484
3	Serbia & Montenegro	1,931	36	Tunisia	475
4	West Bank and Gaza	1,616	37	Burkina Faso	473
5	China	1,476	38	Mali	472
6	India	1,463	39	Hungary	471
7	Indonesia	1,308	40	Lebanon	456
8	Ethiopia	1,307	41	Senegal	449
9	Russia	1,301	42	Colombia	441
10	Egypt	1,286	43	Honduras	435
11	Afghanistan	1,285	44	Angola	421
12	Vietnam	1,277	45	Congo-Brazzaville	420
13	Tanzania	1,233	46	French Polynesia	418
14	Poland	1,160	47	Czech Republic	393
15	Côte d'Ivoire	1,069		Kenya	393
16	Bangladesh	913	49	Bulgaria	381
17	Congo	807	50	Malawi	377
18	Israel	754	51	Brazil	376
19	Romania	701	52	Madagascar	373
20	Bolivia	681	53	Nepal	365
21	South Africa	657	54	Algeria	361
22	Ghana	653	55	Rwanda	356
23	Zambia	641	56	Mauritania	355
24	Uganda	638	57	Sierra Leone	353
25	Morocco	636	58	Sudan	351
	Turkey	636	59	Azerbaijan	349
27	Cameroon	632	60	Sri Lanka	344
28	Bosnia	587	61	New Caledonia	324
29	Yemen	584	62	Albania	317
30	Philippines	560	63	Nigeria	314
31	Jordan	534	64	Georgia	313
32	Nicaragua	517	65	Niger	298
33	Peru	491	66	Thailand	296

Largest bilateral and multilateral donors[a]
% of GDP

1	Saudi Arabia	1.31	13	Canada	0.28
2	Denmark	0.96	14	Germany	0.27
3	Norway	0.89		Portugal	0.27
4	Sweden	0.83	16	Australia	0.26
5	Netherlands	0.81		Austria	0.26
6	Luxembourg	0.77		Spain	0.26
7	Belgium	0.43	19	Japan	0.23
8	Ireland	0.40	20	New Zealand	0.22
9	France	0.38		United Arab Emirates	0.22
10	Finland	0.35	22	Greece	0.21
11	Switzerland	0.32	23	Italy	0.20
12	United Kingdom	0.31	24	Iceland	0.15

Largest recipients of bilateral and multilateral aid
$ per head

1	French Polynesia	1,761	34	Guinea-Bissau	48
2	New Caledonia	1,497	35	Afghanistan	47
3	West Bank and Gaza	523	36	Senegal	46
4	Netherlands Antilles	423	37	Gambia	45
5	Serbia & Montenegro	181		Rwanda	45
6	Bosnia	145	39	Azerbaijan	43
7	Macedonia	136		Mali	43
8	Congo	135	41	Cameroon	42
9	Mauritania	129		Fiji	42
10	Aruba	122	43	Burkina Faso	41
11	Djibouti	121	44	Cambodia	40
12	Mozambique	114	45	Papua New Guinea	39
13	Bahrain	108	46	Croatia	38
14	Jordan	106		Kirgizstan	38
15	Lebanon	104	48	Lesotho	37
16	Albania	100	49	El Salvador	36
17	Nicaragua	99		Malawi	36
18	Armenia	95		Tanzania	36
19	Belize	90	52	Benin	34
20	Bhutan	89	53	Ghana	33
21	Mongolia	86		Guinea	33
	Slovenia	86		Moldova	33
23	Bolivia	80	56	Yemen	32
24	Namibia	75	57	Angola	31
25	Sierra Leone	69	58	Chad	29
26	Honduras	66		Malta	29
27	Côte d'Ivoire	65	60	Uganda	28
28	Zambia	62	61	Suriname	28
29	Georgia	60	62	Tajikistan	27
30	Gabon	57		Niger	27
31	Eritrea	55	64	Burundi	25
32	Laos	51	65	Madagascar	23
33	Tunisia	49		Swaziland	23

a China also provides aid, but does not disclose amounts.

Industry and services

Largest industrial output

$bn

1	United States	2,151		26	Poland	50
2	Japan	1,035		27	Malaysia	45
3	China	647		28	Iran	43
4	Germany	529		29	Ireland	42
5	United Kingdom	367			Turkey	42
6	France	319		31	Israel	41
7	Italy	302		32	Denmark	39
8	Canada	218		33	Venezuela	38
9	South Korea	195		34	Finland	37
10	Spain	178			Portugal	37
11	Mexico	154		36	Argentina	31
12	India	124		37	South Africa	30
13	Australia	109		38	Puerto Rico	29
14	Russia	106			Singapore	29
15	Saudi Arabia	97		40	Algeria	28
16	Netherlands	96			Egypt	28
17	Taiwan	87		42	Greece	26
18	Brazil	82		43	Czech Republic	25
19	Indonesia	77			Philippines	25
20	Switzerland	73		45	Colombia	22
21	Norway	64		46	Hong Kong	21
22	Austria	59		47	Chile	19
	Belgium	59		48	Hungary	17
	Sweden	59		49	New Zealand	16
25	Thailand	54			Romania	16

Highest growth in industrial output

Average annual real % growth, 1992–2002[a]

1	Equatorial Guinea	44.7	11	Georgia	10.4
2	Bosnia	19.0		Laos	10.4
3	Cambodia	15.6	13	Bhutan	9.4
4	Mozambique	15.1		Mali	9.4
5	Eritrea	13.0	15	Albania	8.5
6	Ireland	12.0	16	Syria	7.7
7	China	11.9	17	Ethiopia	7.3
8	Myanmar	11.4	18	Bangladesh	7.2
9	Vietnam	11.2		Malaysia	7.2
10	Uganda	10.7	20	Chad	7.0

Lowest growth in industrial output

Average annual real % growth, 1992–2002[a]

1	Tajikistan	-11.2	11	Zimbabwe	-2.1
2	West Bank and Gaza	-8.6	12	Uruguay	-1.8
3	Kirgizstan	-6.7	13	Macedonia	-1.6
4	Ukraine	-6.3	14	Rwanda	-1.5
5	Moldova	-5.1	15	Bulgaria	-1.4
6	Congo	-3.8	16	Hong Kong	-1.2
7	Sierra Leone	-3.2	17	Iran	-1.1
8	Zambia	-2.3	18	Guinea-Bissau	-1.0
9	Kazakhstan	-2.2	19	Japan	-0.9
	Russia	-2.2		Malawi	-0.9

Largest manufacturing output
$bn

1	United States	1,473		Thailand	43
2	Japan	815	22	Australia	42
3	China	448	23	Belgium[b]	39
4	Germany	407	24	Ireland	33
5	United Kingdom	283	25	Malaysia	29
6	Italy	218		Poland	29
7	France	215	27	Finland	27
8	Canada	152		Israel	27
9	South Korea	139		Puerto Rico[b]	27
10	Mexico	110	30	Turkey	26
11	Russia	96	31	Denmark	24
12	Spain	95		Portugal	24
13	Taiwan	73	33	Singapore	23
14	India	72	34	Argentina	21
15	Switzerland	62	35	Norway	19
16	Netherlands	56		Saudi Arabia	19
17	Sweden	55	37	Philippines	18
18	Brazil	51		South Africa	18
19	Austria	46	39	Egypt	16
20	Indonesia	43	40	Iran	15

Largest services output
$bn

1	United States	6,050	26	Turkey	94
2	Japan	2,886	27	Greece	82
3	Germany	1,237		Saudi Arabia	82
4	United Kingdom	1,009	29	Portugal	77
5	France	929	30	Finland	73
6	Italy	728	31	Indonesia	66
7	Canada	513	32	Israel	64
8	China	424	33	South Africa	61
9	Mexico	402		Thailand	61
10	Spain	392	35	Argentina	56
11	Brazil	284	36	Iran	54
12	Australia	275	37	Singapore	52
13	Netherlands	264	38	Ireland[b]	50
14	South Korea	263	39	Venezuela	48
15	India	236	40	Egypt	42
16	Russia	190	41	Colombia	41
17	Taiwan	189		Malaysia	41
18	Switzerland	173		Philippines	41
19	Belgium	157	44	New Zealand	40
20	Sweden	147	45	Puerto Rico[b]	38
21	Hong Kong	141	46	Hungary	36
22	Austria	120	47	Czech Republic	35
23	Poland	110	48	Peru	33
24	Denmark	105	49	Chile	32
25	Norway	101	50	Pakistan	29

a Or nearest available years.
b 2001

Agriculture

Most economically dependent on agriculture
% of GDP from agriculture

1	Guinea-Bissau	62	24	Bhutan	34
2	Central African Rep	57		Ghana	34
	Myanmar[a]	57		Mali	34
4	Congo	56	27	Burkina Faso	32
5	Sierra Leone	53		Madagascar	32
6	Afghanistan	52		Uganda	32
7	Laos[a]	51	30	Mongolia	30
8	Burundi	49	31	Turkmenistan[b]	29
9	Tanzania	44	32	Papua New Guinea	27
10	Cameroon	43	33	Armenia	26
11	Nepal	41		Côte d'Ivoire	26
	Rwanda	41		Gambia, The	26
13	Ethiopia	40	36	Albania	25
	Niger	40	37	Guinea	24
	Togo	40		Moldova	24
16	Kirgizstan	39		Tajikistan	24
	Sudan	39	40	Bangladesh	23
18	Chad	38		Belize[a]	23
19	Malawi	37		India	23
	Nigeria	37		Mozambique	23
21	Benin	36		Pakistan	23
	Cambodia	36		Syria	23
23	Uzbekistan	35		Vietnam	23

Least economically dependent on agriculture
% of GDP from agriculture

1	Hong Kong	0.1		Italy	2.7
	Singapore	0.1		Netherlands	2.7
3	Bahrain	0.7	26	Oman	3.0
	Luxembourg	0.7	27	Slovenia	3.1
	Puerto Rico[a]	0.7	28	Poland	3.2
6	United Kingdom	1.0	29	Finland	3.4
7	Germany	1.2		Spain	3.4
	Switzerland[a]	1.2	31	New Caledonia[c]	3.7
9	Belgium	1.3	32	Czech Republic	3.8
	Japan	1.3		South Africa	3.8
11	Sweden	1.8	34	Australia	3.9
12	Norway	1.9	35	Mexico	4.0
	Taiwan	1.9		South Korea	4.0
	United States	1.9	37	Slovakia	4.2
15	Canada	2.1	38	Hungary	4.3
16	Jordan	2.2	39	French Polynesia[a]	4.7
17	Austria	2.3		Latvia	4.7
18	Ireland	2.4	41	Saudi Arabia	5.1
19	Botswana	2.5	42	Estonia	5.5
20	Denmark	2.6	43	Panama	5.7
	Malta[a]	2.6	44	Barbados	5.8
	Venezuela	2.6		Portugal	5.8
23	France	2.7		Russia	5.8

a 2000   b 2001   c 1997

Highest growth

Average annual real % growth, 1992–2002[a]

1	Liberia	15.4	10	Peru	6.2
2	United Arab Emirates	13.0	11	Belize	6.0
3	Malawi	8.3	12	Cameroon	5.8
4	Equatorial Guinea	7.9	13	Benin	5.7
5	Sudan	7.7	14	Bosnia	5.0
6	Mozambique	7.1		Yemen	5.0
7	Myanmar	6.5	16	Czech Republic	4.9
8	Zambia	6.4		Laos	4.9
9	Slovakia	6.3	18	Guinea	4.7

Lowest growth

Average annual real % growth, 1992–2002[a]

1	Moldova	-8.5	9	Japan	-2.6
2	West Bank and Gaza	-7.6	10	Luxembourg	-2.5
3	Hong Kong	-5.4	11	Estonia	-2.4
4	Kazakhstan	-4.9	12	Belarus	-2.3
5	Haiti	-4.7	13	United Kingdom	-1.9
6	Eritrea	-4.5	14	Latvia	-1.7
7	Jordan	-4.3		Ukraine	-1.7
8	Singapore	-3.2	16	Tajikistan	-1.6

Biggest producers

'000 tonnes

Cereals

1	China	399,999	6	Indonesia	61,106
2	United States	298,787	7	Brazil	50,237
3	India	211,750	8	Germany	43,391
4	Russia	84,849	9	Bangladesh	39,528
5	France	69,661	10	Ukraine	37,983

Meat

1	China	67,772	6	India	5,762
2	United States	39,195	7	Spain	5,239
3	Brazil	16,605	8	Mexico	4,808
4	France	6,521	9	Russia	4,690
5	Germany	6,503	10	Canada	4,268

Fruit

1	China	70,676	6	Spain	15,739
2	India	46,641	7	Mexico	14,033
3	Brazil	34,370	8	Iran	12,721
4	United States	30,372	9	Philippines	11,440
5	Italy	16,076	10	Turkey	10,726

Vegetables

1	China	383,385	6	Egypt	14,115
2	India	78,191	7	Russia	13,365
3	United States	37,884	8	Japan	12,243
4	Turkey	24,616	9	Spain	11,960
5	Italy	14,155	10	Iran	11,670

a Or nearest available years.

Commodities

Wheat

Top 10 producers '000 tonnes		Top 10 consumers '000 tonnes	
1 EU15	103,200	1 China	108,800
2 China	91,300	2 EU15	96,100
3 India	71,800	3 India	71,200
4 Russia	50,600	4 Russia	38,600
5 United States	44,000	5 United States	30,700
6 Ukraine	20,000	6 Pakistan	18,300
7 Pakistan	18,200	7 Turkey	17,800
8 Turkey	17,300	8 Iran	13,600
9 Canada	16,200	Ukraine	13,600
10 Iran	12,400	10 Egypt	13,400

Rice[a]

Top 10 producers '000 tonnes		Top 10 consumers '000 tonnes	
1 China	122,180	1 China	134,800
2 India	75,700	2 India	83,680
3 Indonesia	33,411	3 Indonesia	36,500
4 Bangladesh	25,360	4 Bangladesh	26,100
5 Vietnam	21,527	5 Vietnam	17,800
6 Thailand	17,124	6 Myanmar	10,100
7 Myanmar	10,440	7 Thailand	9,922
8 Philippines	8,450	8 Japan	8,790
9 Japan	8,089	9 Philippines	9,550
10 Brazil	6,935	10 Brazil	8,100

Sugar[b]

Top 10 producers '000 tonnes		Top 10 consumers '000 tonnes	
1 Brazil	23,600	1 India	17,900
2 India	19,500	2 EU15	15,000
3 EU15	18,200	3 Brazil	10,500
4 China	9,800	4 China	10,000
5 United States	6,800	5 United States	9,100
6 Thailand	6,400	6 Russia	6,500
7 Australia	5,600	7 Mexico	5,100
8 Mexico	5,100	8 Indonesia	3,700
9 Cuba	3,500	9 Pakistan	3,500
10 Pakistan	3,300	10 Japan	2,400

Coarse grains[c]

Top 5 producers '000 tonnes		Top 5 consumers '000 tonnes	
1 United States	245,000	1 United States	215,800
2 China	130,400	2 China	131,800
3 EU15	106,800	3 EU15	101,100
4 Brazil	49,600	4 Brazil	41,100
5 Russia	34,700	5 Mexico	35,000

Tea

Top 10 producers '000 tonnes		*Top 10 consumers* '000 tonnes	
1 India	826	1 India	693
2 China	745	2 China	495
3 Sri Lanka	311	3 Russia	165
4 Kenya	287	4 Turkey	142
5 Indonesia	173	5 United Kingdom	137
6 Turkey	142	6 Japan	136
7 Japan	84	7 Pakistan	98
Vietnam	84	8 United States	93
9 Argentina	58	9 Iran	92
10 Iran	53	10 Iraq	81

Coffee

Top 10 producers '000 tonnes		*Top 10 consumers* '000 tonnes	
1 Brazil	2,909	1 United States	1,182
2 Colombia	703	2 Brazil	810
3 Vietnam	693	3 Germany	566
4 Indonesia	340	4 Japan	405
5 India	275	5 France	334
6 Guatemala	256	6 Italy	320
7 Mexico	240	7 Spain	171
8 Ethiopia	222	8 United Kingdom	126
9 Uganda	175	9 Netherlands	111
10 Peru	174	10 Ethiopia	110

Cocoa

Top 10 producers '000 tonnes		*Top 10 consumers* '000 tonnes	
1 Côte d'Ivoire	1,265	1 United States	663
2 Indonesia	455	2 Germany	283
3 Ghana	341	3 France	215
4 Nigeria	185	4 United Kingdom	207
5 Cameroon	131	5 Russia	180
6 Brazil	124	6 Japan	145
7 Ecuador	81	7 Brazil	105
8 Dominican Republic	45	8 Italy	100
9 Colombia	38	9 Spain	70
Papua New Guinea	38	10 Mexico	65

a Milled.
b Raw.
c Includes: maize (corn), barley, sorghum, rye, oats and millet.

Copper

Top 10 producers[a] '000 tonnes		Top 10 consumers[b] '000 tonnes	
1 Chile	4,581	1 China	2,684
2 Indonesia	1,163	2 United States	2,347
3 United States	1,160	3 Japan	1,164
4 Australia	879	4 Germany	1,066
5 Peru	843	5 South Korea	936
6 Russia	685	6 Italy	673
7 Canada	604	7 Taiwan	656
8 China	556	8 France	561
9 Poland	503	9 Mexico	383
10 Kazakhstan	473	10 Russia	355

Lead

Top 10 producers[a] '000 tonnes		Top 10 consumers[b] '000 tonnes	
1 Australia	683	1 United States	1,682
2 China	568	2 China	921
3 United States	449	3 Germany	388
4 Peru	298	4 South Korea	321
5 Mexico	139	5 United Kingdom	306
6 Canada	97	6 Japan	298
7 Morocco	61	7 Italy	287
8 Poland	57	8 Mexico	261
9 South Africa	50	9 Spain	238
10 Kazakhstan	45	10 France	229

Zinc

Top 10 producers[a] '000 tonnes		Top 10 consumers[c] '000 tonnes	
1 China	1,499	1 China	1,676
2 Australia	1,469	2 United States	1,312
3 Peru	1,222	3 Japan	603
4 Canada	916	4 Germany	496
5 United States	787	5 South Korea	467
6 Mexico	451	6 Italy	375
7 Kazakhstan	393	7 Belgium	357
8 Ireland	253	8 India	315
9 India	234	9 France	303
10 Russia	174	10 Taiwan	302

Tin

Top 5 producers[a] '000 tonnes		Top 5 consumers[b] '000 tonnes	
1 Indonesia	78.6	1 China	53.2
2 China	61.8	2 United States	45.7
3 Peru	38.8	3 Japan	26.8
4 Brazil	13.8	4 Germany	19.5
5 Bolivia	13.2	5 South Korea	17.7

Nickel

Top 10 producers[a] '000 tonnes		*Top 10 consumers[b]* '000 tonnes	
1 Russia	267.3	**1** Japan	169.6
2 Australia	207.0	**2** Germany	116.7
3 Canada	189.3	**3** United States	106.5
4 Indonesia	103.7	**4** Taiwan	103.6
5 New Caledonia	99.9	**5** South Korea	95.6
6 Cuba	75.1	**6** China	85.3
7 China	54.6	**7** Italy	71.6
8 Colombia	44.0	**8** Finland	68.2
9 South Africa	38.5	**9** UnitedKingdom	58.9
10 Brazil	30.0	**10** France	58.2

Aluminium

Top 10 producers[d] '000 tonnes		*Top 10 consumers[e]* '000 tonnes	
1 China	4,335	**1** United States	5,509
2 Russia	3,348	**2** China	4,129
3 Canada	2,709	**3** Japan	2,010
4 United States	2,705	**4** Germany	1,670
5 Australia	1,836	**5** Russia	990
6 Brazil	1,318	**6** South Korea	921
7 Norway	1,096	**7** Italy	851
8 South Africa	704	**8** France	762
9 India	671	**9** Canada	747
10 Germany	653	**10** India	604

Precious metals

Gold[a] Top 10 producers tonnes		*Silver[a]* Top 10 producers tonnes	
1 South Africa	395.2	**1** Peru	2,761
2 United States	285.5	**2** Mexico	2,749
3 Australia	266.1	**3** Australia	2,077
4 China	179.6	**4** China	2,000
5 Russia	171.0	**5** United States	1,419
6 Peru	157.3	**6** Canada	1,408
7 Canada	152.1	**7** Poland	1,221
8 Indonesia	142.2	**8** Chile	1,205
9 Uzbekistan	82.0	**9** Kazakhstan	816
10 Ghana	69.6	**10** Bolivia	461

Platinum Top 3 producers tonnes		*Palladium* Top 3 producers tonnes	
1 South Africa	138.1	**1** South Africa	67.2
2 Russia	29.6	**2** Russia	60.0
3 North America	11.0	**3** North America	30.8

a Mine production. b Refined consumption. c Slab consumption.
d Primary refined production. e Primary refined consumption.

Rubber (natural and synthetic)

Top 10 producers '000 tonnes		Top 10 consumers '000 tonnes	
1 Thailand	2,737	1 China	3,060
2 United States	2,150	2 United States	3,006
3 Indonesia	1,663	3 Japan	1,845
4 China	1,601	4 India	872
5 Japan	1,522	5 Germany	859
6 Russia	919	6 South Korea	710
7 Germany	869	7 France	700
8 India	718	8 Brazil	577
9 France	681	9 Russia	570
10 South Korea	678	10 Spain	476

Raw wool

Top 10 producers[a] '000 tonnes		Top 10 consumers[b] '000 tonnes	
1 Australia	544	1 China	368
2 China	302	2 Italy	134
3 New Zealand	235	3 Russia	89
4 Russia	133	4 India	63
5 Iran	74	5 Turkey	50
6 Argentina	72	6 South Korea	44
7 Turkey	70	7 Iran	38
8 United Kingdom	50	8 United Kingdom	31
9 South Africa	45	9 Japan	29
10 Uruguay	43	10 Algeria	27

Cotton

Top 10 producers '000 tonnes		Top 10 consumers '000 tonnes	
1 China	4,920	1 China	6,500
2 United States	3,747	2 India	2,927
3 India	2,312	3 Pakistan	2,042
4 Pakistan	1,736	4 United States	1,583
5 Uzbekistan	1,022	5 Turkey	1,350
6 Turkey	900	6 Brazil	760
7 Brazil	848	7 Indonesia	500
8 Australia	386	8 Mexico	460
9 Greece	375	9 Thailand	415
10 Syria	245	10 Bangladesh	300

Major oil seeds[c]

Top 5 producers '000 tonnes		Top 5 consumers '000 tonnes	
1 United States	83,780	1 United States	93,290
2 Brazil	53,212	2 China	62,337
3 China	52,170	3 EU15	32,409
4 Argentina	38,705	4 Brazil	31,310
5 India	18,520	5 Argentina	28,010

Oil[d]

Top 15 producers *'000 barrels per day*		*Top 15 consumers* *'000 barrels per day*	
1 Saudi Arabia[e]	8,680	1 United States	19,708
2 United States	7,698	2 China	5,362
3 Russia	7,698	3 Japan	5,337
4 Mexico	3,585	4 Germany	2,709
5 China	3,387	5 Russia	2,469
6 Iran[e]	3,366	6 South Korea	2,288
7 Norway	3,330	7 India	2,090
8 Venezuela[e]	2,942	8 Canada	1,988
9 Canada	2,880	9 France	1,967
10 United Kingdom	2,463	10 Italy	1,943
11 United Arab Emirates[e]	2,270	11 Brazil	1,849
12 Iraq[e]	2,030	12 Mexico	1,791
13 Nigeria[e]	2,013	13 United Kingdom	1,675
14 Kuwait[e]	1,871	14 Spain	1,520
15 Algeria[e]	1,659	15 Saudi Arabia[e]	1,363

Natural gas

Top 10 producers *Billion cubic metres*		*Top 10 consumers* *Billion cubic metres*	
1 Russia	554.9	1 United States	667.5
2 United States	547.7	2 Russia	388.4
3 Canada	183.5	3 United Kingdom	94.5
4 United Kingdom	103.1	4 Germany	82.6
5 Algeria	80.4	5 Canada	80.7
6 Indonesia	70.6	6 Japan	77.4
7 Norway	65.4	7 Ukraine	69.8
8 Iran	64.5	8 Iran	67.9
9 Netherlands	59.9	9 Italy	63.6
10 Saudi Arabia	56.4	10 Saudi Arabia	56.4

Coal

Top 10 producers *Million tonnes oil equivalent*		*Top 10 consumers* *Million tonnes oil equivalent*	
1 China	703.0	1 China	663.4
2 United States	571.7	2 United States	553.8
3 Australia	183.6	3 India	180.8
4 India	168.4	4 Japan	105.3
5 South Africa	126.8	5 Russia	98.5
6 Russia	113.8	6 Germany	84.6
7 Poland	70.8	7 South Africa	81.8
8 Indonesia	63.3	8 Poland	56.4
9 Germany	54.8	9 Australia	49.5
10 Ukraine	43.0	10 South Korea	49.1

a Greasy basis.
b Clean basis.
c Soybeans, sunflower seed, cottonseed, groundnuts and rapeseed.
d Includes crude oil, shale oil, oil sands and natural gas liquids.
e Opec members.

Energy

Largest producers
Million tonnnes oil equivalent, 2001

1	United States	1,711.8	16	South Africa	145.3
2	China	1,138.6	17	United Arab Emirates	144.6
3	Russia	996.1	18	Algeria	144.3
4	Saudi Arabia	476.8	19	Germany	133.7
5	India	438.1	20	France	132.7
6	Canada	379.2	21	Iraq	123.3
7	United Kingdom	261.9	22	Kuwait	108.9
8	Australia	250.4	23	Japan	104.0
9	Iran	246.6	24	Kazakhstan	83.8
10	Indonesia	234.3	25	Ukraine	83.4
11	Mexico	230.2	26	Argentina	82.9
12	Norway	226.6	27	Poland	79.9
13	Venezuela	216.0	28	Malaysia	77.6
14	Nigeria	207.0	29	Libya	74.4
15	Brazil	145.9	30	Colombia	73.9

Largest consumers
Million tonnnes oil equivalent, 2001

1	United States	2,281.4	16	Spain	127.4
2	China	1,139.4	17	Iran	120.0
3	Russia	621.3	18	Australia	115.6
4	India	531.5	19	Saudi Arabia	110.6
5	Japan	520.7	20	South Africa	107.7
6	Germany	351.1	21	Nigeria	95.4
7	France	265.6	22	Poland	90.6
8	Canada	248.2	23	Netherlands	77.2
9	United Kingdom	235.2	24	Thailand	75.5
10	South Korea	194.8	25	Turkey	72.5
11	Brazil	185.0	26	Pakistan	64.5
12	Italy	172.0	27	Belgium	59.0
13	Indonesia	152.3	28	Argentina	57.6
	Mexico	152.3	29	Venezuela	54.9
15	Ukraine	141.6	30	Malaysia	51.6

Energy efficiency[a]

Most efficient
GDP per unit of energy use, 2001

Least efficient
GDP per unit of energy use, 2001

1	Hong Kong	9.9		1	Uzbekistan	0.7
2	Bangladesh	9.7		2	Nigeria	1.1
	Uruguay	9.7		3	Tanzania	1.2
4	Peru	9.4			Zambia	1.2
5	Namibia	9.3		5	Trinidad & Tobago	1.3
6	Morocco	9.0			Turkmenistan	1.3
7	Costa Rica	8.3		7	Ukraine	1.4
8	Colombia	7.9		8	Russia	1.6
9	Italy	7.8		9	Azerbaijan	1.7
10	Denmark	7.3			Kazakhstan	1.7
	Sri Lanka	7.3			Moldova	1.7
					Tajikistan	1.7

a PPP$, per kg of oil equivalent.   b 2000

Highest net energy importers
% of commercial energy use, 2001

1	Hong Kong	100		Portugal	86
	Singapore	100	14	Italy	85
3	Cyprusb	98	15	South Korea	82
	Israel	98	16	Dominican Republic	81
	Luxembourgb	98	17	Japan	80
	Moldova	98	18	Panama	79
7	Lebanon	97	19	Belgium	78
8	Jordan	95	20	Namibia	75
	Morocco	95	21	Armenia	74
10	Ireland	88		Spain	74
	Jamaica	88	23	Austria	68
12	Belarus	86			

Lowest net energy importers
% of commercial energy use, 2001

1	Congo-Brazzaville	-1,368	14	Venezuela	-294
2	Bruneib	-866	15	Turkmenistan	-229
3	Gabon	-769	16	Ecuador	-162
4	Norway	-752	17	Colombia	-153
5	Kuwait	-565	18	Syria	-146
6	Oman	-546	19	Australia	-117
7	Yemen	-537		Nigeria	-117
8	Angola	-415	21	Trinidad & Tobago	-111
9	Algeria	-390	22	Kazakhstan	-108
10	Libya	-365	23	Iran	-106
11	United Arab Emirates	-343	24	Cameroon	-94
12	Iraq	-333	25	Azerbaijan	-69
13	Saudi Arabia	-331			

Largest consumption per head
Kg of oil equivalent, 2001

1	Qatarb	26,773	17	Saudi Arabia	5,195
2	Icelandb	12,246	18	Netherlands	4,814
3	United Arab Emirates	10,860	19	New Zealand	4,714
4	Bahrainb	9,858	20	France	4,487
5	Luxembourgb	8,409	21	Russia	4,293
6	United States	7,996	22	Germany	4,264
7	Canada	7,985	23	South Korea	4,114
8	Kuwait	7,195	24	Japan	4,099
9	Singapore	7,058	25	Czech Republic	4,049
10	Trinidad & Tobago	6,708	26	Oman	4,029
11	Finland	6,518	27	United Kingdom	3,982
12	Australia	5,956	28	Ireland	3,876
13	Norway	5,896	29	Switzerland	3,875
14	Bruneib	5,870	30	Austria	3,825
15	Sweden	5,740	31	Denmark	3,692
16	Belgium	5,735	32	Slovakia	3,480

Note: Consumption data for small countries, especially oil producers, can be unreliable, often leading to unrealistically high consumption per head rates.

Workers of the world

Highest % of population in labour force

1	China	57.8	21	New Zealand	49.9
2	Switzerland	56.7	22	Ethiopia	49.7
3	Thailand	54.7	23	Slovenia	49.2
4	Iceland	54.2	24	Austria	49.1
5	Canada	53.8	25	United States	49.0
	Denmark	53.8	26	Slovakia	48.6
7	Japan	53.1	27	Germany	48.5
8	Norway	52.8	28	Cyprus	48.0
9	Portugal	51.9		Estonia	48.0
	Singapore	51.9		Peru	48.0
11	Hong Kong	51.8	31	Latvia	47.9
12	Netherlands	51.3	32	Brazil	47.9
13	Romania	51.1	33	Russia	47.7
14	Australia	50.6	34	Bahamas	47.6
	Finland	50.6	35	Bahrain	47.4
16	Lithuania	50.5	36	Bangladesh	47.3
17	United Kingdom	50.5		Colombia	47.3
18	Czech Republic	50.3	38	South Korea	47.1
	Macau	50.3	39	Uruguay	46.9
20	Sweden	50.2	40	Kazakhstan	46.8

Most male workforce
Highest % men in workforce

1	Algeria	87.8
2	West Bank and Gaza	86.5
3	Pakistan	84.4
4	Oman	82.4
5	Syria	78.5
6	Bahrain	78.3
7	Egypt	78.1
8	Guatemala	77.4
9	Morocco	74.8
10	Turkey	72.3
11	Nicaragua	69.2
12	Malta	68.3
13	Dominican Republic	68.2
14	Chile	66.7
15	Sri Lanka	66.2
16	Malaysia	65.3
	Mauritius	65.3
	Mexico	65.3
19	Costa Rica	64.6
20	Honduras	64.3
	Panama	64.3
22	Suriname	63.1
23	Bangladesh	62.2
24	Indonesia	61.8
25	Trinidad & Tobago	61.7

Most female workforce
Highest % women in workforce

1	Belarus	52.9
2	Cambodia	51.6
3	Moldova	50.8
4	Malawi	50.2
5	Mongolia	49.6
6	Bahamas	49.4
7	Estonia	48.9
8	Lithuania	48.7
	Ukraine	48.7
10	Latvia	48.4
11	Zimbabwe	48.2
12	Sweden	48.0
13	Finland	47.9
14	Azerbaijan	47.8
15	Russia	47.7
16	Armenia	47.6
17	Georgia	47.3
18	Macau	47.2
19	Bulgaria	47.1
20	Norway	46.9
21	Denmark	46.8
22	Iceland	46.7
23	United States	46.6
24	Romania	46.2
	Slovenia	46.2

Lowest % of population in labour force

1	Oman	20.3		Honduras	38.5
2	West Bank and Gaza	20.4	22	Mexico	39.7
3	Algeria	27.0	23	Malta	40.1
4	Pakistan	29.0	24	Israel	40.4
5	Togo	29.6	25	Georgia	40.5
6	Egypt	30.0	26	Macedonia	41.2
7	Botswana	30.4	27	Malaysia	41.3
	Puerto Rico	30.4	28	Zimbabwe	41.5
9	Syria	31.9	29	Hungary	41.6
10	Congo-Brazzaville	32.3	30	Italy	41.7
11	Morocco	32.5	31	Sri Lanka	42.0
12	Turkey	33.6	32	Greece	42.1
13	Suriname	34.6	33	Costa Rica	42.3
14	Guatemala	35.0	34	Argentina	42.4
15	Nicaragua	36.5	35	Bulgaria	42.9
16	Mongolia	37.1	36	Belgium	43.0
17	Panama	37.6	37	Luxembourg	43.3
18	Armenia	38.1		Philippines	43.3
19	Chile	38.4	39	Dominican Republic	43.7
20	El Salvador	38.5	40	Trinidad & Tobago	43.8

Highest rate of unemployment
% of labour force[a]

1	Namibia	33.8	21	Lithuania	13.8
2	Macedonia	31.9		Serbia & Montenegro	13.8
3	West Bank and Gaza	31.3	23	Jordan	13.2
4	South Africa	29.5		Panama	13.2
5	Algeria	27.3	25	Georgia	12.3
6	Poland	19.9		Iran	12.3
7	Slovakia	18.5		Puerto Rico	12.3
8	Argentina	17.8	28	Nicaragua	12.2
9	Bulgaria	17.6	29	Latvia	12.0
10	Uruguay	17.2	30	Syria	11.7
11	Albania	15.8	31	Morocco	11.6
	Botswana	15.8	32	Yemen	11.5
	Venezuela	15.8	33	Spain	11.4
14	Colombia	15.7	34	Trinidad & Tobago	10.8
	Jamaica	15.7	35	Turkey	10.6
16	Dominican Republic	15.6	36	Barbados	10.3
17	Croatia	14.8		Estonia	10.3
18	Burundi	14.0		Israel	10.3
	Netherlands Antilles	14.0	39	Ukraine	10.2
	Suriname	14.0	40	Philippines	9.8

a ILO definition.
Note: Data refer to the latest year available, 1998–2002.

The business world

Global competitiveness

	Overall	Government	Trade blocks
1	United States	Singapore	United States
2	Singapore	Australia	Japan
3	Canada	Hong Kong	Switzerland
4	Australia	Finland	Sweden
5	Iceland	Denmark	Denmark
6	Hong Kong	Canada	Canada
7	Denmark	Iceland	Finland
8	Finland	Chile	Iceland
9	Luxembourg	Luxembourg	Singapore
10	Ireland	United States	Germany
11	Sweden	Switzerland	Norway
12	Taiwan	New Zealand	Australia
13	Austria	Ireland	Netherlands
14	Switzerland	Austria	France
15	Netherlands	Estonia	Austria
16	Malaysia	Malaysia	Belgium
17	Norway	Norway	Israel
18	New Zealand	Taiwan	Taiwan
19	Germany	Sweden	Luxembourg
20	United Kingdom	Thailand	Hong Kong
21	Japan	China	United Kingdom
22	China	Spain	Ireland
23	Belgium	Netherlands	New Zealand
24	Chile	Slovakia	South Korea
25	Estonia	South Africa	Malaysia
26	Thailand	United Kingdom	Spain
27	France	Jordan	Hungary
28	Spain	Portugal	Czech Republic
29	Israel	India	Estonia
30	India	Germany	Portugal
31	South Korea	Colombia	Italy
32	Portugal	South Korea	Slovenia
33	Slovakia	Japan	Greece
34	Colombia	Russia	Jordan
35	Hungary	France	China
36	Czech Republic	Philippines	Slovakia
37	Greece	Hungary	Russia
38	Slovenia	Belgium	Chile
39	Jordan	Israel	Colombia
40	South Africa	Slovenia	Poland
41	Russia	Czech Republic	Argentina
42	Italy	Greece	Thailand
43	Philippines	Mexico	Romania
44	Brazil	Romania	Turkey

Notes: Rankings reflect assessments for the ability of a country to achieve sustained high rates of GDP growth per head. Column 1 is based on 259 criteria covering: the openness of an economy, the role of the government, the development of financial markets, the quality of infrastructure, technology, business management and judicial and political institutions and labour-market flexibility. Column 2 looks at the extent to which government policies are conducive to competitiveness. Column 3 is based on the extent to which a country is integrated into regional trade blocks.

The business environment

		2004–08 score	1999–2003 score	1999–2003 ranking
1	Canada	8.58	8.55	2
	Netherlands	8.58	8.54	3
3	Finland	8.47	8.26	8
4	United States	8.45	8.61	1
5	Singapore	8.44	8.40	6
6	United Kingdom	8.42	8.52	4
7	Hong Kong	8.41	8.51	5
8	Denmark	8.39	8.00	12
9	Switzerland	8.30	8.33	7
10	Ireland	8.26	8.12	9
	Sweden	8.26	8.00	11
12	France	8.11	7.76	16
13	Germany	8.09	7.81	14
14	Belgium	8.03	7.83	13
15	Norway	8.01	7.41	18
16	Taiwan	7.98	7.36	19
	Australia	7.98	7.78	15
18	New Zealand	7.97	8.10	10
	Chile	7.97	7.33	20
20	Austria	7.87	7.55	17
21	Spain	7.80	7.24	21
22	South Korea	7.48	6.74	24
23	Portugal	7.43	6.70	26
24	Israel	7.36	6.69	27
25	Czech Republic	7.27	6.55	31
26	Italy	7.22	6.74	23
27	Japan	7.20	6.66	28
28	Poland	7.15	6.42	32
29	Hungary	7.14	6.60	30
30	Malaysia	7.02	6.93	22
31	Thailand	6.94	6.73	25
32	Mexico	6.78	6.61	29
33	Greece	6.77	6.15	33
34	Slovakia	6.54	5.78	35
35	Philippines	6.42	5.82	34
36	Brazil	6.40	5.67	37
37	South Africa	6.31	5.51	39
38	China	6.23	5.29	42
39	Bulgaria	6.20	5.29	43
40	India	6.15	5.16	46
41	Sri Lanka	6.08	5.05	48
42	Saudi Arabia	6.00	5.46	41
43	Colombia	5.97	5.47	40
44	Turkey	5.91	5.22	45
45	Argentina	5.87	5.68	36
46	Russia	5.85	5.03	50

Note: Scores reflect the opportunities for, and hindrances to, the conduct of business, measured by countries' rankings in ten categories including market potential, tax and labour-market policies, infrastructure, skills and the political environment. Scores reflect average and forecast average over given date range.

Business creativity and research

Innovation index[a]

1	United States	6.44	23	Slovenia	3.51
2	Taiwan	5.92	24	Ireland	3.48
3	Finland	5.71	25	Spain	3.46
4	Sweden	5.52	26	Estonia	3.38
5	Japan	5.49	27	Russia	3.36
6	Israel	4.80	28	Italy	3.33
7	South Korea	4.69	29	Poland	3.20
8	Switzerland	4.65	30	Lithuania	3.14
9	Canada	4.45	31	Greece	3.02
10	Germany	4.36	32	Portugal	2.98
11	Denmark	4.26	33	Argentina	2.94
12	Norway	4.23	34	Hong Kong	2.86
13	United Kingdom	4.11	35	Chile	2.79
14	Netherlands	4.04		Ukraine	2.79
	Singapore	4.04	37	Hungary	2.76
16	New Zealand	4.02		Thailand	2.76
17	Belgium	4.00	39	Egypt	2.71
18	Australia	3.96	40	Luxembourg	2.68
19	France	3.92	41	Malaysia	2.66
20	Austria	3.87	42	Panama	2.64
21	Iceland	3.70	43	Bulgaria	2.59
22	Latvia	3.52	44	Slovakia	2.58

Information and communications technology index[b]

1	Iceland	6.32	23	France	5.42
2	Finland	6.29	24	Malta	5.37
3	Sweden	6.28	25	Belgium	5.29
4	Denmark	6.25	26	Slovenia	5.28
5	United States	6.16	27	Ireland	5.26
6	Singapore	6.14	28	Italy	5.14
7	Taiwan	6.01	29	Czech Republic	5.04
8	Hong Kong	5.94		Portugal	5.04
9	Norway	5.93	31	Spain	4.99
10	Luxembourg	5.92	32	Malaysia	4.84
11	South Korea	5.88	33	Greece	4.82
12	Switzerland	5.87	34	Latvia	4.73
13	Canada	5.85	35	Hungary	4.68
14	Australia	5.84	36	Chile	4.67
15	Netherlands	5.82	37	Slovakia	4.60
16	United Kingdom	5.81	38	Lithuania	4.58
17	Germany	5.71	39	Croatia	4.54
18	Japan	5.63	40	Mauritius	4.37
19	New Zealand	5.58	41	Poland	4.36
20	Estonia	5.55	42	Uruguay	4.30
21	Israel	5.54	43	Brazil	4.23
22	Austria	5.51	44	South Africa	4.09

a The innovation index is a measure of human resources skills, market incentive structures and interaction between business and scientific sectors.
b The information and communications technology (ICT) index is a measure of ICT usage and includes per capita measures of telephone lines, internet usage, personal computers and mobile phone users.

Total expenditure on R&D
% of GDP, 2001

1	Sweden	3.6		Slovenia	1.3
2	Finland	3.4	24	Ireland	1.2
3	Iceland	3.1	25	China	1.1
4	Japan	3.0		Italy	1.1
5	South Korea	2.9		New Zealand	1.1
6	Israel	2.8	28	Spain	1.0
	United States	2.8	29	Brazil	0.9
8	Switzerland	2.6		Hungary	0.9
9	Germany	2.5		Romania	0.9
10	France	2.2	32	India	0.8
	Taiwan	2.2	33	Greece	0.7
12	Denmark	2.1		Poland	0.7
	Singapore	2.1		Portugal	0.7
14	Belgium	2.0		Slovakia	0.7
	Netherlands	2.0		South Africa	0.7
16	Austria	1.9	38	Chile	0.6
	Canada	1.9		Hong Kong	0.6
18	United Kingdom	1.8		Turkey	0.6
19	Norway	1.7	41	Argentina	0.5
20	Australia	1.6		Malaysia	0.5
21	Russia	1.4		Venezuela	0.5
22	Czech Republic	1.3			

Patents

No. of patents granted to residents
Total, 2000

1	Japan	123,978
2	United States	83,090
3	South Korea	34,052
4	Taiwan	20,094
5	Germany	18,328
6	Russia	16,340
7	France	11,290
8	United Kingdom	4,491
9	Italy	3,983
10	China	3,742
11	Netherlands	2,917
12	Sweden	2,336
13	Spain	1,752
14	Switzertland	1,371
15	Australia	1,313
16	Austria	1,248
17	Canada	1,138
18	Poland	1,045
19	Belgium	844
20	Israel	433

No. of patents in force
Per 100,000 inhabitants, 2000

1	Luxembourg	6,722
2	Switzerland	1,214
3	Sweden	1,097
4	Belgium	835
5	Japan	820
6	Netherlands	756
7	Taiwan	645
8	Canada	639
9	France	631
10	Ireland	619
11	Denmark	555
12	Singapore	549
13	United Kingdom	523
14	Australia	486
15	United States	471
16	Germany	459
17	South Korea	457
18	Finland	394
19	Spain	360
20	Norway	354

Business costs and corruption

Office rents

Occupation cost[a], $ per square metre, January 2004

1	London (West End), UK	1,606	15	Luxembourg City, Lux.	647

1	London (West End), UK	1,606
2	Tokyo (Inner Central), Japan	1,271
3	London (City), UK	1,243
4	Tokyo (Outer Central), Japan	1,135
5	Paris, France	1,016
6	Birmingham, UK	774
7	Dublin, Ireland	750
8	Milan, Italy	735
9	Edinburgh, UK	722
10	Manchester, UK	717
11	Moscow, Russia	700
12	Zurich, Switzerland	680
13	Glasgow, UK	669
14	Frankfurt, Germany	651
15	Luxembourg City, Lux.	647
16	Rome, Italy	636
17	Mumbai, India	612
18	Geneva, Switzerland	600
19	Munich, Germany	584
20	Stockholm, Sweden	570
21	New York (Midtown Manhattan), USA	563
22	Seoul, South Korea	560
23	Madrid, Spain	553
24	Sydney, Australia	527
25	Athens, Greece	523
26	Washington, DC, (Central), USA	512
27	Brussels, Belgium	510
28	Boston (Central), USA	474

Employment costs

Pay, social security and other benefits, $ per hr. worked for a production worker

1	Norway	27.40	11	Japan	18.80
2	Germany	26.07	12	United Kingdom	17.48
3	Denmark	24.20	13	France	17.33
4	Switzerland	24.09	14	Canada	16.03
5	Belgium	22.69	15	Australia	15.56
6	Netherlands	21.64	16	Ireland	15.02
7	Finland	21.47	17	Italy	14.86
8	United States	21.33	18	Spain	11.99
9	Austria	20.99	19	Greece	8.88
10	Sweden	20.15		New Zealand	8.88

Business software piracy

% of software that is pirated

1	Vietnam	95		El Salvador	68
2	China	92		Malaysia	68
3	Indonesia	89		Philippines	68
	Russia	89	23	Kenya	67
	Ukraine	89		Nigeria	67
6	Pakistan	80	25	Honduras	66
7	Nicaragua	77	26	Jordan	64
	Thailand	77	27	Greece	63
9	Bahrain	76	28	Argentina	62
	Qatar	76		Croatia	62
11	Bolivia	74	30	Costa Rica	61
	Lebanon	74		Dominican Republic	61
13	Kuwait	73		Guatemala	61
14	Paraguay	71		Mauritius	61
15	India	70	34	Peru	60
	Oman	70		Uruguay	60
	Romania	70	36	Ecuador	59
	Zimbabwe	70		Slovenia	59
19	Bulgaria	68			

Corruption perceptions index[b]

2003, 10 = least corrupt

Least			Most		
1	Finland	9.7	1	Bangladesh	1.3
2	Iceland	9.6	2	Nigeria	1.4
3	Denmark	9.5	3	Haiti	1.5
	New Zealand	9.5	4	Myanmar	1.6
5	Singapore	9.4		Paraguay	1.6
6	Sweden	9.3	6	Angola	1.8
7	Netherlands	8.9		Azerbaijan	1.8
8	Australia	8.8		Cameroon	1.8
	Norway	8.8		Georgia	1.8
	Switzerland	8.8		Tajikistan	1.8
11	Canada	8.7	11	Indonesia	1.9
	Luxembourg	8.7		Kenya	1.9
	United Kingdom	8.7	13	Côte d'Ivoire	2.1
14	Austria	8.0		Kirgizstan	2.1
	Hong Kong	8.0		Libya	2.1
16	Germany	7.7		Papua New Guinea	2.1
17	Belgium	7.6	17	Congo	2.2
18	Ireland	7.5		Ecuador	2.2
	United States	7.5		Iraq	2.2
20	Chile	7.4		Sierra Leone	2.2
21	Israel	7.0		Uganda	2.2
	Japan	7.0	22	Bolivia	2.3
23	France	6.9		Honduras	2.3
	Spain	6.9		Macedonia	2.3
25	Portugal	6.6		Serbia & Montenegro	2.3
26	Oman	6.3		Sudan	2.3
27	Bahrain	6.1		Ukraine	2.3
	Cyprus	6.1		Zimbabwe	2.3
29	Slovenia	5.9	29	Guatemala	2.4
30	Botswana	5.7		Kazakhstan	2.4
	Taiwan	5.7		Moldova	2.4
32	Qatar	5.6		Uzbekistan	2.4
33	Estonia	5.5		Venezuela	2.4
	Uruguay	5.5		Vietnam	2.4
35	Italy	5.3	35	Albania	2.5
	Kuwait	5.3		Argentina	2.5
37	Malaysia	5.2		Ethiopia	2.5
	United Arab Emirates	5.2		Gambia, The	2.5
39	Tunisia	4.9		Pakistan	2.5
40	Hungary	4.8		Philippines	2.5
41	Lithuania	4.7		Tanzania	2.5
	Namibia	4.7		Zambia	2.5
43	Cuba	4.6	43	Algeria	2.6
	Jordan	4.6		Madagascar	2.6
	Trinidad & Tobago	4.6		Nicaragua	2.6
46	Saudi Arabia	4.5		Yemen	2.6

a Total rent, taxes and operating expenses.
b This index ranks countries based on how much corruption is perceived by business people, academics and risk analysts to exist among politicians and public officials.

Businesses and banks

Largest businesses

By sales, \$bn

1	Wal-Mart Stores	United States	246.5
2	General Motors	United States	186.8
3	Exxon Mobil	United States	182.5
4	Royal Dutch/Shell Group	United Kingdom/Netherlands	179.4
5	BP	United Kingdom	178.7
6	Ford Motor	United States	163.9
7	DaimlerChrysler	United States	141.4
8	Toyota Motor	Japan	131.8
9	General Electric	United States	131.7
10	Mitsubishi	Japan	109.4
11	Mitsui	Japan	108.6
12	Allianz	Germany	101.9
13	Citigroup	United States	100.8
14	Total Fina Elf	France	96.9
15	ChevronTexaco	United States	92.0
16	Nippon Telegraph & Telephone	Japan	89.6
17	ING Group	Netherlands	88.1
18	Itochu	Japan	85.9
19	IBM	United States	83.1
20	Volkswagen	Germany	82.2
21	Siemens	Germany	77.2
22	Sumitomo	Japan	75.7
23	Marubeni	Japan	72.2
24	Verizon Communications	United States	67.6
25	American Intl. Group	United States	67.5
26	Hitachi	Japan	67.2
27	U.S. Postal Service	United States	66.5
28	Honda Motor	Japan	65.4
29	Carrefour	France	65.0
30	Altria Group	United States	62.2
31	AXA	France	62.1
32	Sony	Japan	61.3
33	Nippon Life Insurance	Japan	61.2
34	Matsushita Electric Industrial	Japan	60.7
35	Royal Ahold	Netherlands	59.5
36	ConocoPhillips	United States	58.4
37	Home Depot	United States	58.2
38	Nestle	Switzerland	57.3
39	McKesson	United States	57.1
40	Hewlett-Packard	United States	56.6
41	Nissan Motor	Japan	56.0
42	Vivendi Universal	France	55.0
43	Boeing	United States	54.1
44	Assicurazioni Generali	Italy	53.6

Notes: Industrial and service corporations. Figures refer to the year ended December 31, 2002, except for Japanese companies, where figures refer to year ended March 31, 2003. They include sales of consolidated subsidiaries but exclude excise taxes, thus differing, in some instances, from figures published by the companies themselves.

Largest banks

By capital, $m

1	Citigroup	United States	59,012
2	Bank of America Corp	United States	43,012
3	HSBC Holdings	United Kingdom	38,949
4	J.P. Morgan Chase	United States	37,570
5	Crédit Agricole Groupe	France	35,661
6	Mizuho Financial Group	Japan	29,092
7	Royal Bank of Scotland	United Kingdom	27,652
8	Sumitomo Mitsui Financial Group	Japan	27,099
9	Mitsubishi Tokyo Financial Group	Japan	26,039
10	BNP Paribas	France	24,119
11	Bank One Corp	United States	23,918
12	Deutsche Bank	Germany	23,849
13	HBOS	United Kingdom	23,836
14	Barclays Bank	United Kingdom	22,895
15	Bank of China	China	21,916
16	Industrial and Commercial Bank of China	China	21,530
17	Wells Fargo & Co.	United States	21,512
18	Wachovia Corporation	United States	21,411
19	UFJ Holding	Japan	21,310
20	HypoVereinsbank	Germany	20,057
21	UBS	Switzerland	19,503
22	ING Bank	Netherlands	18,960
23	ABN-Amro Bank	Netherlands	18,014
24	Rabobank Nederland	Netherlands	17,902
25	Agricultural Bank of China	China	16,435
26	Société Générale	France	16,001
27	Santander Central Hispano	Spain	15,556
28	Washington Mutual	United States	15,351
29	Lloyds TSB Group	United Kingdom	15,297
30	FleetBoston Financial Corp	United States	15,049
31	MetLife	United States	14,806
32	Banco Bilbao Vizcaya Argentaria	Spain	14,346
33	Banca Intesa	Italy	14,151
34	Credit Suisse Group	Switzerland	14,093
35	Crédit Mutuel	France	13,156
36	Groupe Caisse d'Epargne	France	13,084
37	China Construction Bank	China	12,955
38	Fortis Bank	Belgium	12,809
39	Norinchukin Bank	Japan	12,695
40	US Bancorp	United States	12,606
41	Commerzbank	Germany	12,260
42	Abbey National	United Kingdom	11,680
43	UniCredito	Italy	11,300
44	Groupe Banques Populaires	France	10,926
45	Dexia	Belgium	10,693
46	National Australia Bank	Australia	10,452

Notes: Capital is essentially equity and reserves.
Figures for Japanese banks refer to the year ended March 31, 2003. Figures for all other countries refer to the year ended December 31, 2002.

Stockmarkets

Largest market capitalisation
$m, end 2002

1	United States	11,052,403	27	Denmark	76,788
2	Japan	2,126,075	28	Saudi Arabia	74,855
3	United Kingdom	1,864,134	29	Greece	68,741
4	France	966,962	30	Norway	67,300
5	Germany	685,970	31	Ireland	59,938
6	Canada	575,316	32	Chile	47,584
7	Switzerland	553,758	33	Thailand	46,084
8	Italy	477,075	34	Israel	45,371
9	Hong Kong	463,108	35	Portugal	42,846
10	China	463,080	36	Philippines	39,021
11	Spain	461,559	37	Turkey	33,958
12	Netherlands	401,465	38	Austria	31,664
13	Australia	380,969	39	Indonesia	29,991
14	Taiwan	261,474	40	Poland	28,750
15	South Korea	249,639	41	Egypt	26,094
16	South Africa	184,622	42	Luxembourg	22,587
17	Sweden	177,065	43	New Zealand	21,745
18	Finland	138,833	44	Kuwait[a]	20,772
19	India	131,011	45	Czech Republic	15,893
20	Belgium	127,556	46	Zimbabwe	15,632
21	Russia	124,198	47	Iran	14,344
22	Malaysia	123,872	48	Peru	13,363
23	Brazil	123,807	49	Hungary	13,110
24	Argentina	103,434	50	Pakistan	10,200
25	Mexico	103,137	51	Colombia	9,664
26	Singapore	101,900	52	Morocco	8,591

Highest growth in market capitalisation, $ terms
% increase, 1997–2002

1	Bulgaria	36,550	21	Latvia	112
2	Macedonia	2,175	22	Nepal	109
3	Zimbabwe	694		Trinidad & Tobago	109
4	Romania	627	24	Greece	101
5	El Salvador	442	25	Qatar[c]	99
	South Korea	442	26	Thailand	96
7	Moldova	440	27	Finland	89
8	Bolivia	348	28	Argentina	75
9	Iceland	240		Kirgizstan[d]	75
10	Cayman Islands	231	30	Spain	59
11	Barbados	202	31	Nigeria	57
12	Malta	200	32	Bermuda	54
13	Tanzania[b]	194	33	France	43
14	Jamaica	185	34	Italy	38
15	Slovenia	183	35	Malaysia	32
16	Botswana	181	36	Panama	31
17	Costa Rica[c]	147	37	Jordan	30
18	Poland	137	38	Australia	29
19	China	124	39	Saudi Arabia	26
20	Estonia	121	40	Egypt	25

Highest growth in value traded, $ terms
% increase, 1997–2002

1	Kazakhstan	29,850	23	Pakistan	129
2	Barbados	3,496	24	Spain	124
3	Macedonia	2,175	25	Russia	123
4	Iceland	1,762	26	Saudi Arabia	116
5	Bulgariab	1,333	27	Ireland	102
6	Moldova	440	28	Thailand	97
7	Israel	416	29	Jamaica	96
8	South Korea	408	30	West Bank and Gaza	80
9	Finland	385	31	South Africa	76
10	Zimbabwe	361	32	Kirgizstand	75
11	Nepal	300	33	Bangladesh	73
12	Nigeria	260	34	Australia	72
13	Qatarc	251	35	Netherlands	62
14	United Kingdom	228	36	El Salvador	60
15	Slovenia	186	37	Iran	58
16	Italy	172	38	Romania	50
17	Tanzaniad	171	39	Latvia	48
18	Jordan	167	40	Canada	38
19	United States	148	41	Ukraineb	37
20	Malta	141	42	Switzerland	33
21	France	132	43	Trinidad & Tobago	28
22	Germany	130			

Highest growth in number of listed companies
% increase, 1997–2002

1	Romania	6,308	24	Singapore	43
2	Bulgaria	2,260	25	West Bank and Gazae	42
3	Macedonia	1,850	26	Iceland	39
4	Kazakhstan	1,533		Moldova	39
5	Spain	678	28	Tunisia	38
6	Cyprus	214	29	Slovenia	35
7	Canada	176	30	Trinidad & Tobago	29
8	Bolivia	173	31	Japan	28
9	Tanzaniab	150	32	Iran	27
10	Malta	100	33	Swaziland	25
11	South Korea	97	34	Panama	24
12	Egypt	76	35	Italy	23
13	China	66	36	Latvia	22
14	Taiwan	58		Malaysia	22
15	Zambia	57		Qatarc	22
16	Poland	51	39	Finland	19
17	Botswana	50		Switzerland	19
	Uzbekistan	50		Zimbabwe	19
19	El Salvador	48	42	Bangladesh	18
	Greece	48	43	Australia	17
21	Ukraineb	47		Indonesia	17
22	Hong Kong	44	45	Ghana	14
	Lebanon	44		Jordan	14

a 2000   b 1998–2002   c 1997–2000   d 1999–2002   e 1997–2001

Transport: *roads and cars*

Longest road networks
Km, 2001 or latest

1	United States	6,304,193	21	Sweden	212,961
2	India	3,319,644	22	Bangladesh	207,486
3	Brazil	1,724,929	23	Philippines	201,994
4	China	1,698,012	24	Austria	200,000
5	Japan	1,166,340	25	Romania	198,603
6	Canada	901,903	26	Nigeria	194,394
7	France	894,000	27	Ukraine	169,630
8	Australia	811,603	28	Hungary	167,839
9	Spain	663,795	29	Iran	167,157
10	Russia	537,289	30	Congo	157,000
11	Italy	479,688	31	Saudi Arabia	152,044
12	United Kingdom	371,913	32	Belgium	149,028
13	Poland	364,697	33	Czech Republic	127,728
14	South Africa	362,099	34	Greece	117,000
15	Turkey	354,373	35	Netherlands	116,500
16	Indonesia	342,700	36	Colombia	112,988
17	Mexico	329,532	37	Algeria	104,000
18	Pakistan	257,683	38	Sri Lanka	96,695
19	Germany	230,735	39	Venezuela	96,155
20	Argentina	215,471	40	Vietnam	93,300

Densest road networks
Km of road per km^2 land area, 2001 or latest

1	Macau	19.6	21	Sri Lanka	1.5
2	Malta	7.1		United Kingdom	1.5
3	Bahrain	5.2	23	Bangladesh	1.4
4	Belgium	4.9	24	Ireland	1.3
5	Singapore	4.8		Spain	1.3
6	Barbados	3.7	26	Cyprus	1.2
7	Japan	3.1		Estonia	1.2
8	Netherlands	2.8		Lithuania	1.2
9	Puerto Rico	2.6		Poland	1.2
10	Austria	2.4	30	Latvia	1.1
11	Luxembourg	2.0	31	India	1.0
12	Hungary	1.8		Mauritius	1.0
13	Denmark	1.7		Slovenia	1.0
	Hong Kong	1.7		Taiwan	1.0
	Jamaica	1.7	35	Greece	0.9
	Switzerland	1.7		Slovakia	0.9
17	Czech Republic	1.6		South Korea	0.9
	France	1.6	38	Israel	0.8
	Italy	1.6		Portugal	0.8
	Trinidad & Tobago	1.6		Romania	0.8

Most crowded road networks
Number of vehicles per km of road network, 2001 or latest

1	Hong Kong	286.7	26	Switzerland	54.0
2	United Arab Emirates	231.6	27	Russia	47.3
3	Germany	194.5	28	Mexico	47.0
4	Lebanon	190.6	29	Slovenia	45.8
5	Singapore	168.9	30	Guatemala	44.8
6	Macau	163.5	31	Puerto Rico	44.5
7	Kuwait	155.7	32	Croatia	44.1
8	Qatar	154.5	33	Barbados	43.2
9	Taiwan	148.6	34	Jordan	40.4
10	South Korea	138.4		Tunisia	40.4
11	Thailand	108.6	36	France	37.8
12	Israel	105.9	37	Greece	36.6
13	Malta	103.0	38	El Salvador	36.1
14	Malaysia	74.8	39	Belgium	35.4
15	Italy	73.3	40	Macedonia	34.9
16	Brunei	73.2	41	Serbia	34.8
17	Uruguay	63.1	42	United States	34.1
18	Portugal	62.5	43	Cyprus	33.7
19	Japan	62.3	44	Slovakia	33.4
	United Kingdom	62.3	45	Poland	32.5
21	Mauritius	61.2	46	Denmark	31.1
22	Bahrain	61.1	47	Cambodia	30.9
23	Bulgaria	59.6	48	Finland	30.6
24	Netherlands	57.9	49	Argentina	30.4
25	Luxembourg	54.7	50	Dominican Republic	29.8

Most used road networks
'000 vehicle-km per year per km of road network, 2001 or latest

1	Indonesia	8,134	16	Luxembourg	740
2	Hong Kong	5,888	17	Greece	678
3	Taiwan	2,753	18	Japan	665
4	Germany	2,555	19	Chile	631
5	Israel	2,240		Denmark	631
6	Portugal	1,397	21	Sweden	602
7	Bahrain	1,367	22	Finland	591
8	Malta	1,246	23	France	581
9	United Kingdom	1,243	24	Cambodia	563
10	Belgium	1,062	25	Croatia	536
11	Netherlands	944	26	China	495
12	Pakistan	910	27	Macedonia	489
13	Ethiopia	835	28	Slovenia	467
14	South Korea	773	29	El Salvador	423
15	Tunisia	770	30	United States	421

Highest car ownership
Number of cars per 1,000 people, 2001 or latest

1	Lebanon	732		Kuwait	359
2	New Zealand	578	27	Ireland	349
3	Brunei	576	28	Estonia	339
	Luxembourg	576	29	Czech Republic	335
5	Iceland	561	30	Portugal	321
6	Italy	542	31	Lithuania	317
7	Germany	516	32	Poland	259
8	Austria	495	33	Greece	254
9	Malta	494	34	Bahrain	248
10	Switzerland	493	35	Croatia	247
11	Australia	488	36	Hungary	237
12	United States	481	37	Slovakia	236
13	France	477	38	Latvia	235
14	Belgium	462	39	Bulgaria	234
15	Canada	458	40	Israel	233
16	Sweden	450	41	Puerto Rico	230
17	Slovenia	426	42	Qatar	219
18	Japan	413	43	Taiwan	212
19	Norway	411	44	South Korea	171
20	Spain	408	45	Bahamas	161
21	Finland	403	46	Libya	154
22	Cyprus	400		Uruguay	154
23	Netherlands	384	48	Serbia & Montenegro	150
	United Kingdom	384	49	Belarus	145
25	Denmark	359		Malaysia	145

Lowest car ownership
Number of cars per 1,000 people, 2001 or latest

1	Somalia	0.1	17	Liberia	2.6
	Tajikistan	0.1	18	Burundi	2.8
3	Armenia	0.3	19	Mali	2.9
	Central African Rep	0.3	20	Chad	3.2
	Mozambique	0.3	21	Laos	3.4
6	Bangladesh	0.5	22	Burkina Faso	3.6
7	Myanmar	0.6	23	Niger	3.8
8	Tanzania	0.8	24	Sierra Leone	3.9
9	Ethiopia	0.9	25	Madagascar	4.1
10	Guatemala	1.0	26	Haiti	4.4
11	Afghanistan	1.4	27	Ghana	4.7
	Rwanda	1.4	28	Pakistan	5.0
13	Eritrea	1.5	29	India	5.2
14	Uganda	1.8	30	Guinea-Bissau	5.7
15	Guinea	2.0		Lesotho	5.7
16	Malawi	2.3	32	China	6.7

Most accidents
Number of people injured per 100m vehicle-km, 2001 or latest

1	Malawi	2,730	27	Saudi Arabia	89
2	Rwanda	1,764	28	Philippines	86
3	South Korea	510	29	Germany	81
4	Costa Rica	406		Macedonia	81
5	Kenya	363	31	United States	74
6	India	333	32	Spain	73
7	Honduras	317	33	Ghana	72
8	Egypt	222	34	Mexico	66
9	Sri Lanka	205	35	Yemen	59
10	Portugal	194	36	Iceland	58
11	Morocco	183	37	Bahrain	57
12	Turkey	179	38	Hungary	56
13	Hong Kong	176		Senegal	56
14	Japan	149	40	Iran	53
15	Kirgizstan	134		Oman	53
16	Colombia	126		Switzerland	53
17	Latvia	125	43	Malta	42
18	Italy	122	44	Thailand	40
19	Canada	121	45	Slovakia	39
20	Czech Republic	113	46	Ireland	38
21	Belgium	108	47	Estonia	37
22	Slovenia	106	48	Norway	34
23	Israel	100	49	New Zealand	33
	South Africa	100	50	Mauritius	32
25	United Kingdom	94		Sweden	32
26	Mongolia	90		Zimbabwe	32

Most deaths
Number of people killed per 100m vehicle-km, 2001 or latest

1	Malawi	1,117		Saudi Arabia	11
2	India	65		Yemen	11
3	Egypt	44	19	Mexico	10
4	Kenya	41	20	Albania	8
5	Latvia	25	21	South Africa	7
6	Kirgizstan	24		Suriname	7
7	Sri Lanka	23	23	Portugal	6
8	Mongolia	22		Romania	6
9	Colombia	17		Turkey	6
	Morocco	17	26	Czech Republic	5
	South Korea	17		Iran	5
12	Honduras	16	28	Ecuador	4
13	Philippines	14		Macedonia	4
14	Thailand	13		Oman	4
15	Ghana	12		Senegal	4
16	Costa Rica	11			

Transport: *planes and trains*

Most air travel
Million passenger-km[a] per year

1	United States	1,132,266		16	Malaysia	44,836
2	Japan	215,520		17	Thailand	36,630
3	United Kingdom	172,845		18	Switzerland	29,386
4	China	117,243		19	Mexico	28,066
5	Germany	117,099		20	Belgium	27,940
6	France	93,171		21	Saudi Arabia	26,797
7	Australia	76,795		22	South Africa	26,445
8	Hong Kong	71,998		23	India	24,756
9	Singapore	71,224		24	United Arab Emirates	24,652
10	Canada	70,048		25	New Zealand	22,829
11	South Korea	66,306		26	Argentina	19,533
12	Netherlands	58,852		27	Indonesia	18,210
13	Russia	52,850		28	Turkey	17,726
14	Spain	51,470		29	Austria	17,017
15	Italy	48,938		30	Ireland	16,539

Busiest airports
Total passengers, m

				Total cargo, m tonnes		
1	Atlanta, Hartsfield	79.1		1	Memphis, Intl.	3.39
2	Chicago, O'Hare	69.1		2	Hong Kong, Intl.	2.67
3	London, Heathrow	63.3		3	Tokyo, Narita	2.15
4	Tokyo, Haneda	63.3		4	Anchorage, Intl.	2.10
5	Los Angeles, Intl.	55.0		5	Seoul, Inchon	1.84
6	Dallas, Ft. Worth	52.9		6	Los Angeles, Intl.	1.81
7	Frankfurt, Main	48.3		7	Frankfurt, Main	1.65
8	Paris, Charles de Gaulle	48.0		8	Miami, Intl.	1.64
9	Amsterdam, Schipol	40.0		9	New York, JFK	1.63
10	Phoenix, Skyharbor Intl.	37.4			Singapore, Changi	1.63
11	Denver, Intl.	37.3		11	Louisville, Standiford F.	1.62
12	Las Vegas, McCarran Intl.	36.0		12	Chicago, O'Hare	1.60

Average daily aircraft movements, take-offs and landings

1	Chicago, O'Hare	2,527		11	Detroit, Metro	1,343
2	Atlanta, Hartsfield	2,482		12	Houston, George Bush Intercont.	1,288
3	Dallas, Ft. Worth	2,084		13	Los Angeles, Van Nuys	1,278
4	Los Angeles, Intl.	1,708		14	London, Heathrow	1,269
5	Phoenix, Skyharbor Intl.	1,488		15	Frankfurt, Main	1,258
6	Paris, Charles de Gaulle	1,412		16	Philadelphia, Intl.	1,223
7	Minneapolis, St Paul	1,401		17	Charlotte/Douglas, Intl.	1,202
8	Cincinnati, Intl.	1,377		18	Miami, Intl.	1,149
9	Denver, Intl.	1,368		19	Amsterdam, Schipol	1,120
10	Las Vegas, McCarran Intl.	1,367		20	Newark	1,107

a   Air passenger–km data refer to the distance travelled by each aircraft of national origin.

Longest railway networks
'000 km

1	United States	235.1	21	Australia	9.5
2	Russia	85.5		Czech Republic	9.5
3	India	63.1	23	Turkey	8.7
4	Canada	62.7	24	Hungary	8.0
5	China	59.5	25	Pakistan	7.8
6	Germany	35.9	26	Iran	6.2
7	Argentina	34.2	27	Finland	5.9
8	France	29.4	28	Austria	5.7
9	Mexico	26.5	29	Belarus	5.5
10	South Africa	22.7	30	Egypt	5.2
11	Brazil	22.1	31	Philippines	4.9
	Ukraine	22.1	32	Cuba	4.8
13	Japan	20.2	33	Sudan	4.6
	Poland	20.2	34	North Korea	4.5
15	United Kingdom	17.1	35	Bulgaria	4.3
16	Italy	16.3	36	Indonesia	4.2
17	Spain	13.9	37	Norway	4.1
18	Kazakhstan	13.6		Serbia & Montenegro	4.1
19	Romania	11.4		Uzbekistan	4.1
20	Sweden	9.9	40	New Zealand	3.9

Most rail passengers
Km per person per year

1	Switzerland	2,077	11	Italy	815
2	Japan	1,900	12	Belgium	802
3	Belarus	1,435	13	Hungary	753
4	France	1,237	14	Kazakhstan	701
5	Germany	1,169	15	United Kingdom	671
6	Russia	1,059	16	Luxembourg	670
7	Austria	1,039	17	Sweden	665
8	Denmark	1,036	18	Czech Republic	643
9	Ukraine	1,017	19	Finland	636
10	Netherlands	893	20	South Korea	609

Most rail freight
Million tonnes-km per year

1	United States	2,200,123	11	Poland	46,560
2	Russia	1,510,200	12	Australia	40,092
3	China	1,507,817	13	Belarus	34,169
4	India	333,728	14	Italy	23,420
5	Canada	313,048	15	Japan	21,950
6	Ukraine	193,141	16	United Kingdom	19,561
7	Kazakhstan	133,088	17	Uzbekistan	18,428
8	South Africa	105,719	18	Austria	17,637
9	Germany	72,731	19	Czech Republic	17,042
10	France	50,036	20	Iran	15,842

Transport: *shipping*

Largest merchant fleets
Number of vessels not less than 100 GRT and built before end of 2002[a]
By country of :

		registration	ownership			registration	ownership
1	Japan	7,151	2,948	46	Portugal	331	74
2	Panama	6,302	5	47	Bangladesh	327	36
3	United States	6,185	1,549	48	Nigeria	311	48
4	Russia	4,950	2,539	49	Georgia	303	3
5	China	3,376	2,416	50	Iceland	301	76
6	Indonesia	2,700	616	51	North Korea	292	95
7	South Korea	2,604	865	52	Azerbaijan	288	149
8	Singapore	1,761	758	53	Saudi Arabia	285	126
9	Philippines	1,703	350	54	Finland	280	126
10	UK	1,594	793	55	Venezuela	275	60
11	Greece	1,558	3,025	56	Croatia	259	95
12	Liberia	1,553	0	57	South Africa	251	27
13	Norway	1,548	1,653	58	Ireland	236	58
14	Italy	1,504	656	59	Romania	232	91
15	Spain	1,413	334	60	Belgium	222	165
16	Netherlands	1,313	742	61	Neth. Antilles	213	0
17	Malta	1,301	18	62	Ecuador	211	28
18	Bahamas	1,297	24	63	Kuwait	208	32
19	Cyprus	1,198	114	64	Ghana	207	16
20	Honduras	1,143	3	65	Senegal	187	1
21	Turkey	1,113	576	66	Estonia	178	76
22	India	1,028	394		Syria	178	78
23	Malaysia	972	335	68	Lithuania	176	71
24	Canada	916	323	69	New Zealand	170	45
25	Hong Kong	901	485	70	Cayman Islands	159	0
26	Ukraine	829	390	71	Latvia	156	103
27	Germany	782	2,464	72	Bulgaria	151	98
28	Vietnam	735	174	73	Faroe Islands	142	0
29	Peru	718	23		Mauritania	142	0
30	France	711	265	75	Libya	138	14
31	Thailand	671	254	76	Algeria	137	55
32	Cambodia	663	0	77	Bolivia	136	0
33	Mexico	654	97	78	Namibia	129	6
34	Australia	643	88	79	Mozambique	128	1
35	Taiwan	637	537	80	Mongolia	124	0
36	Sweden	581	319	81	Angola	122	7
37	Chile	532	80		Myanmar	122	28
38	Argentina	497	86	83	Colombia	121	19
39	Morocco	483	36	84	Bahrain	120	11
40	Brazil	482	151	85	Papua New Guin.	112	15
41	Denmark	435	686	86	Bermuda	106	0
42	Iran	382	156	87	Madagascar	103	9
43	Poland	373	124	88	Cuba	90	53
44	United Arab Em.	363	206		Uruguay	90	19
45	Egypt	346	114	90	Iraq	85	28

a Gross Tonnage (GRT) = total volume within the hull and above deck. 1 GRT=100 cu ft.

Tourism

Most tourist arrivals
Number of arrivals, '000

1	France	77,012	21	Russia	7,943
2	Spain	51,748	22	Saudi Arabia	7,511
3	United States	41,892	23	Singapore	6,996
4	Italy	39,799	24	Croatia	6,944
5	China	36,803	25	Belgium	6,724
6	United Kingdom	24,180	26	Macau	6,565
7	Canada	20,057	27	South Africa	6,550
8	Mexico	19,667	28	Ireland	6,476
9	Austria	18,611	29	Ukraine	6,326
10	Germany	17,969	30	United Arab Emirates	5,445
11	Hong Kong	16,566	31	South Korea	5,347
12	Hungary	15,870	32	Japan	5,239
13	Greece	14,180	33	Tunisia	5,064
14	Poland	13,980	34	Indonesia	5,033
15	Malaysia	13,292	35	Egypt	4,906
16	Turkey	12,782	36	Australia	4,841
17	Portugal	11,666	37	Bahamas	4,508
18	Thailand	10,873	38	Norway	4,321
19	Switzerland	10,000	39	Morocco	4,193
20	Netherlands	9,595	40	Finland	4,023

Biggest tourist spenders
$m

1	United States	58,716	11	Netherlands	9,607
2	Germany	47,041	12	Belgium	8,930
3	United Kingdom	35,096	13	Russia	7,563
4	Japan	29,094	14	Poland	7,030
5	Spain	20,788	15	Switzerland	6,790
6	France	17,586	16	Sweden	5,831
7	Italy	14,507	17	South Korea	5,817
8	Canada	10,209	18	Taiwan	5,656
9	China	10,181	19	Mexico	5,136
10	Austria	9,877	20	Singapore	4,813

Largest tourist receipts
$m

1	United States	66,547	11	Canada	9,700
2	Spain	33,609	12	Turkey	9,010
3	France	32,329	13	Mexico	8,858
4	Italy	26,915	14	Australia	8,087
5	China	20,385	15	Thailand	7,902
6	Germany	19,158	16	Netherlands	7,706
7	United Kingdom	17,591	17	Switzerland	7,628
8	Austria	11,237	18	Belgium	6,892
9	Hong Kong	10,117	19	Malaysia	6,785
10	Greece	9,741	20	Portugal	5,919

Education

Highest primary enrolment

Number enrolled as % of relevant age group

1	Brazil	155		Libya	116
2	Gabon	144	17	Ecuador	115
3	Peru	127		Lesotho	115
	Suriname	127	19	China	114
5	Swaziland	125		Israel	114
6	Dominican Republic	124	21	Laos	113
	Togo	124		Mexico	113
8	Portugal	121		Paraguay	113
9	Argentina	120		Philippines	113
	Equatorial Guinea	120	25	Algeria	112
11	Ireland	119		Colombia	112
	Rwanda	119		Namibia	112
13	Nepal	118		Panama	112
14	Tunisia	117	29	Aruba	111
15	Bolivia	116		South Africa	111

Lowest primary enrolment

Number enrolled as % of relevant age group, 2000 or latest available

1	Afghanistan	15	15	Chad	73
2	Niger	35	16	Angola	74
3	Burkina Faso	44	17	Central African Rep	75
4	Congo-Brazzaville	47		Pakistan	75
5	Eritrea	59		Senegal	75
	Sudan	59	20	Ukraine	78
7	Mali	61		Zambia	78
8	Tanzania	63	22	Côte d'Ivoire	79
9	Ethiopia	64		Yemen	79
10	Burundi	65	24	Ghana	80
11	Serbia & Montenegro	66	25	Gambia, The	82
12	Guinea	67	26	Guinea-Bissau	83
13	Saudi Arabia	68		Mauritania	83
14	Oman	72			

Highest tertiary enrolment[a]

Number enrolled as % of relevant age group, 2000 or latest available

1	South Korea	78	11	United Kingdom	60
2	United States	73	12	Canada	59
3	Norway	70		Denmark	59
	Sweden	70		Spain	59
5	New Zealand	69	15	Austria	58
6	Russia	64		Belgium	58
7	Australia	63		Estonia	58
	Greece	63	18	Belarus	56
	Latvia	63		Poland	56
10	Slovenia	61	20	Netherlands	55

Notes: Latest available year 1999–2001. The gross enrolment ratios shown are the actual number enrolled as a percentage of the number of children in the official primary age group. They may exceed 100 when children outside the primary age group are receiving primary education either because they have not moved on to secondary education or because they have started primary education early.

Least literate
% adult literacy rate, latest year 1999–2002

1	Niger	17.1	16	Haiti	51.9
2	Mali	19.0	17	Liberia	55.9
3	Senegal	39.3	18	Togo	59.6
4	Benin	39.8	19	Sudan	59.9
5	Bangladesh	41.1	20	India	61.3
6	Mauritania	41.2	21	Malawi	61.8
7	Ethiopia	41.5	22	Laos	66.4
8	Nepal	44.0	23	Nigeria	66.8
9	Chad	45.8	24	Cameroon	67.9
10	Mozambique	46.5	25	Algeria	68.9
11	Côte d'Ivoire	47.6	26	Uganda	68.9
12	Central African Rep	48.6	27	Rwanda	69.2
13	Yemen	49.0	28	Cambodia	69.4
14	Burundi	50.4	29	Guatemala	69.9
15	Morocco	50.7	30	Tunisia	73.2

Highest education spending
% of GDP

1	Zimbabwe	10.4	14	New Zealand	6.6
2	Lesotho	10.0	15	Barbados	6.5
	Yemen	10.0		Mongolia	6.5
4	Saudi Arabia	9.5	17	Jamaica	6.4
5	Cuba	9.0	18	Kenya	6.2
6	Denmark	8.3	19	Belarus	6.0
7	Namibia	8.1		Iceland	6.0
8	Malaysia	7.9	21	Belgium	5.9
9	Sweden	7.7		Finland	5.9
10	Estonia	7.5		Latvia	5.9
11	Israel	7.3	24	Austria	5.8
12	Norway	6.9		France	5.8
13	Tunisia	6.8		Portugal	5.8

Lowest education spending
% of GDP

1	Equatorial Guinea	0.6	14	Botswana	2.1
2	Haiti	1.1		Guinea-Bissau	2.1
3	Indonesia	1.3		Tanzania	2.1
	Myanmar	1.3	17	China	2.2
	Sri Lanka	1.3	18	Bangladesh	2.3
6	Ecuador	1.6		Niger	2.3
7	Guatemala	1.7		Papua New Guinea	2.3
8	Pakistan	1.8		Uganda	2.3
9	Central African Rep	1.9		Zambia	2.3
	Guinea	1.9	23	Dominican Republic	2.4
	United Arab Emirates	1.9		Mozambique	2.4
12	Cambodia	2.0		Tajikistan	2.4
13	Chad	2.0			

a Tertiary education includes all levels of post-secondary education including courses
  leading to awards not equivalent to a university degree, courses leading to a first
  university degree and postgraduate courses.

Life expectancy

Highest life expectancy
Years, 2000–05

1	Andorra[a]	83.5		Guadeloupe	78.3
2	Japan	81.6		Netherlands	78.3
3	Sweden	80.1		New Zealand	78.3
4	Hong Kong	79.9	29	Channel Islands	78.2
5	Iceland	79.8		United Kingdom	78.2
6	Cayman Islands[a]	79.7	31	Costa Rica	78.1
7	Canada	79.3		Singapore	78.1
	Spain	79.3	33	Finland	78.0
9	Australia	79.2		Virgin Islands	78.0
	Israel	79.2	35	Bermuda[a]	77.4
11	Martinique	79.1	36	Barbados	77.2
	Switzerland	79.1	37	United States	77.1
13	France	79.0	38	Ireland	77.0
14	Faroe Islands[a]	78.9	39	Taiwan[a]	76.9
	Macau	78.9	40	Cuba	76.7
	Norway	78.9	41	Denmark	76.6
17	Aruba[a]	78.8		Kuwait	76.6
	Belgium	78.8	43	Brunei	76.3
19	Italy	78.7	44	Netherlands Antilles	76.3
20	Austria	78.5		Slovenia	76.3
21	Luxembourg	78.4	46	Portugal	76.2
	Malta	78.4	47	Chile	76.1
23	Cyprus	78.3	48	Jamaica	75.7
	Germany	78.3	49	Puerto Rico	75.6
	Greece	78.3	50	South Korea	75.5

Highest male life expectancy
Years, 2000–05

1	Andorra[a]	80.6	9	Macau	76.5
2	Japan	77.9	10	Australia	76.4
3	Iceland	77.6	11	Cyprus	76.0
	Sweden	77.6		Norway	76.0
5	Hong Kong	77.3	13	Malta	75.9
6	Cayman Islands[a]	77.1		Singapore	75.9
	Israel	77.1		Spain	75.9
8	Canada	76.7		Switzerland	75.9

Highest female life expectancy
Years, 2000–05

1	Andorra[a]	86.6		Martinique	82.3
2	Japan	85.1		Switzerland	82.3
3	France	82.8	12	Australia	82.0
	Hong Kong	82.8		Virgin Islands	82.0
	Spain	82.8	14	Belgium	81.9
6	Sweden	82.6		Canada	81.9
7	Faroe Islands[a]	82.4		Iceland	81.9
8	Aruba[a]	82.3		Italy	81.9
	Cayman Islands[a]	82.3		Norway	81.9

a 2003 estimate. b 2001

Lowest life expectancy

Years, 2000–05

1	Zambia	32.4		Uganda	46.2
2	Zimbabwe	33.1	27	South Africa	47.7
3	Sierra Leone	34.2	28	Somalia	47.9
4	Swaziland	34.4	29	Congo-Brazzaville	48.2
5	Lesotho	35.1	30	Mali	48.6
6	Malawi	37.5	31	Equatorial Guinea	49.1
7	Mozambique	38.1		Guinea	49.1
8	Rwanda	39.3	33	Haiti	49.5
9	Central African Rep	39.5	34	Togo	49.7
10	Botswana	39.7	35	Benin	50.6
11	Angola	40.1	36	Nigeria	51.5
12	Burundi	40.9	37	Mauritania	52.5
13	Côte d'Ivoire	41.0	38	Eritrea	52.7
14	Liberia	41.4	39	Senegal	52.9
15	Congo	41.8	40	Madagascar	53.6
16	Afghanistan	43.1	41	Gambia, The	54.1
17	Tanzania	43.3	42	Laos	54.5
18	Namibia	44.3	43	Sudan	55.6
19	Kenya	44.6	44	Gabon	56.6
20	Chad	44.7	45	Myanmar	57.3
21	Guinea-Bissau	45.3	46	Cambodia	57.4
22	Ethiopia	45.5	47	Papua New Guinea	57.6
23	Burkina Faso	45.7	48	Ghana	57.9
24	Cameroon	46.2	49	Nepal	59.9
	Niger	46.2	50	Yemen	60.0

Lowest male life expectancy

Years, 2000–05

1	Lesotho	32.3	11	Botswana	38.9
2	Zambia	32.7	12	Burundi	40.4
3	Sierra Leone	33.1	13	Liberia	40.7
4	Swaziland	33.3	14	Congo	40.8
5	Zimbabwe	33.7		Côte d'Ivoire	40.8
6	Mozambique	36.6	16	Tanzania	42.5
7	Malawi	37.3	17	Namibia	42.9
8	Central African Rep	38.5	18	Afghanistan	43.0
9	Angola	38.8	19	Kenya	43.5
	Rwanda	38.8	20	Chad	43.7

Lowest female life expectancy

Years, 2000–05

1	Zambia	32.1	10	Central African Rep	40.6
2	Zimbabwe	32.6	11	Côte d'Ivoire	41.2
3	Swaziland	35.4	12	Burundi	41.4
4	Sierra Leone	35.5	13	Angola	41.5
5	Lesotho	37.7	14	Liberia	42.2
	Malawi	37.7	15	Congo	42.8
7	Mozambique	39.6	16	Afghanistan	43.3
8	Rwanda	39.7	17	Tanzania	44.1
9	Botswana	40.5			

Death rates and infant mortality

Highest death rates
Number of deaths per 1,000 population, 2000–05

#	Country	Rate	#	Country	Rate
1	Sierra Leone	29.3	49	Senegal	12.2
2	Zambia	28.0	50	Eritrea	11.9
3	Zimbabwe	27.0	51	Croatia	11.8
4	Lesotho	25.7	52	Sudan	11.7
5	Swaziland	25.4	53	Lithuania	11.6
6	Malawi	24.1	54	Gabon	11.5
7	Angola	23.6	55	Denmark	11.3
8	Mozambique	23.5	56	Myanmar	11.2
9	Central African Rep	22.1	57	North Korea	11.0
10	Rwanda	21.8	58	Italy	10.9
11	Afghanistan	21.5	59	Czech Republic	10.8
	Liberia	21.5		Portugal	10.8
13	Botswana	21.4	61	Moldova	10.7
	Congo	21.4	62	Germany	10.6
15	Burundi	20.6		Serbia & Montenegro	10.6
16	Côte d'Ivoire	20.0		Sweden	10.6
17	Guinea-Bissau	19.6	65	Greece	10.5
18	Chad	19.5	66	United Kingdom	10.4
19	Niger	19.1	67	Channel Islands	10.1
20	Tanzania	18.1	68	Belgium	10.0
21	Namibia	17.9		Cambodia	10.0
22	Ethiopia	17.7		Ghana	10.0
	Somalia	17.7		Poland	10.0
24	Burkina Faso	17.4	72	Austria	9.9
25	Cameroon	16.9		Georgia	9.9
	South Africa	16.9		Norway	9.9
27	Equatorial Guinea	16.7	75	Finland	9.8
	Kenya	16.7		Slovakia	9.8
	Uganda	16.7		Slovenia	9.8
30	Mali	16.2		Switzerland	9.8
31	Guinea	16.1	79	Nepal	9.7
32	Congo-Brazzaville	15.4	80	Pakistan	9.6
33	Bulgaria	15.1	81	Kazakhstan	9.5
34	Togo	14.7	82	Papua New Guinea	9.4
35	Haiti	14.6	83	France	9.3
	Russia	14.6	84	Yemen	9.2
37	Benin	14.3	85	Spain	9.1
38	Mauritania	14.2		Uruguay	9.1
	Ukraine	14.2	87	Netherlands	8.9
40	Nigeria	13.7	88	Iraq	8.8
41	Estonia	13.6	89	Faroe Islands [a]	8.7
	Latvia	13.6	90	Bhutan	8.6
43	Hungary	13.5	91	India	8.5
44	Belarus	13.2	92	Macedonia	8.4
	Madagascar	13.2	93	Bangladesh	8.3
46	Gambia, The	12.7		Ireland	8.3
47	Laos	12.6		Puerto Rico	8.3
48	Romania	12.5		United States	8.3

Note: Both death and, in particular, infant mortality rates can be underestimated in certain countries where not all deaths are officially recorded.   a 2003 estimate.

Highest infant mortality
Number of deaths per 1,000 live births, 2000–05

1	Sierra Leone	177.2	21	Tanzania	99.8
2	Afghanistan	161.7	22	Mauritania	96.7
3	Liberia	147.4	23	Burkina Faso	93.2
4	Angola	140.3	24	Benin	92.7
5	Niger	125.7	25	Lesotho	92.1
6	Mozambique	122.0	26	Madagascar	91.5
7	Guinea-Bissau	120.0	27	Cameroon	88.1
8	Congo	119.6	28	Laos	88.0
9	Mali	118.7	29	Pakistan	86.5
10	Somalia	117.7	30	Uganda	86.1
11	Malawi	115.4	31	Congo-Brazzaville	84.0
12	Chad	115.3	32	Myanmar	83.5
13	Rwanda	111.5	33	Iraq	83.3
14	Burundi	107.4	34	Togo	81.5
15	Zambia	104.8	35	Gambia, The	80.5
16	Guinea	101.7	36	Nigeria	78.8
17	Côte d'Ivoire	101.3	37	Swaziland	78.3
18	Equatorial Guinea	100.9	38	Sudan	77.0
19	Central African Rep	100.4	39	Cambodia	73.2
	Ethiopia	100.4	40	Eritrea	73.0

Lowest death rates
No. deaths per 1,000 pop., 2000–05

1	Kuwait	1.9
2	United Arab Emirates	2.4
3	Brunei	2.8
4	Bahrain	3.1
5	Oman	3.3
6	Qatar	3.7
	Saudi Arabia	3.7
8	Costa Rica	3.9
	Syria	3.9
10	Libya	4.2
11	Jordan	4.3
	West Bank and Gaza	4.3
13	Malaysia	4.6
	Venezuela	4.6
15	Cayman Islands[a]	4.7
	Macau	4.7
17	French Polynesia	4.8
18	Guam	4.9
	New Caledonia	4.9
20	Mexico	5.0
	Panama	5.0
22	Nicaragua	5.1
	Paraguay	5.1
	Philippines	5.1
25	Singapore	5.2

Lowest infant mortality
No. deaths per 1,000 live births, 2000–05

1	Singapore	2.9
2	Japan	3.2
3	Iceland	3.4
	Sweden	3.4
5	Finland	4.0
6	Andorra[a]	4.1
	Hong Kong	4.1
8	Belgium	4.2
9	Germany	4.5
	Netherlands	4.5
	Norway	4.5
12	Austria	4.7
13	Switzerland	4.8
14	Denmark	5.0
	France	5.0
	South Korea	5.0
17	Spain	5.1
18	Canada	5.3
19	Italy	5.4
	Luxembourg	5.4
	United Kingdom	5.4
22	Australia	5.5
	Channel Islands	5.5
	Slovenia	5.5
25	Czech Republic	5.6

a 2003 estimate.

Death and disease

Breast cancer

Deaths per 100,000 pop., 2000

1	Denmark	26.5
2	Iceland	24.9
3	Belgium	24.5
4	United Kingdom	24.2
5	Hungary	24.0
6	Switzerland	23.5
7	Germany	23.4
8	Netherlands	23.3
9	Malta	23.2
10	Austria	21.7
11	Italy	20.7
12	Luxembourg	20.1
13	Uruguay	19.9
14	France	19.4
15	Czech Republic	19.3
16	New Zealand	18.5
17	Canada	18.1
	Norway	18.1
	Slovenia	18.1
20	Croatia	17.7
21	Barbados	17.5

Lung cancer

Deaths per 100,000 pop., 2000

1	Hungary	79.0
2	Belgium	67.5
3	Denmark	66.2
4	United Kingdom	63.3
5	Croatia	58.3
6	Italy	57.0
7	Netherlands	56.9
8	United States	56.7
9	Canada	56.6
10	Czech Republic	55.9
11	Greece	53.6
12	Hong Kong	52.9
13	Poland	51.5
14	Luxembourg	51.1
15	Estonia	49.8
16	Germany	48.5
17	Slovenia	48.1
18	Russia	44.6
19	Spain	44.3
20	Japan	42.4
21	Latvia	42.2

Malaria

Deaths per 100,000 pop., 2000

1	Congo	452
2	Angola	383
3	Niger	329
4	Sierra Leone	321
5	Mozambique	263
6	Mali	260
7	Chad	232
8	Burkina Faso	223
9	Malawi	212
10	Nigeria	209
11	Guinea	206
12	Benin	190
13	Rwanda	186
14	Tanzania	181
15	Equatorial Guinea	165
16	Liberia	164
17	Zambia	158
18	Uganda	151
19	Burundi	149
20	Guinea-Bissau	139
21	Madagascar	138
22	Central African Rep	132
23	Côte d'Ivoire	118

Tuberculosis

Deaths per 100,000 pop., 2000

1	Somalia	115
2	Afghanistan	96
3	Swaziland	92
4	Cambodia	91
5	Zambia	89
6	Mali	73
7	Indonesia	67
8	Angola	64
9	Sierra Leone	63
	Togo	63
11	Philippines	61
	Uganda	61
13	Haiti	58
14	Congo	57
	Côte d'Ivoire	57
	Papua New Guinea	57
17	Bangladesh	56
18	Gambia, The	55
	Liberia	55
	Mauritania	55
	Rwanda	55
22	Madagascar	54
	Nigeria	54

Note: Statistics are not available for all countries. The number of cases diagnosed and reported depends on the quality of medical practice and administration and can be under-reported in a number of countries.

Diabetes
Cases per 100,000 pop., 2000

1	United Arab Emirates	13,230
2	Malta	9,994
3	Mauritius	9,491
4	Andorra	8,426
5	Greece	8,032
6	Singapore	7,976
7	Italy	7,394
8	Belarus	7,244
9	Spain	6,807
10	Qatar	6,616
11	Portugal	6,601
12	Canada	6,468
13	Cyprus	6,284
14	United States	6,191
15	Bulgaria	5,993
16	Bahrain	5,667
17	Brunei	5,419
18	Japan	5,313
19	Kuwait	5,265
20	Romania	4,879

Measles immunisation
Lowest % of children under 12 months, 2002

1	Mali	33
2	Central African Rep	35
3	Congo-Brazzaville	37
4	Nigeria	40
5	Afghanistan	44
6	Congo	45
	Somalia	45
8	Burkina Faso	46
9	Guinea-Bissau	47
10	Niger	48
11	Sudan	49
12	Cambodia	52
	Ethiopia	52
14	Haiti	53
15	Guinea	54
	Senegal	54
17	Chad	55
	Gabon	55
	Laos	55
20	Côte d'Ivoire	56

HIV/AIDS
Prevalence among population aged 15–49, %, 2000

1	Botswana	37.5
2	Swaziland	31.2
3	Lesotho	29.9
4	Zimbabwe	24.8
5	Namibia	20.8
6	South Africa	19.6
7	Zambia	16.8
8	Malawi	16.0
9	Central African Rep	12.8
10	Kenya	12.3
11	Mozambique	11.9
12	Côte d'Ivoire	9.7
13	Equatorial Guinea	9.2
14	Cameroon	7.4
15	Tanzania	7.1
16	Rwanda	7.0
17	Burundi	6.4
18	Uganda	5.8
19	Nigeria	5.7
20	Congo-Brazzaville	5.5
	Haiti	5.5
22	Ethiopia	5.0
	Gabon	5.0
24	Chad	4.9
25	Togo	4.8

AIDS
Estimated deaths per 100,000 pop., 2001

1	Botswana	1,673
2	Zimbabwe	1,556
3	Swaziland	1,279
4	Lesotho	1,215
5	Zambia	1,127
6	South Africa	822
7	Namibia	727
8	Malawi	691
9	Rwanda	616
10	Burundi	615
11	Kenya	607
12	Central African Rep	582
13	Côte d'Ivoire	459
14	Tanzania	389
15	Burkina Faso	371
16	Haiti	363
17	Congo-Brazzaville	354
18	Uganda	350
19	Cameroon	349
20	Mozambique	322
21	Togo	258
22	Ethiopia	248
23	Sierra Leone	240
24	Congo	228
25	Bahamas	198

Health

Highest health spending
As % of GDP

1	United States	13.9
2	Lebanon	12.4
3	Cambodia	11.8
4	Switzerland	11.1
5	Uruguay	10.9
6	Germany	10.8
7	Suriname	9.8
8	France	9.6
9	Argentina	9.5
	Canada	9.5
11	Jordan	9.5
12	Greece	9.4
13	Australia	9.2
	Portugal	9.2
15	Croatia	9.0
	Iceland	9.0
17	Belgium	8.9
	Malta	8.9
	Netherlands	8.9
20	Israel	8.7
	Sweden	8.7
22	South Africa	8.6
23	Denmark	8.4
	Italy	8.4
	Slovenia	8.4
26	New Zealand	8.3
27	Serbia & Montenegro	8.2

Lowest health spending
As % of GDP

1	Azerbaijan	0.9
2	Madagascar	2.0
3	Congo	2.1
	Myanmar	2.1
5	Indonesia	2.4
6	North Korea	2.5
7	Chad	2.6
	Somalia	2.6
9	Togo	2.8
10	Libya	2.9
11	Oman	3.0
12	Brunei	3.1
	Kazakhstan	3.1
	Laos	3.1
15	Iraq	3.2
	Qatar	3.2
17	Cameroon	3.3
	Philippines	3.3
	Swaziland	3.3
20	Mauritius	3.4
	Nigeria	3.4
	Tajikistan	3.4
23	Bangladesh	3.5
	Congo-Brazzavila	3.5
	Guinea	3.5
	Sudan	3.5
	United Arab Emirates	3.5

Highest population per doctor

1	Niger	33,333
2	Nepal	25,000
3	Papua New Guinea	14,286
4	Senegal	11,111
5	Madagascar	7,143
6	Yemen	5,000
7	Cambodia	3,333
	Myanmar	3,333
9	Sri Lanka	2,703
10	Vietnam	2,083
11	West Bank and Gaza	2,000
12	Iraq	1,818
13	Costa Rica	1,111
14	Algeria	1,000
15	Syria	769

	Turkey	769
17	Oman	752
18	Albania	719
19	South Korea	714
20	China	694
21	Bosnia	690
22	Mexico	667
23	Singapore	613
24	Romania	529
25	Japan	526
26	United Kingdom	500
27	Canada	476
28	Tajikistan	472
29	Macedonia	457
	Slovenia	457

Most hospital beds
Beds per 1,000 pop.

1	Switzerland	17.9	30	Moldova	5.9
2	Japan	16.5	31	Kirgizstan	5.5
3	Norway	14.6	32	Uzbekistan	5.3
4	Belarus	12.6	33	Slovenia	5.2
5	Netherlands	10.8	34	Malta	5.0
	Russia	10.8	35	Greece	4.9
7	Ireland	9.7		Italy	4.9
8	Lithuania	9.2		Poland	4.9
9	Germany	9.1	38	Macedonia	4.8
10	Czech Republic	8.8	39	Denmark	4.5
11	Ukraine	8.7	40	Armenia	4.3
12	Austria	8.6		Georgia	4.3
13	Azerbaijan	8.5	42	Spain	4.1
14	France	8.2		United Kingdom	4.1
	Hungary	8.2	44	Portugal	4.0
	Latvia	8.2	45	Canada	3.9
17	Australia	7.9	46	Sweden	3.6
18	Slovakia	7.8		United States	3.6
19	Finland	7.5	48	Albania	3.3
	Romania	7.5	49	Bosnia	3.2
21	Bulgaria	7.2	50	Turkey	2.6
22	Kazakhstan	7.0	51	China	2.5
23	Estonia	6.7	52	Andorra	2.3
	Ethiopia	6.7	53	Oman	2.2
25	Tajikistan	6.4	54	Algeria	2.1
26	Israel	6.2	55	Costa Rica	1.7
	New Caledonia	6.2	56	Iraq	1.5
28	South Korea	6.1	57	Syria	1.4
29	Croatia	6.0	58	Malawi	1.3

Lowest population per doctor

1	Belarus	222		Denmark	294
2	Greece	227	17	France	303
3	Italy	233		Germany	303
4	Russia	238		Netherlands	303
5	Lithuania	248		Spain	303
6	Belgium	256	21	Austria	313
7	Georgia	258		Portugal	313
8	Israel	267	23	Estonia	319
9	Kazakhstan	277	24	Finland	323
10	Slovakia	278	25	Norway	333
11	Azerbaijan	279		Sweden	333
12	Iceland	286	27	Ukraine	336
	Switzerland	286	28	Uzbekistan	341
14	Bulgaria	291	29	Latvia	344
15	Czech Republic	294		Malta	344

Note: Data for these six health rankings refer to the latest year available, 1998–2002.

Marriage and divorce

Highest marriage rates
Number of marriages per 1,000 population

1	Bermuda	16.7		Costa Rica	6.4
2	Barbados	13.1		Denmark	6.4
3	Cyprus	12.3		Singapore	6.4
4	Egypt	10.6	36	Malta	6.2
5	Jamaica	10.4		Réunion	6.2
6	Ethiopia	10.2	38	Bosnia	6.1
7	Fiji	10.1	39	Croatia	6.0
8	Guam	9.7		Moldova	6.0
9	Bangladesh	9.5	41	Japan	5.9
10	Bahamas	9.3		Ukraine	5.9
	Sri Lanka	9.3	43	Trinidad & Tobago	5.8
12	Mauritius	9.2	44	Algeria	5.6
13	Cayman Islands	8.7		El Salvador	5.6
14	Syria	8.5		Iceland	5.6
15	Iran	8.4		Romania	5.6
	United States	8.4		Turkmenistan	5.6
17	Turkey	8.3	49	Bahrain	5.5
18	Taiwan	7.5		Kazakhstan	5.5
19	Albania	7.4		Norway	5.5
	Belarus	7.4		Poland	5.5
21	Uzbekistan	7.1	53	Australia	5.4
22	Aruba	7.0		Kirgizstan	5.4
	Brunei	7.0	55	French Polynesia	5.3
	Macedonia	7.0		Mongolia	5.3
	Puerto Rico	7.0		New Zealand	5.3
26	Indonesia	6.7	58	Ecuador	5.2
	Mexico	6.7		Jordan	5.2
	Philippines	6.7		Serbia & Montenegro	5.2
	Thailand	6.7		Spain	5.2
30	Portugal	6.6		Suriname	5.2
31	South Korea	6.5		Tunisia	5.2
32	China	6.4		United Kingdom	5.2

Lowest marriage rates
Number of marriages per 1,000 population

1	Macau	2.8	12	Slovenia	3.6
2	Armenia	2.9	13	Argentina	3.7
	Georgia	2.9		Greenland	3.7
4	Saudi Arabia	3.0		Panama	3.7
5	Latvia	3.1	16	Bulgaria	3.8
	Malaysia	3.1	17	Libya	3.9
7	Colombia	3.3	18	Dominican Republic	4.0
	United Arab Emirates	3.3		Estonia	4.0
9	Andorra	3.4		Honduras	4.0
	Qatar	3.4		Hong Kong	4.0
11	Tajikistan	3.5		Venezuela	4.0

Note: The data are based on latest available figures and hence will be affected by the population age structure at the time. Marriage rates refer to registered marriages only and, therefore, reflect the customs surrounding registry and efficiency of administration.

Highest divorce rates
Number of divorces per 1,000 population

1	United States	4.7	32	Costa Rica	2.0
2	Puerto Rico	4.6		Israel	2.0
3	Guam	4.3		Kazakhstan	2.0
4	Belarus	4.2		Romania	2.0
	Cayman Islands	4.2		Uruguay	2.0
6	Aruba	3.4	37	France	1.9
	Cuba	3.4		Japan	1.9
8	New Zealand	3.3		Netherlands	1.9
	Ukraine	3.3		Taiwan	1.9
10	Czech Republic	3.2	41	Hong Kong	1.8
	Lithuania	3.2		Singapore	1.8
12	Estonia	3.1	43	Iceland	1.7
	United Kingdom	3.1		Slovakia	1.7
14	Bermuda	3.0	45	Cyprus	1.6
15	Russia	2.9		Kuwait	1.6
16	Australia	2.8		Portugal	1.6
17	Denmark	2.7		South Korea	1.6
	Finland	2.7	49	Egypt	1.5
	Moldova	2.7		Tajikistan	1.5
	Switzerland	2.7	51	Bahamas	1.4
21	Ethiopia	2.6	52	Bahrain	1.3
	Netherlands Antilles	2.6		Bulgaria	1.3
23	Hungary	2.5		Guadeloupe	1.3
24	Belgium	2.4		Jordan	1.3
	Latvia	2.4		Réunion	1.3
	Luxembourg	2.4	57	Dominican Republic	1.2
	Norway	2.4		Turkmenistan	1.2
28	Canada	2.3	59	Kirgizstan	1.1
	Germany	2.3		Poland	1.1
30	Austria	2.2		Qatar	1.1
31	Sweden	2.1		United Arab Emirates	1.1

Lowest divorce rates
Number of divorces per 1,000 population

1	Guatemala	0.1		Brazil	0.7
2	Colombia	0.2		Ecuador	0.7
3	Libya	0.3		Martinique	0.7
	Mongolia	0.3		Syria	0.7
5	Armenia	0.4	20	Albania	0.8
	Georgia	0.4		Brunei	0.8
	Jamaica	0.4		China	0.8
8	Bosnia	0.5		Iran	0.8
	Chile	0.5		Italy	0.8
	Macedonia	0.5		Macau	0.8
	Mexico	0.5		New Caledonia	0.8
12	El Salvador	0.6		Panama	0.8
	Nicaragua	0.6		Saudi Arabia	0.8
	Turkey	0.6		Spain	0.8
15	Azerbaijan	0.7		Uzbekistan	0.8

Households and prices

Biggest households[a]
Population per dwelling

1	Kuwait	8.3		Lesotho	5.6
2	Saudi Arabia	8.2		Sri Lanka	5.6
3	Pakistan	7.6	29	Central African Rep	5.5
4	Gabon	6.9		Chad	5.5
5	United Arab Emirates	6.7		Gambia, The	5.5
6	Algeria	6.3		Iran	5.5
7	Bosnia	6.2		Iraq	5.5
	Congo-Brazzaville	6.2		Laos	5.5
9	Burundi	6.1		Mozambique	5.5
	Jordan	6.1		Uzbekistan	5.5
	North Korea	6.1		Yemen	5.5
	Swaziland	6.1	38	Bangladesh	5.4
13	Papua New Guinea	6.0		Fiji	5.4
	Réunion	6.0	40	Madagascar	5.3
	Rwanda	6.0		Mauritius	5.3
	Sierra Leone	6.0		Morocco	5.3
	Sudan	6.0		New Caledonia	5.3
18	French Polynesia	5.9		Tanzania	5.3
	Guam	5.9	45	Afghanistan	5.2
	India	5.9		Azerbaijan	5.2
	Malawi	5.9		Haiti	5.2
22	Ghana	5.8		Liberia	5.2
	Niger	5.8		Mongolia	5.2
	Togo	5.8		Nigeria	5.2
25	Senegal	5.7		Uganda	5.2
26	Guinea	5.6			

Highest cost of living[b]
December 2003, USA=100

1	Japan	138	17	Australia	93
2	Norway	123		Belgium	93
3	Denmark	116	19	Russia	92
	France	116	20	China	90
5	Hong Kong	113		Côte d'Ivoire	90
6	Switzerland	109	22	Israel	89
	United Kingdom	109		Taiwan	89
8	Iceland	106	24	Italy	88
9	Austria	104	25	Luxembourg	86
10	Finland	103	26	Spain	85
11	Netherlands	100	27	Canada	82
12	Sweden	99		Mexico	82
13	Singapore	98		New Zealand	82
14	South Korea	97	30	Jordan	81
15	Germany	95		Turkey	81
16	Ireland	94			

a Latest available year.
b The cost of living index shown is compiled by The Economist Intelligence Unit for use
by companies in determining expatriate compensation: it is a comparison of the cost
of maintaining a typical international lifestyle in the country rather than a
comparison of the purchasing power of a citizen of the country. The index is based on
typical urban prices an international executive and family will face abroad. The prices

Smallest households[a]
Population per dwelling

1	Sweden	2.0		New Zealand	2.8
2	Denmark	2.1		Poland	2.8
3	Finland	2.2		Russia	2.8
	Germany	2.2	30	Croatia	2.9
	Norway	2.2		Cyprus	2.9
6	Iceland	2.3		Luxembourg	2.9
	Netherlands	2.3		Portugal	2.9
	Switzerland	2.3		Romania	2.9
9	Austria	2.4	35	Greece	3.0
	Belgium	2.4	36	Mali	3.1
	Estonia	2.4		Slovenia	3.1
	France	2.4	38	Belarus	3.2
	Latvia	2.4		Ireland	3.2
	United Kingdom	2.4		Spain	3.2
15	Uruguay	2.5	41	Hong Kong	3.3
16	Australia	2.6		Malta	3.3
	Canada	2.6		Myanmar	3.3
	Italy	2.6		Serbia & Montenegro	3.3
	Japan	2.6		South Korea	3.3
	Lithuania	2.6		Taiwan	3.3
	Ukraine	2.6	47	Macau	3.4
	United States	2.6		Singapore	3.4
23	Bulgaria	2.7	49	Albania	3.5
	Hungary	2.7		Brazil	3.5
	Slovakia	2.7		Oman	3.5
26	Czech Republic	2.8			

Lowest cost of living[b]
December 2003, USA=100

1	Iran	32	16	Bangladesh	57
2	Philippines	39	17	Chile	58
3	Paraguay	40		Uzbekistan	58
4	Pakistan	44	19	Cambodia	59
5	India	45	20	Peru	61
6	Egypt	51		Thailand	61
7	Argentina	52		Venezuela	61
	Zambia	52	23	Brunei	62
9	Costa Rica	53		Hungary	62
	Romania	53		Kenya	62
11	Algeria	54		Malaysia	62
	Sri Lanka	54	27	Syria	63
13	Brazil	56		Vietnam	63
	Colombia	56	29	Ukraine	64
	Uraguay	56	30	South Africa	65

are for products of international comparable quality found in a supermarket or department store. Prices found in local markets and bazaars are not used unless the available merchandise is of the specified quality and the shopping area itself is safe for executive and family members. New York City prices are used as the base, so United States = 100.

Consumer goods ownership

TV

Colour TVs per 100 households

1	Belgium	99.6	26	Norway	92.7
2	United States	99.5	27	Denmark	92.4
3	Taiwan	99.4	28	Jordan	92.2
4	Ireland	99.3	29	Australia	91.7
5	Hong Kong	99.1	30	Greece	91.4
	Japan	99.1	31	Malaysia	90.2
5	Saudi Arabia	99.1	32	Argentina	90.1
8	Canada	98.7	33	Tunisia	89.9
9	Singapore	98.6	34	Mexico	89.7
	United Kingdom	98.6	35	Kuwait	89.4
11	Netherlands	98.5	36	Czech Republic	89.3
12	Spain	98.4	37	Hungary	89.2
13	Finland	98.3	38	Slovenia	88.6
14	Austria	97.8	39	Croatia	87.9
15	Portugal	97.7	40	Brazil	86.6
16	New Zealand	97.4	41	Slovakia	86.1
17	Sweden	97.2	42	Colombia	85.8
18	Germany	97.1	43	Estonia	85.1
19	Switzerland	96.8	44	Poland	82.8
20	Israel	96.5	45	Thailand	82.3
21	United Arab Emirates	96.1	46	Belarus	77.8
22	France	95.9	47	Russia	76.3
23	Italy	94.2	48	Ukraine	75.7
24	South Korea	93.1	49	Lithuania	72.6
25	Venezuela	92.8	50	Algeria	71.7

Telephone

Telephone lines per 100 people

1	Bermuda	86.2	23	Guam	50.9
2	Cayman Islands	84.9	24	Slovenia	50.6
3	Luxembourg	79.7		Spain	50.6
4	Switzerland	74.4	26	Ireland	50.2
5	Sweden	73.6	27	Barbados	49.4
6	Norway	73.4	27	Belgium	49.4
7	Denmark	68.9	29	Greece	49.1
8	Cyprus	68.8	30	Austria	48.9
9	Iceland	65.3		South Korea	48.9
10	Germany	65.1	32	Faroe Islands	48.2
11	United States	64.6	33	Italy	48.1
12	Canada	63.6	34	Israel	46.7
13	Virgin Islands	63.5	35	Singapore	46.3
14	Netherlands	61.8	36	Guadeloupe	45.7
15	United Kingdom	59.1	37	New Zealand	44.8
16	Taiwan	58.2	38	Andorra	43.8
17	France	56.9	39	Martinique	43.0
18	Hong Kong	56.5	40	Portugal	42.1
19	Japan	55.8	41	Croatia	41.7
20	Australia	53.9	42	Réunion	41.0
21	Finland	52.4	43	Bahamas	40.6
22	Malta	52.3	44	Macau	39.9

CD player
CD players per 100 households

1	Denmark	89.3	13	Japan	65.8
2	Netherlands	89.0	14	Finland	64.6
3	Norway	88.2	15	Switzerland	60.1
4	New Zealand	86.4	16	United States	56.8
5	Germany	85.4	17	Singapore	56.4
6	United Kingdom	84.1	18	Hong Kong	56.1
7	Sweden	83.5	19	Ireland	40.9
8	Australia	82.3	20	Spain	39.8
9	Canada	76.1	21	Portugal	39.0
10	Austria	70.8	22	Peru	31.7
11	Taiwan	69.1	23	Saudi Arabia	31.5
12	Belgium	67.4	24	Hungary	30.1

Computer
Computers per 100 people

1	Switzerland	70.9	18	United Kingdom	40.6
2	United States	65.9	19	Taiwan	39.5
3	Singapore	62.2	20	Japan	38.2
4	Sweden	62.1	21	Austria	36.9
5	Luxembourg	59.4	22	France	34.7
6	Denmark	57.7	23	Slovenia	30.1
7	Australia	56.5	24	Cyprus	27.0
8	South Korea	55.6	25	Malta	25.5
9	Norway	52.8	26	Israel	24.3
10	Canada	48.7	27	Belgium	24.1
11	Netherlands	46.7	28	Italy	23.1
12	Iceland	45.1	29	Estonia	21.0
13	Finland	44.2	30	Macau	20.8
14	Germany	43.1	31	Costa Rica	19.7
15	Hong Kong	42.2	32	Spain	19.6
16	Ireland	42.1	33	Slovakia	18.0
17	New Zealand	41.4	34	Qatar	17.8

Mobile telephone
Subscribers per 100 people

1	Taiwan	106.2	16	Spain	82.4
2	Luxembourg	106.1	17	Martinique	79.0
3	Israel	95.5	18	Switzerland	78.9
4	Hong Kong	94.3	19	Austria	78.6
5	Italy	93.9		Belgium	78.6
6	Iceland	90.6	21	Ireland	76.3
7	Sweden	88.9	22	Netherlands	74.5
8	Finland	86.7	23	Germany	72.8
9	Czech Republic	84.9	24	Malta	69.9
10	Greece	84.5	25	Guadeloupe	69.7
11	Norway	84.4	26	United Arab Emirates	69.6
12	United Kingdom	84.1	27	South Korea	68.0
13	Slovenia	83.5	28	Hungary	67.6
14	Denmark	83.3	29	Réunion	65.9
15	Portugal	82.5	30	Estonia	65.0

Books and newspapers

Book sales

$m

1	United States	29,548
2	Japan	19,148
3	Germany	9,845
4	United Kingdom	4,676
5	Mexico	3,464
6	China	3,171
7	France	2,724
8	Italy	2,583
9	Spain	2,402
10	Canada	1,677
11	Australia	1,187
12	Belgium	979
13	India	781
14	South Korea	723
15	Sweden	697
16	Colombia	673
17	Switzerland	672
18	Venezuela	641
19	Norway	626
20	Taiwan	618
21	Finland	510
22	Singapore	427
23	Netherlands	421
24	Poland	418
25	Portugal	381
26	Denmark	361
27	Chile	352
28	Austria	340
29	Vietnam	335
30	Argentina	276

Per head, $

1	Japan	150
2	Norway	139
3	Germany	120
4	Singapore	102
	United States	102
6	Finland	98
7	Belgium	95
8	Switzerland	93
9	Sweden	79
10	United Kingdom	78
11	New Zealand	70
12	Denmark	68
13	Australia	61
14	Ireland	60
	Spain	60
16	Canada	54
17	France	46
18	Italy	45
19	Austria	42
20	Portugal	38
21	Mexico	34
22	Taiwan	27
23	Netherlands	26
	Venezuela	26
25	Israel	25
26	Czech Republic	24
	Greece	24
28	Chile	23
29	Hungary	16
30	Colombia	15
	South Korea	15

Daily newspapers

Copies per '000 population, latest year

1	Norway	561
2	Japan	555
3	Finland	445
4	Sweden	417
5	Switzerland	365
6	Austria	297
	United Kingdom	297
8	Luxembourg	295
9	Germany	283
10	Denmark	270
11	Netherlands	269
12	Singapore	249
13	Hong Kong	210
14	New Zealand	198
15	United States	191

16	Estonia	182
17	Bulgaria	179
18	Slovenia	172
19	Czech Republic	164
20	Hungary	161
	Latvia	161
22	Canada	160
23	Australia	154
24	Ireland	152
25	Belgium	144
26	France	132
27	Croatia	127
28	Spain	108
29	Italy	103
30	Malaysia	101

Music and the internet

Music sales[a]

$m, 2003			$ per head, 2003	
1	United States	11,847.9	1 Norway	57
2	Japan	4,909.7	2 United Kingdom	54
3	United Kingdom	3,215.7	3 Iceland	52
4	France	2,114.7	4 Qatar	46
5	Germany	2,022.1	5 United States	41
6	Canada	676.0	6 Japan	39
7	Australia	673.8	7 Switzerland	36
8	Italy	644.6	8 Australia	35
9	Spain	595.9	Austria	35
10	Netherlands	498.8	France	35
11	Mexico	346.5	11 Sweden	34
12	Russia	326.2	12 Denmark	33
13	Brazil	304.9	Ireland	33
14	Sweden	295.0	14 Netherlands	31
15	Austria	282.1	15 New Zealand	29
16	Switzerland	256.3	16 Finland	27
17	Norway	255.7	17 Germany	25
18	Belgium	250.7	18 Belgium	24
19	China	198.3	19 Canada	22
20	Denmark	176.9	20 Portugal	15
21	South Korea	162.4	Spain	15
22	South Africa	160.4	22 Hong Kong	13

Internet hosts

By country, January 2004			Per 1,000 pop., January 2004	
1	United States[b]	153,941,781	1 United States[b]	533.6
2	Japan	12,962,065	2 Denmark	276.9
3	Italy	5,469,578	3 Finland	235.4
4	United Kingdom	3,715,752	4 Norway	225.2
5	Germany	3,421,455	5 Netherlands	213.7
6	Netherlands	3,419,182	6 Sweden	175.0
7	Canada	3,210,081	7 Australia	146.0
8	Brazil	3,163,349	8 Switzerland	141.5
9	Australia	2,847,763	9 Belgium	141.2
10	Taiwan	2,777,085	10 New Zealand	124.8
11	France	2,770,836	11 Taiwan	123.4
12	Sweden	1,539,917	12 Austria	121.3
13	Denmark	1,467,415	13 Singapore	115.4
14	Belgium	1,454,350	14 Canada	102.6
15	Mexico	1,333,406	15 Japan	101.7
16	Poland	1,296,766	16 Israel	100.6
17	Finland	1,224,155	17 Italy	95.3
18	Spain	1,127,366	18 Hong Kong	84.6
19	Switzerland	1,018,445	19 United Kingdom	62.2
20	Norway	1,013,273	20 France	46.4
21	Austria	982,246	21 Germany	41.7
22	Argentina	742,358	22 Poland	33.7
23	Israel	634,001	23 Hungary	31.7

a Vinyl, tape, CD, DVD and video.
b Includes all hosts ending ".com", ".net" and ".org", which exaggerates the numbers.

Teenagers

15-year-olds who watch TV 4+ hours a day on weekdays

Males, %			Females, %		
1	Ukraine	45.4	1	Ukraine	39.2
2	Estonia	40.8	2	Israel	33.4
3	Latvia	40.7	3	Portugal	32.0
4	Lithuania	39.1	4	Latvia	31.6
5	Russia	34.7	5	United Kingdom	29.5
6	Israel	33.7	6	Estonia	29.2
7	Poland	33.3	7	Italy	27.3
8	Macedonia	32.4		Russia	27.3
9	Croatia	31.4	9	Norway	26.7
10	United States	31.2		United States	26.7
11	United Kingdom	30.9	11	Spain	26.3
12	Czech Republic	30.5	12	Lithuania	25.4
13	Netherlands	29.6	13	Croatia	25.2
14	Norway	29.0	14	Greenland	24.1
15	Portugal	28.2	15	Czech Republic	23.5

15-year-olds who drink soft drinks every day

Males, %			Females, %		
1	Israel	58.7	1	Israel	54.4
2	Netherlands	57.8	2	Slovenia	41.8
3	Belgium	53.0	3	Ireland	41.0
4	Ireland	48.7	4	Netherlands	40.6
5	Greenland	48.5	5	United States	39.8
6	United States	47.1	6	United Kingdom	36.8
7	Slovenia	46.1	7	Malta	35.9
8	United Kingdom	45.9	8	Belgium	34.7
9	Malta	45.0	9	Macedonia	34.0
10	Switzerland	42.7	10	Hungary	33.5
11	Macedonia	41.6	11	Croatia	32.2
12	Spain	38.1	12	Greenland	31.4
13	Germany	37.7	13	Switzerland	28.8
14	Canada	36.6	14	Czech Republic	27.2
15	Czech Republic	34.7	15	Spain	26.1

15-year-olds who are obese[a]

Males, %			Females, %		
1	United States	10.5	1	United States	5.3
2	Malta	9.3	2	Malta	4.8
3	Canada	4.3	3	Canada	4.6
	United Kingdom	4.3	4	United Kingdom	2.7
5	Hungary	3.7	5	France	2.4
6	Austria	3.3	6	Belgium	1.8
7	Spain	2.9		Hungary	1.8
8	Finland	2.8		Ireland	1.8
9	Greece	2.7	9	Finland	1.4
	Greenland	2.7	10	Greenland	1.2
	Israel	2.7		Macedonia	1.2
12	Italy	2.5		Switzerland	1.2
13	Germany	2.1			
14	Norway	2.0			

15-year-olds who communicate electronically every day[b]

Males, %			Females, %		
1	Greece	50.0	1	Greece	62.7
2	Greenland	46.9	2	Croatia	60.1
	Norway	46.9	3	Italy	58.8
4	Denmark	45.4	4	Norway	57.1
5	Israel	44.2	5	Denmark	56.5
6	Croatia	41.9		Israel	56.5
7	United Kingdom	39.8	7	Russia	55.4
8	Russia	39.3	8	United States	52.8
9	Malta	38.3	9	Macedonia	52.6
10	Canada	37.4	10	Canada	51.4
11	Slovenia	35.9	11	Slovenia	50.0
12	Macedonia	35.5		United Kingdom	50.0
13	Belgium	34.3	13	Switzerland	49.9
14	Sweden	34.2	14	Greenland	48.2
	Switzerland	34.2	15	Austria	47.6

15-year-olds who drink alcohol weekly[c]

Males, %			Females, %		
1	Malta	55.8	1	United Kingdom	48.3
2	Netherlands	55.6	2	Netherlands	47.3
3	United Kingdom	55.0	3	Denmark	43.6
4	Denmark	49.7	4	Malta	39.8
5	Italy	48.3	5	Germany	33.3
6	Germany	45.7	6	Austria	33.1
7	Slovenia	41.5	7	Belgium	29.0
8	Belgium	41.0	8	Italy	28.1
9	Switzerland	39.1	9	Switzerland	27.6
10	Greece	37.5	10	Slovenia	26.4
11	Austria	35.9	11	Czech Republic	25.8
	Croatia	35.9	12	Spain	25.3
13	Hungary	33.7	13	Croatia	24.8
14	Canada	33.6	14	Canada	22.7

15-year-olds who have used cannabis within the past year

Males, %			Females, %		
1	Canada	43.3	1	Canada	37.5
2	Switzerland	40.3	2	Switzerland	35.3
3	United States	36.5	3	United Kingdom	31.7
4	United Kingdom	36.3	4	Greenland	31.1
5	Greenland	36.1	5	Spain	30.0
6	Spain	31.6	6	United States	26.2
7	France	31.2	7	France	23.8
8	Czech Republic	30.9	8	Czech Republic	23.2
9	Slovenia	27.3	9	Slovenia	21.4
10	Ireland	25.5	10	Belgium	20.2
11	Belgium	25.1	11	Netherlands	19.2
12	Portugal	24.9	12	Denmark	18.5

Note: Tables cover Europe and North America only.
a According to body-mass-index measures – see Glossary, page 246.
b Telephone, e-mail or text c Any alcoholic drink.

Nobel prize winners: *1901–2002*

Peace

1	United States	17
2	United Kingdom	11
3	France	9
4	Sweden	5
5	Belgium	4
	Germany	4
7	Norway	3
	South Africa	3
9	Argentina	2
	Austria	2
	Israel	2
	Russia	2
	Switzerland	2

Economics[a]

1	United States	27
2	United Kingdom	8
3	Norway	2
	Sweden	2
5	France	1
	Germany	1
	Netherlands	1
	Russia	1

Literature

1	France	14
2	United States	12
3	United Kingdom	9
4	Germany	7
5	Sweden	6
6	Italy	5
7	Spain	5
8	Norway	3
9	Poland	3
10	Russia	3

Physiology or medicine

1	United States	48
2	United Kingdom	21
3	Germany	14
4	Sweden	7
5	France	6
	Switzerland	6
7	Austria	5
	Denmark	5
9	Belgium	3
	Italy	3

Physics

1	United States	45
2	United Kingdom	19
3	Germany	17
4	France	8
5	Netherlands	6
	Russia	6
7	Japan	4
	Sweden	4
	Switzerland	4
10	Austria	3
	Italy	3
12	Canada	2
	Denmark	2
14	Colombia	1
	India	1
	Ireland	1
	Pakistan	1
	Poland	1

Chemistry

1	United States	39
2	United Kingdom	22
3	Germany	14
4	France	6
	Switzerland	6
6	Sweden	5
7	Canada	4
	Japan	4
9	Argentina	1
	Austria	1
	Belgium	1
	Czech Republic	1
	Denmark	1
	Finland	1
	Italy	1
	Netherlands	1
	Norway	1
	Russia	1

a Since 1969.
Notes: Prizes by country of residence at time awarded. When prizes have been shared in the same field, one credit given to each country. Only top rankings in each field are included.

Olympic medal winners

Summer games, 1896–2000

		Gold	Silver	Bronze
1	United States	872	659	581
2	Soviet Union[a]	517	423	382
3	Germany	374	392	417
4	France	189	195	216
5	United Kingdom	188	243	232
6	Italy	179	144	155
7	Hungary	150	134	158
8	Sweden	138	157	176
9	Australia	103	110	139
10	Finland	101	81	114
11	Japan	98	97	103
12	China	80	79	64
13	Romania	74	83	108
14	Netherlands	61	66	85
15	Cuba	57	47	41
16	Poland	56	72	113
17	Canada	52	80	99
18	Bulgaria	48	82	65
19	Switzerland	47	74	62
20	Denmark	41	63	58

Winter games, 1924–2002

		Gold	Silver	Bronze
1	Germany	108	105	87
2	Norway	94	94	75
3	Soviet Union[a]	87	63	67
4	United States	69	72	52
5	Finland	42	51	49
6	Austria	41	57	63
7	Sweden	39	30	29
8	Switzerland	32	33	38
9	Italy	31	31	27
10	Canada	31	28	37
11	Russia	27	20	13
12	Netherlands	22	28	19
13	France	22	22	28
14	South Korea	11	5	4
15	Japan	8	10	13
16	United Kingdom	8	4	15
17	Croatia	3	1	0
18	China	2	12	8
19	Czech Republic	2	1	2
20	Australia	2	0	1

a Includes unified team in 1992.

Drinking and smoking

Beer drinkers
Litres consumed per head

1	Czech Republic	155.0
2	Ireland	147.1
3	Germany	121.5
4	Austria	109.3
5	Luxembourg	108.2
6	United Kingdom	100.6
7	Denmark	96.7
8	Belgium	96.0
9	Australia	92.4
10	Slovakia	92.3
11	United States[a]	82.0
12	Finland	81.2
	Venezuela[a]	81.2
14	Netherlands	79.2
15	New Zealand	77.8
16	Spain	73.4
17	Estonia	71.0
18	Hungary[a]	70.9
19	Poland	70.7
20	Canada	69.9
21	Romania	59.0
22	Portugal	58.6
23	Sweden	55.9

Wine drinkers
Litres consumed per head

1	Luxembourg	59.1
2	France	56.0
3	Italy	51.0
4	Portugal	43.0
5	Switzerland	41.8
6	Argentina	36.1
7	Hungary[a]	36.0
8	Greece[a]	33.9
9	Uruguay[a]	32.8
10	Denmark	32.0
11	Austria	29.8
12	Spain	29.6
13	Romania	25.3
14	Germany	24.2
15	Finland	23.5
16	Bulgaria[a]	21.3
17	Australia[a]	20.6
18	Malta[a]	20.5
19	United Kingdom	19.6
20	Netherlands	19.0
21	New Zealand	18.9
22	Belgium[a]	17.0
23	Cyprus[a]	16.9

Alcoholic drinks
Litres of pure alcohol consumed per head

1	Luxembourg	11.9
2	Hungary	11.1
3	Czech Republic	10.8
	Ireland	10.8
5	Germany	10.4
6	France	10.3
7	Portugal	9.7
8	Spain	9.6
	United Kingdom	9.6
10	Denmark	9.5
11	Austria	9.2
12	Cyprus	9.1
13	Switzerland	9.0
14	Slovakia	8.8
15	Russia	8.6
16	Romania	8.5
17	Netherlands	8.0
18	Belgium	7.9
19	Greece	7.8
20	Finland	7.7
	Latvia	7.7
22	Italy	7.4
23	Australia	7.3

Smokers
Av. ann. consumption of cigarettes per head per day

1	Greece	8.7
2	Bulgaria	8.2
3	Bosnia	6.6
4	Japan	6.4
5	Macedonia	6.3
	Slovenia	6.3
	Spain	6.3
8	Belgium	6.0
9	Albania	5.7
10	Russia	5.5
	South Korea	5.5
12	Czech Republic	5.3
13	Hungary	5.2
	Switzerland	5.2
	Ukraine	5.2
16	Austria	5.1
	Serbia	5.1
18	Cyprus	5.0
	Poland	5.0
20	Croatia	4.9
	Latvia	4.9
	Taiwan	4.9

a Estimate.

Crime and punishment

Serious assault[a]

No. per 100,000 pop., latest avail. yr.

1	Australia	737
2	Sweden	667
3	South Africa	598
4	Belgium	553
5	Ghana	473
6	Swaziland	466
7	Fiji	379
8	Jamaica	352
9	Netherlands	326
10	United States	319
11	France	226
12	Zimbabwe	226
13	Lebanon	222
14	Barbados	201
15	El Salvador	173
16	Uruguay	168
17	Germany	161
18	Canada	149
19	Côte d'Ivoire	140
20	Ireland	138

Theft[a]

No. per 100,000 pop., latest avail. yr.

1	Australia	6,653
2	Netherlands	5,788
3	United Kingdom	4,542
4	Norway	4,330
5	Belgium	4,258
6	France	3,993
7	Austria	3,808
8	United States	3,805
9	Germany	3,743
10	Iceland	3,722
11	Switzerland	3,714
12	South Africa	3,566
13	Finland	3,528
14	Denmark	3,456
15	Luxembourg	3,319
16	Israel	3,221
17	Estonia	2,821
18	Canada	2,758
19	Malta	2,549
20	Uruguay	2,513

Prisoners

Total prison pop., latest available year

1	United States	2,033,331
2	China[b]	1,549,000
3	Russia	846,967
4	India	313,635
5	Thailand	258,076
6	Brazil	248,989
7	Ukraine	198,900
8	South Africa	180,952
9	Iran	163,526
10	Mexico	154,765
11	Rwanda[b]	112,000
12	Pakistan[b]	87,000
13	Indonesia	84,357
14	United Kingdom	83,409
15	Germany	81,176
16	Poland	80,693
17	Egypt[b]	80,000
18	Philippines	70,383
19	Japan	69,502
20	Ethiopia[b]	65,000
21	Bangladesh	64,866

Per 100,000 pop., latest available year

1	United States	701
2	Russia	584
3	Belarus	554
4	Bermuda	532
5	Virgin Islands	522
6	Cayman Islands	501
7	Turkmenistan	489
8	Suriname	437
9	Ukraine	417
10	Bahamas	410
11	South Africa	402
12	Thailand	401
13	Kirgizstan	390
14	Singapore	388
15	Kazakhstan[b]	386
16	Puerto Rico	378
17	Barbados	367
18	Netherlands Antilles	364
19	Panama	354
20	Latvia	351
	Trinidad & Tobago	351

a Crime statistics are based on offences recorded by the police. The number will therefore depend partly on the efficiency of police administration systems, the definition of offences and the proportion of crimes reported, and therefore may not be strictly comparable.
b Estimate.

Stars...

Space missions

Firsts and selected events

1957 Man-made satellite   Dog in space, Laika
1961 Human in space, Yuri Gagarin
Entire day in space, Gherman Titov
1963 Woman in space, Valentina Tereshkova
1964 Space crew, one pilot and two passengers
1965 Space walk, Alexei Leonov
Computer guidance system
Eight days in space achieved (needed to travel to moon and back)
1966 Docking between space craft and target vehicle
Autopilot re-entry and landing
1968 Live television broadcast from space
Moon orbit
1969 Astronaut transfer from one craft to another in space
Moon landing
1971 Space station, Salyut
Drive on the moon
1973 Space laboratory, Skylab
1978 Non-American, non-Soviet, Vladimir Remek (Czechoslovakia)
1982 Space shuttle, Columbia (first craft to carry four crew members)
1983 Five crew mission
1984 Space walk, untethered
Capture, repair and redeployment of satellite in space
Seven crew mission
1986 Space shuttle explosion, Challenger
Mir space station activated
1990 Hubble telescope deployed
2001 Dennis Tito, first paying space tourist
2003 Space shuttle explosion, Columbia. Shuttle programme suspended.
China's first manned space flight, Yang Liwei

Space vehicle launches

By host country

2002			2003		
1	Russia	23	**1**	United States	24
2	United States	18	**2**	Russia	19
3	France	11	**3**	China	6
4	China	3	**4**	France	4
5	Japan	2	**5**	India	2
6	India	1		Japan	2
	Israel	1			

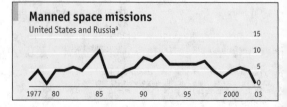

Manned space missions
United States and Russia[a]

1977 80   85   90   95   2000 03

...and Wars

Defence spending
As % of GDP

1	North Korea	25.0	21	Turkey	5.1
2	Congo-Brazzaville	21.7	22	Myanmar	5.0
3	Eritrea	16.0		Suriname	5.0
4	Oman	13.4	24	Sudan	4.9
5	Saudi Arabia	12.0	25	Russia	4.8
6	Kuwait	10.7	26	Iran	4.6
7	Qatar	10.6	27	Botswana	4.5
8	Syria	10.3		Liberia	4.5
9	Angola	9.8	29	Greece	4.4
10	Israel	9.7	30	Chile	4.1
11	Jordan	9.3		China	4.1
12	Ethiopia	8.0		Rwanda	4.1
13	Vietnam	7.1	33	Bahrain	4.0
14	Armenia	6.4		Somalia	4.0
15	Algeria	5.9		United Arab Emirates	4.0
16	Burundi	5.9	36	Cuba	3.9
17	Yemen	5.7		Egypt	3.9
18	Serbia & Montenegro	5.3		Pakistan	3.9
19	Brunei	5.2	39	Bosnia	3.8
	Singapore	5.2		Libya	3.8

Armed forces
'000

		Regulars	Reserves			Regulars	Reserves
1	China	2,270	550	21	France	260	100
2	United States	1,414	1,259	22	Ethiopia	253	
3	India	1,298	535	23	Japan	240	47
4	North Korea	1,082	4,700	24	Italy	217	65
5	Russia	988	2,400	25	United Kingdom	210	257
6	South Korea	686	4,500	26	Saudi Arabia	200	
7	Pakistan	620	513	27	Morocco	196	150
8	Iran	520	350	28	Mexico	193	300
9	Turkey	515	379	29	Greece	178	291
10	Vietnam	484	3,000	30	Spain	178	329
11	Myanmar	444		31	Eritrea	172	120
12	Egypt	443	254	32	Poland	163	234
13	Iraq	389	650	33	Israel	162	425
14	Taiwan	370	1,657	34	Colombia	158	61
15	Syria	319	354	35	Algeria	137	150
16	Thailand	306	200	36	Bangladesh	137	
17	Ukraine	302	1,000	37	Sri Lanka	128	6
18	Indonesia	297	400	38	Cambodia	125	
19	Germany	296	390	39	Sudan	117	
20	Brazil	288	1,115	40	Peru	110	188

a Previously Soviet Union; United States only from 1984; up to May 2003.

Environment

Environmental sustainability index[a]

Highest			Lowest		
1	Finland	73.9	1	Kuwait	23.9
2	Norway	73.0	2	United Arab Emirates	25.7
3	Sweden	72.6	3	North Korea	32.3
4	Canada	70.6	4	Iraq	33.2
5	Switzerland	66.5	5	Saudi Arabia	34.2
6	Uruguay	66.0	6	Haiti	34.8
7	Austria	64.2	7	Ukraine	35.0
8	Iceland	63.9	8	South Korea	35.9
9	Costa Rica	63.2	9	Sierra Leone	36.5
10	Latvia	63.0	10	Nigeria	36.7
11	Hungary	62.7	11	Somalia	37.1
12	Croatia	62.5	12	Turkmenistan	37.3
13	Botswana	61.8	13	Liberia	37.7
14	Slovakia	61.6	14	China	38.5
15	Argentina	61.5	15	Guinea-Bissau	38.8
16	Australia	60.3		Madagascar	38.8
17	Estonia	60.0	17	Mauritania	38.9
	Panama	60.0	18	Belgium	39.1
19	New Zealand	59.9	19	Libya	39.3
20	Brazil	59.6	20	Niger	39.4

Rural population density, highest
People per sq. km. of arable land, 2001

1	Puerto Rico	2,681	25	Slovenia	581
2	Papua New Guinea	2,060	26	Tanzania	575
3	Sri Lanka	1,607	27	Switzerland	571
4	Oman	1,533	28	Philippines	564
5	Egypt	1,306	29	China	561
6	Bangladesh	1,228	30	Malaysia	554
7	Vietnam	923	31	Ethiopia	517
	Yemen	923	32	Guatemala	516
9	United Arab Emirates	773	33	Laos	495
10	Rwanda	743	34	South Korea	491
11	Mauritius	701	35	Tajikistan	485
12	Burundi	699	36	Liberia	461
13	Costa Rica	697	37	India	460
14	Congo-Brazzaville	690	38	Jordan	449
15	Kuwait	684	39	Trinidad & Tobago	441
16	Eritrea	679	40	Swaziland	440
17	Nepal	668	41	Kenya	439
18	Haiti	664	42	Pakistan	438
19	Jamaica	648	43	Colombia	420
20	Sierra Leone	644	44	Malawi	406
21	Somalia	622	45	Uganda	401
22	Guinea	614	46	Lesotho	380
23	Japan	603	47	Madagascar	378
24	Indonesia	591	48	Gambia, The	372

a Based on 20 key indicators, including: environmental systems and stresses; human vulnerability to environmental risks; institutional capacities on environmental issues; shared resources

Rural population

Highest av. ann. growth, 1980–2002, %

1	Yemen	3.2
2	Gambia, The	2.8
	Niger	2.8
4	Uganda	2.7
5	Syria	2.6
	Zambia	2.6
7	Cambodia	2.5
	Chad	2.5
	Côte d'Ivoire	2.5
	Iraq	2.5
	Namibia	2.5
	Tajikistan	2.5
	Turkmenistan	2.5

Lowest av. ann. growth, 1980–2002, %

1	Portugal	-3.2
	South Korea	-3.2
3	Lebanon	-2.8
4	Belgium	-2.4
5	Uruguay	-2.3
6	Gabon	-2.0
7	Libya	-1.7
8	Kuwait	-1.6
9	Belarus	-1.5
10	Germany	-1.4
11	Bulgaria	-1.3
	Serbia & Montenegro	-1.3

Use of fertilisers[a]

Hundreds of grams per ha. of arable land, 1999–2001

1	Singapore	30,423
2	Costa Rica	7,096
3	United Arab Emirates	7,090
4	Malaysia	6,695
5	Ireland	5,871
6	New Zealand	5,317
7	Netherlands	4,755
8	South Korea	4,539
9	Egypt	4,401
10	Slovenia	4,384
11	Mauritius	3,667
12	Belgium	3,549
13	Vietnam	3,407
14	United Kingdom	3,251
15	Japan	3,162

16	Lebanon	3,105
17	Sri Lanka	2,768
18	Israel	2,696
19	China	2,562
20	Chile	2,421
21	Colombia	2,397
22	France	2,367
	Germany	2,367
24	Switzerland	2,277
25	Norway	2,196
26	Italy	2,078
27	Oman	1,690
28	Spain	1,674
29	Bangladesh	1,662
30	Uzbekistan	1,637

Healthy cities index[b]

New York =100, November 2003

Highest

1	Calgary, Canada	121.0
2	Honolulu, United States	120.0
3	Helsinki, Finland	119.5
4	Ottawa, Canada	118.5
5	Minneapolis, United States	117.0
	Oslo, Norway	117.0
	Stockholm, Sweden	117.0

Lowest

1	Baku, Azerbaijan	25.5
2	Antananarivo, Madag.	26.0
3	Dhaka, Bangladesh	29.0
4	Brazzaville, Congo-Braz.	32.0
5	Baghdad, Iraq	32.5
	Ndjamena, Chad	32.5
7	Ouagadougou, Burk. F.	34.0
	Bangui, Cent. Afr. Rep.	34.0
9	Dar es Salaam, Tanzania	34.5
10	Addis Ababa, Ethiopia	35.0
11	Niamey, Niger	35.5

a Nitrogenous, potash and phosphates. Excludes traditional nutrients such as animal and plant manures
b Criteria include: waste removal; air pollution; water potability; infectious disease; hospitals

Water pollutants

'000 kg of organic emissions per day, highest			*Kg of organic emissions per day per industrial worker, highest*	
1	China	6,204.2	1	Senegal	0.36
2	United States	1,968.2	2	Namibia	0.35
3	India	1,582.3	3	Gambia, The	0.34
4	Russia	1,485.8	4	Sierra Leone	0.32
5	Japan	1,332.3	5	Mozambique	0.31
6	Germany	792.2		Panama	0.31
7	Indonesia	752.8	7	Albania	0.29
8	Brazil	629.4		Jamaica	0.29
9	United Kingdom	569.7		Malawi	0.29
10	Ukraine	499.9		Moldova	0.29
11	Italy	495.4	11	Guatemala	0.28
12	Poland	388.2		Paraguay	0.28
13	Spain	374.6		Trinidad & Tobago	0.28
14	Thailand	355.8		Uruguay	0.28
15	Canada	307.3	15	Ecuador	0.27
16	South Korea	303.1	16	Gabon	0.26
17	Mexico	296.1	17	Bolivia	0.25
18	France	278.9		Kenya	0.25
19	Bangladesh	273.1		Tanzania	0.25
20	Czech Republic	258.4		Yemen	0.25
21	South Africa	234.0	21	Algeria	0.24
22	Egypt	203.6		Burundi	0.24
23	Philippines	202.0		Chile	0.24
24	Argentina	177.9		Côte d'Ivoire	0.24
25	Turkey	170.7	25	Ethiopia	0.23
26	Malaysia	158.8		Swaziland	0.23
27	Hungary	152.5	27	Burkina Faso	0.22
28	Netherlands	124.2		New Zealand	0.22
29	Switzerland	123.8		Zambia	0.22

Rural population with access to improved water source[a]
Lowest, 2000, %

1	Afghanistan	11	16	Cameroon	39
2	Ethiopia	12	17	Angola	40
3	Romania	16		Mauritania	40
4	Congo-Brazzaville	17		Rwanda	40
5	Cambodia	26	20	Mozambique	41
6	Chad	26	21	Eritrea	42
	Congo	26		Kenya	42
8	Laos	29	23	Malawi	44
9	Mongolia	30	24	Armenia	45
	Oman	30		Haiti	45
11	Madagascar	31	26	Sierra Leone	46
12	Papua New Guinea	32	27	Gabon	47
13	Guinea	36		Tajikistan	47
14	Burkina Faso	37		Uganda	47
15	Togo	38			

a Such as household connections, public standpipes, protected wells.

Total forested areas, largest
Hectares, m, 2000

1	Russia	851.4	21	Mozambique	30.6
2	Brazil	543.9		Papua New Guinea	30.6
3	Canada	244.6	23	Sweden	27.1
4	United States	226.0	24	Cameroon	23.8
5	China	163.5	25	Paraguay	23.4
6	Australia	154.6	26	Central African Rep	22.9
7	Congo	135.2	27	Congo-Brazzaville	22.1
8	Indonesia	110.0	28	Finland	21.9
9	Angola	69.8	29	Gabon	21.8
10	Peru	65.2	30	Malaysia	19.3
11	India	64.1	31	Zimbabwe	19.0
12	Sudan	61.6	32	Kenya	17.1
13	Mexico	55.2	33	Chile	15.5
14	Bolivia	53.1	34	France	15.3
15	Colombia	49.6	35	Thailand	14.8
16	Venezuela	49.5	36	Spain	14.4
17	Tanzania	38.8	37	Suriname	14.1
18	Myanmar	34.9	38	Nigeria	13.5
19	Argentina	34.6	39	Mali	13.2
20	Zambia	31.2	40	Chad	12.7

Largest forest harvest[a]
Cubic metres, m, annual average between 1999–2001

1	United States	493.0	16	France	42.5
2	India	296.4	17	Myanmar	38.3
3	China	287.9	18	Uganda	37.3
4	Brazil	234.0	19	Chile	36.1
5	Canada	182.6	20	Pakistan	33.3
6	Russia	154.7	21	South Africa	30.6
7	Indonesia	124.0		Vietnam	30.6
8	Ethiopia	89.8	23	Australia	29.3
9	Nigeria	68.7	24	Bangladesh	28.5
10	Congo	68.5	25	Thailand	25.9
11	Sweden	61.6	26	Poland	25.2
12	Finland	53.4	27	Tanzania	23.1
13	Mexico	45.4	28	Ghana	21.9
14	Philippines	43.8	29	Kenya	21.6
15	Germany	43.6	30	Malaysia	20.5

Exports of forest products
$bn, annual average, 1999–2001

1	Canada	26.7	8	Austria	4.2
2	United States	15.1	9	Russia	3.7
3	Finland	10.7	10	China	3.5
	Germany	10.7	11	Belgium	3.4
5	Sweden	9.7	12	Malaysia	2.9
6	France	5.6	13	Netherlands	2.8
7	Indonesia	5.1	14	Brazil	2.7

a Industrial roundwood and wood fuel.

Number of mammal species under threat
Highest, 2002

1	Indonesia	147		Tanzania	42
2	China	94	16	Colombia	41
3	India	88	17	Cameroon	40
4	Brazil	81		Congo	40
5	Mexico	70		Vietnam	40
6	Australia	63	20	Myanmar	39
7	Papua New Guinea	58	21	Japan	37
8	Kenya	51		Thailand	37
9	Madagascar	50		United States	37
	Malaysia	50	24	Ethiopia	35
	Philippines	50	25	Argentina	34
12	Peru	49	26	Ecuador	33
13	Russia	45	27	Laos	31
14	South Africa	42		Nepal	31

Number of bird species under threat
Highest, 2002

1	China	183		Malaysia	37
2	Brazil	114		Thailand	37
	Indonesia	114		Vietnam	37
4	Colombia	78	18	Myanmar	35
5	Peru	76	19	Japan	34
6	India	72	20	Tanzania	33
7	Philippines	67	21	Papua New Guinea	32
8	New Zealand	63	22	Bolivia	28
9	Ecuador	62		Congo	28
10	United States	55		South Africa	28
11	Argentina	39	25	Madagascar	27
	Mexico	39	26	Paraguay	26
13	Russia	38	27	Nepal	25
14	Australia	37		South Korea	25

Most area under protected status[a]
'000 hectares

1	Brazil	153,299.1	15	Bolivia	21,102.1
2	United States	149,796.9	16	Congo	19,392.5
3	Russia	128,699.0	17	Ethiopia	18,619.8
4	Colombia	85,527.9	18	Botswana	17,491.5
5	Saudi Arabia	82,153.7	19	Argentina	17,435.2
6	China	72,754.8	20	India	15,643.9
7	Venezuela	64,438.8	21	Angola	12,547.8
8	Canada	62,879.1	22	Sudan	12,479.0
9	Australia	58,153.8	23	Chad	11,977.3
10	Tanzania	37,428.0	24	Algeria	11,888.4
11	Zambia	31,225.3	25	Germany	11,660.7
12	Indonesia	23,893.2	26	Iran	10,554.3
13	Mongolia	21,791.2	27	Central African Rep	10,333.5
14	Peru	21,609.0	28	Niger	9,964.1

a Includes national parks, wilderness and conservation areas, and managed habitats.
Marine areas are not included.

Country
profiles

ALGERIA

Area	2,381,741 sq km	Capital	Algiers
Arable as % of total land	3	Currency	Algerian dinar (AD)

People

Population	31.4m	Life expectancy: men	68.1 yrs
Pop. per sq km	13.2	women	71.3 yrs
Av. ann. growth		Adult literacy	68.9%
in pop. 2000–05	1.67%	Fertility rate (per woman)	2.8
Pop. under 15	35.1%	Urban population	57.7%
Pop. over 60	6.0%		per 1,000 pop.
No. of men per 100 women	102	Crude birth rate	22.8
Human Development Index	70.4	Crude death rate	5.5

The economy

GDP	AD4,455bn	GDP per head	$1,780
GDP	$55.9bn	GDP per head in purchasing	
Av. ann. growth in real		power parity (USA=100)	15.3
GDP 1992–2002	2.3%	Economic freedom index	3.31

Origins of GDP		Components of GDP	
	% of total		% of total
Agriculture	10.0	Private consumption	44.3
Industry, of which:	52.7	Public consumption	15.3
manufacturing	7.9	Investment	19.1
Services	37.3	Exports	35.6
		Imports	-25.6

Structure of employment

	% of total		% of labour force
Agriculture	...	Unemployed 2002	27.3
Industry	...	Av. ann. rate 1995–2002	27.4
Services	...		

Energy

	m TOE		
Total output	144.3	Net energy imports as %	
Total consumption	23.9	of energy use	-390
Consumption per head,			
kg oil equivalent	955		

Inflation and finance

Consumer price		av. ann. increase 1996–2001	
inflation 2003	2.6%	Narrow money (M1)	16.0%
Av. ann. inflation 1998–2003	2.2%	Broad money	17.8%
Money market rate, 2003	3.96%		

Exchange rates

	end 2003		December 2003
AD per $	72.61	Effective rates	1995 = 100
AD per SDR	107.90	– nominal	73.26
AD per €	91.49	– real	92.28

Trade

Principal exports		Principal imports	
	$bn fob		*$bn cif*
Minerals & metals	26.0	Intermediate & other goods	28.2
Rural goods	15.7	Consumption goods	20.9
Manufacturing goods	15.0	Capital goods	15.8
Other goods	8.4	Other	5.3
Total incl. others	**65.0**	Total incl. others	**72.6**

Main export destinations		Main origins of imports	
	% of total		*% of total*
Developing countries	47.3	Developing countries	31.4
Japan	18.8	EU15	23.0
Asean[a]	12.2	United States	18.2
EU15	12.0	Asean[a]	14.8
United States	9.7	Japan	12.6

Balance of payments, reserves and aid, $bn

Visible exports fob	65.1	Capital balance	17.8
Visible imports fob	-70.5	Overall balance	0.1
Trade balance	-5.4	Change in reserves	2.9
Invisibles inflows	26.1	Level of reserves	
Invisibles outflows	-37.8	end Dec.	21.6
Net transfers	-0.1	No. months of import cover	2.4
Current account balance	-17.3	Aid given	0.92
– as % of GDP	-4.2	– as % of GDP	0.26

Health and education

Health spending, % of GDP	9.2	Education spending, % of GDP	4.6
Doctors per 1,000 pop.	2.5	Enrolment, %: primary	102
Hospital beds per 1,000 pop.	7.9	secondary	161
Improved-water source access,		tertiary	63
% of pop.	100		

Society

No. of households	7.5m	Colour TVs per 100 households	91.7
Av. no. per household	2.6	Telephone lines per 100 pop.	53.9
Marriages per 1,000 pop.	5.4	Mobile telephone subscribers	
Divorces per 1,000 pop.	2.8	per 100 pop.	63.7
Cost of living, Dec. 2003		Computers per 100 pop.	56.5
New York = 100	93	Internet hosts per 1,000 pop.	146.0

a Brunei, Indonesia, Laos, Malaysia, Myanmar, Philippines, Singapore, Thailand, Vietnam.

AUSTRIA

Area	83,855 sq km	Capital	Vienna
Arable as % of total land	17	Currency	Euro (€)

People

Population	8.1m	Life expectancy: men	75.4 yrs
Pop. per sq km	96.6	women	81.5 yrs
Av. ann. growth		Adult literacy	99.0%
in pop. 2000–05	0.05%	Fertility rate (per woman)	1.3
Pop. under 15	16.7%	Urban population	67.4%
Pop. over 60	20.7%		per 1,000 pop.
No. of men per 100 women	96	Crude birth rate	8.6
Human Development Index	92.9	Crude death rate	9.9

The economy

GDP	€217bn	GDP per head	$25,190
GDP	$204bn	GDP per head in purchasing	
Av. ann. growth in real		power parity (USA=100)	80.1
GDP 1992–2002	2.0%	Economic freedom index	2.08

Origins of GDP

	% of total
Agriculture	2.4
Industry, of which:	31.5
manufacturing	...
Services	66.1

Components of GDP

	% of total
Private consumption	56.8
Public consumption	18.6
Investment	22.4
Exports	52.8
Imports	-50.6

Structure of employment

	% of total		% of labour force
Agriculture	6	Unemployed 2002	4.0
Industry	30	Av. ann. rate 1995–2002	3.9
Services	64		

Energy

	m TOE		
Total output	9.7	Net energy imports as %	
Total consumption	30.7	of energy use	68
Consumption per head,			
kg oil equivalent	3,825		

Inflation and finance

Consumer price		av. ann. increase 1997–2002	
inflation 2003	1.4%	Euro area:	
Av. ann. inflation 1998–2003	1.7%	Narrow money (M1)	9.0%
Interbank rate, 2003	2.34%	Broad money	6.4%
		Household saving rate, 2002	7.6%

Exchange rates

	end 2003		December 2003
€ per $	0.79	Effective rates	1995 = 100
€ per SDR	1.18	– nominal	96.5
		– real	88.5

Trade

Principal exports		Principal imports	
	$bn fob		*$bn cif*
Machinery & transport		Machinery & transport	
equipment	31.3	equipment	28.7
Consumer goods	9.5	Consumer goods	11.3
Chemicals	7.4	Chemicals	8.1
Food, drink & tobacco	3.8	Raw materials	8.1
Paper	3.4	Food, drink & tobacco	4.3
Total incl. others	**70.6**	Total incl. others	**72.6**

Main export destinations		Main origins of imports	
	% of total		*% of total*
EU15	60.3	EU15	66.0
Germany	32.0	Germany	40.3
Italy	8.5	Italy	7.1
United States	5.1	United States	4.8
		France	3.9

Balance of payments, reserves and aid, $bn

Visible exports fob	73.7	Capital balance	-5.5
Visible imports fob	-70.1	Overall balance	-1.7
Trade balance	3.6	Change in reserves	-2.4
Invisibles inflows	48.4	Level of reserves	
Invisibles outflows	-49.8	end Dec.	13.2
Net transfers	-1.6	No. months of import cover	1.3
Current account balance	0.6	Aid given	0.49
– as % of GDP	0.3	– as % of GDP	0.26

Health and education

Health spending, % of GDP	8.0	Education spending, % of GDP	5.8
Doctors per 1,000 pop.	3.2	Enrolment, %: primary	104
Hospital beds per 1,000 pop.	8.6	secondary	99
Improved-water source access,		tertiary	58
% of pop.	100		

Society

No. of households	3.3m	Colour TVs per 100 households	97.8
Av. no. per household	2.4	Telephone lines per 100 pop.	48.9
Marriages per 1,000 pop.	4.2	Mobile telephone subscribers	
Divorces per 1,000 pop.	2.2	per 100 pop.	78.6
Cost of living, Dec. 2003		Computers per 100 pop.	36.9
New York = 100	104	Internet hosts per 1,000 pop.	121.3

BANGLADESH

Area	143,998 sq km	Capital	Dhaka
Arable as % of total land	62	Currency	Taka (Tk)

People

Population	143.4m	Life expectancy: men	61.0 yrs
Pop. per sq km	995.8	women	61.8 yrs
Av. ann. growth		Adult literacy	41.1%
in pop. 2000–05	2.02%	Fertility rate (per woman)	3.5
Pop. under 15	39.2%	Urban population	25.6%
Pop. over 60	5.0%		per 1,000 pop.
No. of men per 100 women	105	Crude birth rate	28.9
Human Development Index	50.2	Crude death rate	8.3

The economy

GDP	Tk2,732bn	GDP per head	$330
GDP	$47.6bn	GDP per head in purchasing	
Av. ann. growth in real		power parity (USA=100)	4.9
GDP 1992–2002	4.9%	Economic freedom index	3.70

Origins of GDP

Components of GDP[a]

	% of total		% of total
Agriculture	22.7	Private consumption	76.8
Industry, of which:	26.4	Public consumption	5.0
manufacturing	15.9	Investment	23.1
Services	50.9	Exports	14.3
		Imports	-19.0

Structure of employment

	% of total		% of labour force
Agriculture	63	Unemployed 2001	2.3
Industry	10	Av. ann. rate 1995–2001	2.4
Services	27		

Energy

	m TOE		
Total output	16.2	Net energy imports as %	
Total consumption	20.4	of energy use	21
Consumption per head,			
kg oil equivalent	153		

Inflation and finance

Consumer price		av. ann. increase 1997–2002	
inflation 2003	4.6%	Narrow money (M1)	10.8%
Av. ann. inflation 1998–2003	3.7%	Broad money	14.8%
Deposit rate, 2003	7.82%		

Exchange rates

	end 2003		December 2003
Tk per $	58.78	Effective rates	1995 = 100
Tk per SDR	87.35	– nominal	...
Tk per €	74.06	– real	...

Trade

Principal exports[a]		Principal imports[a]	
	$bn fob		*$bn cif*
Clothing	3.4	Machinery & transport	
Fish & fish products	0.2	equipment	2.5
Jute goods	0.2	Textiles & yarn	2.1
Leather	0.2	Fuels	0.8
		Cereal & dairy products	0.5
Total incl. others	**4.6**	Total incl. others	**8.0**

Main export destinations		Main origins of imports	
	% of total		*% of total*
United States	27.6	India	14.7
Germany	10.4	China	11.6
United Kingdom	9.8	Singapore	11.6
France	5.7	Japan	7.6
Italy	4.0	Hong Kong	5.4

Balance of payments, reserves and debt, $bn

Visible exports fob	6.1	Overall balance	0.5
Visible imports fob	-7.7	Change in reserves	0.4
Trade balance	-1.6	Level of reserves	
Invisibles inflows	1.0	end Dec.	1.7
Invisibles outflows	-1.8	No. months of import cover	2.2
Net transfers	3.2	Foreign debt	17.0
Current account balance	0.7	– as % of GDP	35
– as % of GDP	1.6	– as % of total exports	182
Capital balance	0.1	Debt service ratio	8

Health and education

Health spending, % of GDP	3.5	Education spending, % of GDP	2.3
Doctors per 1,000 pop.	...	Enrolment, %: primary	100
Hospital beds per 1,000 pop.	...	secondary	46
Improved-water source access,		tertiary	7
% of pop.	97		

Society

No. of households	24.4m	Colour TVs per 100 households	2.7
Av. no. per household	5.4	Telephone lines per 100 pop.	0.5
Marriages per 1,000 pop.	9.5	Mobile telephone subscribers	
Divorces per 1,000 pop.	...	per 100 pop.	0.8
Cost of living, Dec. 2003		Computers per 100 pop.	0.3
New York = 100	57	Internet hosts per 1,000 pop.	...

a Fiscal year ending June 30 2002.

BELGIUM

Area	30,520 sq km	Capital	Brussels
Arable as % of total land	26	Currency	Euro (€)

People

Population	10.3m	Life expectancy: men	75.7 yrs
Pop. per sq km	337.5	women	81.9 yrs
Av. ann. growth		Adult literacy	99.0%
in pop. 2000–05	0.21%	Fertility rate (per woman)	1.7
Pop. under 15	17.4%	Urban population	97.4%
Pop. over 60	22.1%		per 1,000 pop.
No. of men per 100 women	96	Crude birth rate	10.8
Human Development Index	93.7	Crude death rate	10.0

The economy

GDP	€261bn	GDP per head	$23,820
GDP	$245bn	GDP per head in purchasing	
Av. ann. growth in real		power parity (USA=100)	77.9
GDP 1992–2002	2.0%	Economic freedom index	2.19

Origins of GDP		Components of GDP	
	% of total		% of total
Agriculture	1.6	Private consumption	54.9
Industry, of which:	26.8	Public consumption	22.6
manufacturing	...	Investment	19.9
Services	71.6	Exports	77.5
		Imports	-74.8

Structure of employment

	% of total		% of labour force
Agriculture	2	Unemployed 2002	7.5
Industry	27	Av. ann. rate 1995–2002	8.3
Services	71		

Energy

	m TOE		
Total output	13.0	Net energy imports as %	
Total consumption	59.0	of energy use	78
Consumption per head,			
kg oil equivalent	5,735		

Inflation and finance

Consumer price		av. ann. increase 1997–2002	
inflation 2003	1.6%	Euro area:	
Av. ann. inflation 1998–2003	1.9%	Narrow money (M1)	9.0%
Treasury bill rate, 2003	2.23%	Broad money	6.4%
		Household saving rate, 2002	14.4%

Exchange rates

	end 2003		December 2003
€ per $	0.79	Effective rates	1995 = 100
€ per SDR	1.18	– nominal	94.8
		– real	88.4

Trade

Principal exports		Principal imports	
	$bn fob		*$bn cif*
Chemicals	47.1	Chemicals	42.3
Transport equipment	30.9	Machinery	31.7
Machinery	29.3	Transport equipment	24.6
Food & animals	19.2	Food & animals	17.5
Total incl. others	**215.1**	Total incl. others	**198.6**

Main export destinations		Main origins of imports	
	% of total		*% of total*
Germany	18.6	Netherlands	17.3
France	16.3	Germany	15.7
Netherlands	11.7	France	12.6
United Kingdom	9.6	United Kingdom	7.3
EU15	72.8	EU15	71.1

Balance of payments, reserves and aid, $bn

Visible exports fob	168.2	Capital balance	-14.5
Visible imports fob	-159.5	Overall balance	0.0
Trade balance	8.7	Change in reserves	1.1
Invisibles inflows	73.4	Level of reserves	
Invisibles outflows	-64.7	end Dec.	14.7
Net transfers	-4.3	No. months of import cover	0.8
Current account balance	13.1	Aid given	1.00
– as % of GDP	4.6	– as % of GDP	0.43

Health and education

Health spending, % of GDP	8.9	Education spending, % of GDP	5.9
Doctors per 1,000 pop.	3.9	Enrolment, %: primary	105
Hospital beds per 1,000 pop.	...	secondary	...
Improved-water source access,		tertiary	57
% of pop.	...		

Society

No. of households	4.3m	Colour TVs per 100 households	99.6
Av. no. per household	2.4	Telephone lines per 100 pop.	49.4
Marriages per 1,000 pop.	4.1	Mobile telephone subscribers	
Divorces per 1,000 pop.	2.4	per 100 pop.	78.6
Cost of living, Dec. 2003		Computers per 100 pop.	24.1
New York = 100	93	Internet hosts per 1,000 pop.	141.1

BRAZIL

Area	8,511,965 sq km	Capital	Brasilia
Arable as % of total land	7	Currency	Real (R)

People

Population	174.7m	Life expectancy: men	64.0 yrs
Pop. per sq km	20.5	women	72.6 yrs
Av. ann. growth		Adult literacy	86.4%
in pop. 2000–05	1.24%	Fertility rate (per woman)	2.2
Pop. under 15	29.3%	Urban population	81.7%
Pop. over 60	7.8%		per 1,000 pop.
No. of men per 100 women	97	Crude birth rate	19.7
Human Development Index	77.7	Crude death rate	7.1

The economy

GDP	R1,321bn	GDP per head	$2,590
GDP	$452bn	GDP per head in purchasing	
Av. ann. growth in real		power parity (USA=100)	20.6
GDP 1992–2002	2.9%	Economic freedom index	3.10

Origins of GDP		Components of GDP	
	% of total		% of total
Agriculture	8.7	Private consumption	58.0
Industry, of which:	38.3	Public consumption	20.1
manufacturing	...	Investment	19.8
Services	52.9	Exports	15.5
		Imports	-13.4

Structure of employment

	% of total		% of labour force
Agriculture	21	Unemployed 2001	9.4
Industry	20	Av. ann. rate 1995–2001	8.1
Services	59		

Energy

	m TOE		
Total output	145.9	Net energy imports as %	
Total consumption	185.0	of energy use	21
Consumption per head,			
kg oil equivalent	1,074		

Inflation and finance

Consumer price		av. ann. increase 1997–2002	
inflation 2003	14.7%	Narrow money (M1)	17.9%
Av. ann. inflation 1998–2003	8.3%	Broad money	15.1%
Money market rate, 2003	23.37%		

Exchange rates

	end 2003		December 2003
R per $	2.89	Effective rates	1995 = 100
R per SDR	4.29	– nominal	...
R per €	3.64	– real	...

Trade

Principal exports	$bn fob	Principal imports	$bn cif
Transport equipment & parts	9.9	Machines & electrical equipment	13.3
Metal goods	6.3	Chemical products	8.5
Soyabeans etc.	5.9	Oil & derivatives	6.3
Chemical products	1.2	Transport equipment & parts	5.1
Total incl. others	**60.4**	Total incl. others	**49.6**

Main export destinations	% of total	Main origins of imports	% of total
United States	25.2	United States	28.9
Argentina	9.0	Argentina	15.7
Germany	5.3	Germany	10.9
China	4.5	Japan	6.4

Balance of payments, reserves and debt, $bn

Visible exports fob	60.4	Overall balance	-11.3
Visible imports fob	-47.2	Change in reserves	2.0
Trade balance	13.1	Level of reserves	
Invisibles inflows	12.9	end Dec.	37.8
Invisibles outflows	-36.1	No. months of import cover	5.4
Net transfers	2.4	Foreign debt	227.9
Current account balance	-7.7	– as % of GDP	45
– as % of GDP	-1.7	– as % of total exports	316
Capital balance	-2.7	Debt service ratio	72

Health and education

Health spending, % of GDP	7.6	Education spending, % of GDP	4.7
Doctors per 1,000 pop.	...	Enrolment, %: primary	162
Hospital beds per 1,000 pop.	...	secondary	108
Improved-water source access, % of pop.	87	tertiary	17

Society

No. of households	50.5m	Colour TVs per 100 households	86.6
Av. no. per household	3.5	Telephone lines per 100 pop.	22.3
Marriages per 1,000 pop.	4.4	Mobile telephone subscribers	
Divorces per 1,000 pop.	0.7	per 100 pop.	20.1
Cost of living, Dec. 2003		Computers per 100 pop.	7.5
New York = 100	56	Internet hosts per 1,000 pop.	18.1

BULGARIA

Area	110,994 sq km	Capital	Sofia
Arable as % of total land	40	Currency	Lev (BGL)

People

Population	7.8m	Life expectancy: men	67.4 yrs
Pop. per sq km	70.3	women	74.6 yrs
Av. ann. growth		Adult literacy	98.6%
in pop. 2000–05	-0.85%	Fertility rate (per woman)	1.1
Pop. under 15	15.8%	Urban population	67.4%
Pop. over 60	21.7%		per 1,000 pop.
No. of men per 100 women	94	Crude birth rate	7.9
Human Development Index	79.5	Crude death rate	15.1

The economy

GDP	BGL32.3bn	GDP per head	$1,990
GDP	$15.5bn	GDP per head in purchasing	
Av. ann. growth in real		power parity (USA=100)	19.5
GDP 1992–2002	0.7%	Economic freedom index	3.08

Origins of GDP

Components of GDP

	% of total		% of total
Agriculture	12.5	Private consumption	77.3
Industry, of which:	27.8	Public consumption	10.0
manufacturing	...	Investment	19.7
Services	59.7	Exports	53.1
		Imports	-59.7

Structure of employment

	% of total		% of labour force
Agriculture	26	Unemployed 2002	17.6
Industry	28	Av. ann. rate 1995–2002	15.3
Services	46		

Energy

	m TOE		
Total output	10.3	Net energy imports as %	
Total consumption	19.5	of energy use	47
Consumption per head,			
kg oil equivalent	2,428		

Inflation and finance

Consumer price		*av. ann change 1997–2002*	
inflation 2003	2.2%	Narrow money (M1)	17.9%
Av. ann. inflation 1998–2003	5.6%	Broad money	19.9%
Money market rate 2003	1.95%		

Exchange rates

	end 2003		December 2003
BGL per $	1.55	Effective rates	1995 = 100
BGL per SDR	2.30	– nominal	7.29
BGL per €	1.95	– real	149.61

Trade

Principal exports		Principal imports	
	$bn fob		*$bn cif*
Clothing	1.2	Mineral fuels	1.3
Metals (excl. iron & steel)	0.4	Machinery & equipment	0.8
Chemicals	0.3	Textiles	0.8
Iron & steel	0.3	Chemicals	0.5
Total incl. others	**5.7**	Total incl. others	**7.9**

Main export destinations		Main origins of imports	
	% of total		*% of total*
Italy	15.4	Germany	14.3
Germany	9.5	Russia	14.3
Greece	9.3	Italy	11.3
Turkey	9.1	France	6.0

Balance of payments, reserves and debt, $bn

Visible exports fob	5.7	Overall balance	0.7
Visible imports fob	-7.3	Change in reserves	1.2
Trade balance	-1.6	Level of reserves	
Invisibles inflows	2.9	end Dec.	4.8
Invisibles outflows	-2.6	No. months of import cover	5.9
Net transfers	0.5	Foreign debt	10.5
Current account balance	-0.7	– as % of GDP	77
– as % of GDP	-4.4	– as % of total exports	132
Capital balance	1.7	Debt service ratio	17

Health and education

Health spending, % of GDP	4.8	Education spending, % of GDP	3.4
Doctors per 1,000 pop.	3.4	Enrolment, %: primary	103
Hospital beds per 1,000 pop.	7.2	secondary	94
Improved-water source access,		tertiary	41
% of pop.	100		

Society

No. of households	3.0m	Colour TVs per 100 households	63.1
Av. no. per household	2.7	Telephone lines per 100 pop.	36.8
Marriages per 1,000 pop.	3.8	Mobile telephone subscribers	
Divorces per 1,000 pop.	1.3	per 100 pop.	33.3
Cost of living, Dec. 2003		Computers per 100 pop.	5.2
New York = 100	...	Internet hosts per 1,000 pop.	6.6

CAMEROON

Area	475,442 sq km	Capital	Yaoundé
Arable as % of total land	13	Currency	CFA franc (CFAfr)

People

Population	15.5m	Life expectancy: men	45.1 yrs
Pop. per sq km	32.6	women	47.4 yrs
Av. ann. growth		Adult literacy[a]	67.9%
in pop. 2000–05	1.83%	Fertility rate (per woman)	4.6
Pop. under 15	43.2%	Urban population	49.7%
Pop. over 60	4.5%		per 1,000 pop.
No. of men per 100 women	99	Crude birth rate	35.4
Human Development Index	49.9	Crude death rate	16.9

The economy

GDP	CFAfr6,642bn	GDP per head	$580
GDP	$9.1bn	GDP per head in purchasing	
Av. ann. growth in real		power parity (USA=100)	5.3
GDP 1992–2002	3.1%	Economic freedom index	3.63

Origins of GDP[b]

	% of total
Agriculture	27
Industry, of which:	30
manufacturing	...
Services	43

Components of GDP[b]

	% of total
Private consumption	68.7
Public consumption	9.4
Investment	23.3
Exports	20.8
Imports	-22.2

Structure of employment

	% of total		% of labour force
Agriculture	70	Unemployed 2002	...
Industry	11	Av. ann. rate 1995–2002	...
Services	19		

Energy

	m TOE		
Total output	12.3	Net energy imports as %	
Total consumption	6.4	of energy use	-94
Consumption per head,			
kg oil equivalent	417		

Inflation and finance

		av. ann. change 1997–2002	
Consumer price			
inflation 2002	2.8%	Narrow money (M1)	13.9%
Av. ann. inflation 1998–2002	1.7%	Broad money	14.2%
Deposit rate, 2003	5.00%		

Exchange rates

	end 2003		December 2003
CFAfr per $	519.36	Effective rates	1995 = 100
CFAfr per SDR	771.76	– nominal	107.6
CFAfr per €	654.39	– real	106.4

Trade

Principal exports		Principal imports	
	$bn fob		*$bn cif*
Crude oil	0.8	Food & consumer goods	1.6
Timber	0.3	Capital goods	0.4
Cocoa	0.2	Intermediate goods	0.1
Total incl. others	**1.9**	Total incl. others	**2.2**

Main export destinations		Main origins of imports	
	% of total		*% of total*
Italy	16.5	France	28.4
Spain	15.9	Nigeria	12.8
France	12.7	United States	8.0

Balance of payments[c], reserves and debt, $bn

Visible exports fob	2.3	Overall balance[d]	-0.3
Visible imports fob	-1.4	Change in reserves	0.3
Trade balance	0.9	Level of reserves	
Invisibles inflows	0.6	end Dec.	0.6
Invisibles outflows	-1.2	No. months of import cover	1.9
Net transfers	0.1	Foreign debt	8.5
Current account balance	0.5	– as % of GDP	102
– as % of GDP	5.6	– as % of total exports	321
Capital balance[d]	-0.1	Debt service ratio	14

Health and education

Health spending, % of GDP	3.3	Education spending, % of GDP	5.4
Doctors per 1,000 pop.	...	Enrolment, %: primary	108
Hospital beds per 1,000 pop.	...	secondary	20
Improved-water source access,		tertiary	5
% of pop.	58		

Society

No. of households	4.1m	Colour TVs per 100 households	2.3
Av. no. per household	4.0	Telephone lines per 100 pop.	0.7
Marriages per 1,000 pop.	...	Mobile telephone subscribers	
Divorces per 1,000 pop.	...	per 100 pop.	4.3
Cost of living, Dec. 2003		Computers per 100 pop.	0.6
New York = 100	...	Internet hosts per 1,000 pop.	...

a 2001
b Fiscal year ending June 30 2002.
c 2000
d Fiscal year ending June 30 2000.

CANADA

Area[a]	9,970,610 sq km	Capital	Ottawa
Arable as % of total land	5	Currency	Canadian dollar (C$)

People

Population	31.3m	Life expectancy: men	76.7 yrs
Pop. per sq km	3.1	women	81.9 yrs
Av. ann. growth		Adult literacy	99.0%
in pop. 2000–05	0.77%	Fertility rate (per woman)	1.5
Pop. under 15	19.0%	Urban population	78.9%
Pop. over 60	16.7%		per 1,000 pop.
No. of men per 100 women	98	Crude birth rate	10.3
Human Development Index	93.7	Crude death rate	7.5

The economy

GDP	C$1,121bn	GDP per head	$22,820
GDP	$714bn	GDP per head in purchasing	
Av. ann. growth in real		power parity (USA=100)	80.1
GDP 1992–2002	3.5%	Economic freedom index	1.98

Origins of GDP

Components of GDP

	% of total		% of total
Agriculture	2.2	Private consumption	57.0
Industry, of which:	28.9	Public consumption	18.8
manufacturing & mining	20.6	Investment	20.1
Services	68.9	Exports	41.2
		Imports	-37.0

Structure of employment

	% of total		% of labour force
Agriculture	3	Unemployed 2002	7.7
Industry	23	Av. ann. rate 1995–2002	8.3
Services	74		

Energy

	m TOE		
Total output	379.2	Net energy imports as %	
Total consumption	248.2	of energy use	-53
Consumption per head,			
kg oil equivalent	7,985		

Inflation and finance

Consumer price		av. ann. increase 1997–2002	
inflation 2003	2.8%	Narrow money (M1)	9.6%
Av. ann. inflation 1998–2003	2.4%	Broad money	6.7%
Money market rate, 2003	2.93%	Household saving rate, 2002	4.2%

Exchange rates

	end 2003		December 2003
C$ per $	1.29	Effective rates	1995 = 100
C$ per SDR	1.92	– nominal	105.8
C$ per €	1.63	– real	108.8

Trade

Principal exports	$bn fob	Principal imports	$bn fob
Motor vehicles & parts	61.9	Machinery & industrial equipment	67.4
Machinery & industrial equipment	60.3	Motor vehicles & parts	51.9
Industrial goods	44.2	Industrial goods	43.8
Energy products	32.1	Consumer goods	29.6
Forest products	23.4	Agric. products	13.9
Agricultural products	19.4	Energy products	10.5
Total incl. others	**261.7**	Total incl. others	**226.9**

Main export destinations	% of total	Main origins of imports	% of total
United States	84.8	United States	71.5
Japan	2.4	Japan	3.3
United Kingdom	1.4	United Kingdom	2.9
EU15 (excl. UK)	3.7	EU15 (excl. UK)	7.3

Balance of payments, reserves and aid, $bn

Visible exports fob	264.1	Capital balance	-8.6
Visible imports fob	-227.2	Overall balance	-0.2
Trade balance	36.8	Change in reserves	2.9
Invisibles inflows	57.4	Level of reserves	
Invisibles outflows	-80.2	end Dec.	37.2
Net transfers	0.9	No. months of import cover	1.5
Current account balance	14.9	Aid given	2.01
– as % of GDP	2.1	– as % of GDP	0.28

Health and education

Health spending, % of GDP	9.5	Education spending, % of GDP	5.2
Doctors per 1,000 pop.	2.1	Enrolment, %: primary	99
Hospital beds per 1,000 pop.	3.9	secondary	103
Improved-water source access,		tertiary	60
% of pop.	100		

Society

No. of households	12.1m	Colour TVs per 100 households	98.7
Av. no. per household	2.6	Telephone lines per 100 pop.	63.6
Marriages per 1,000 pop.	4.6	Mobile telephone subscribers	
Divorces per 1,000 pop.	2.3	per 100 pop.	37.7
Cost of living, Dec. 2003		Computers per 100 pop.	48.7
New York = 100	82	Internet hosts per 1,000 pop.	102.6

a Including freshwater.

CHILE

Area	756,945 sq km	Capital	Santiago
Arable as % of total land	3	Currency	Chilean peso (Ps)

People

Population	15.6m	Life expectancy: men		73 yrs
Pop. per sq km	20.6		women	79 yrs
Av. ann. growth		Adult literacy		95.7%
in pop. 2000–05	1.23%	Fertility rate (per woman)		2.4
Pop. under 15	28.4%	Urban population		86.1%
Pop. over 60	10.3%			per 1,000 pop.
No. of men per 100 women	98	Crude birth rate		18.2
Human Development Index	83.1	Crude death rate		5.6

The economy

GDP	44,198bn pesos	GDP per head	$4,110
GDP	$64.2bn	GDP per head in purchasing	
Av. ann. growth in real		power parity (USA=100)	26.1
GDP 1992–2002	5.0%	Economic freedom index	1.91

Origins of GDP		Components of GDP	
	% of total		% of total
Agriculture	6.4	Private consumption	63.2
Industry, of which:	38.8	Public consumption	12.6
manufacturing	17.7	Investment	21.9
Services	54.8	Exports	34.1
		Imports	-31.8

Structure of employment

	% of total		% of labour force
Agriculture	14	Unemployed 2002	7.8
Industry	24	Av. ann. rate 1995–2002	6.9
Services	62		

Energy

	m TOE		
Total output	8.7	Net energy imports as %	
Total consumption	23.8	of energy use	64
Consumption per head,			
kg oil equivalent	1,545		

Inflation and finance

Consumer price		av. ann. increase 1997–2002	
inflation 2003	2.8%	Narrow money (M1)	7.5%
Av. ann. inflation 1998–2003	3.2%	Broad money	5.2%
Money market rate, 2003	2.72%		

Exchange rates

	end 2003		December 2003
Ps per $	599.42	Effective rates	1995 = 100
Ps per SDR	890.72	– nominal	77.8
Ps per Ecu	755.27	– real	88.0

Trade

Principal exports		Principal imports	
	$bn fob		*$bn cif*
Copper	6.3	Intermediate goods	9.7
Fruit	1.3	Capital goods	3.3
Paper products	1.1	Consumer goods	2.8
Total incl. others	**18.2**	**Total incl. others**	**17.2**

Main export destinations		Main origins of imports	
	% of total		*% of total*
United States	19.0	Argentina	17.6
Japan	10.5	United States	15.3
China	6.7	Brazil	9.3
United Kingdom	4.3	China	6.3

Balance of payments, reserves and debt, $bn

Visible exports fob	18.3	Overall balance	0.2
Visible imports fob	-15.8	Change in reserves	0.9
Trade balance	2.5	Level of reserves	
Invisibles inflows	5.1	end Dec.	15.3
Invisibles outflows	-8.6	No. months of import cover	7.5
Net transfers	0.4	Foreign debt	41.9
Current account balance	-0.6	– as % of GDP	63
– as % of GDP	-0.9	– as % of total exports	174
Capital balance	1.0	Debt service ratio	32

Health and education

Health spending, % of GDP	7.0	Education spending, % of GDP	4.2
Doctors per 1,000 pop.	...	Enrolment, %: primary	103
Hospital beds per 1,000 pop.	...	secondary	75
Improved-water source access,		tertiary	38
% of pop.	93		

Society

No. of households	4.0m	Colour TVs per 100 households	60.9
Av. no. per household	3.9	Telephone lines per 100 pop.	23.0
Marriages per 1,000 pop.	4.7	Mobile telephone subscribers	
Divorces per 1,000 pop.	0.5	per 100 pop.	42.8
Cost of living, Dec. 2003		Computers per 100 pop.	11.9
New York = 100	58	Internet hosts per 1,000 pop.	13.0

CHINA

Area	9,560,900 sq km	Capital	Beijing
Arable as % of total land	15	Currency	Yuan

People

Population	1,294.4m	Life expectancy: men	68.9 yrs
Pop. per sq km	135.4	women	73.3 yrs
Av. ann. growth		Adult literacy[a]	90.9%
in pop. 2000–05	0.73%	Fertility rate (per woman)	1.8
Pop. under 15	24.8%	Urban population	36.7%
Pop. over 60	10.1%		per 1,000 pop.
No. of men per 100 women	106	Crude birth rate	14.5
Human Development Index	72.1	Crude death rate	7.0

The economy

GDP	Yuan10,479bn	GDP per head	$980
GDP	$1,266bn	GDP per head in purchasing	
Av. ann. growth in real		power parity (USA=100)	12.5
GDP 1992–2002	9.3%	Economic freedom index	3.64

Origins of GDP		**Components of GDP**	
	% of total		% of total
Agriculture	15.4	Private consumption	46.3
Industry, of which:	51.1	Public consumption	13.2
manufacturing	35.4	Investment	40.2
Services	33.5	Exports	28.9
		Imports	-25.9

Structure of employment

	% of total		% of labour force
Agriculture	50	Unemployed 2001	3.1
Industry	23	Av. ann. rate 1995–2001	3.0
Services	27		

Energy

	m TOE		
Total output	1,138.6	Net energy imports as %	
Total consumption	1,139.4	of energy use	0
Consumption per head,			
kg oil equivalent	896		

Inflation and finance

Consumer price		av. ann. increase 1997–2002	
inflation 2002	-0.8%	Narrow money (M1)	15.9%
Av. ann. inflation 1998–2002	-0.4%	Broad money	15.2%
Deposit rate, 2003	1.98%		

Exchange rates

	end 2003		December 2003
Yuan per $	8.28	Effective rates	1995 = 100
Yuan per SDR	12.30	– nominal	107.32
Yuan per €	10.43	– real	110.43

Trade

Principal exports		Principal imports	
	$bn fob		*$bn cif*
Apparel & clothing	41.3	Electrical machinery	55.4
Office equipment	36.2	Petroleum products	17.2
Telecoms equipment	32.0	Office equipment	17.1
Electrical machinery	31.9	Other machinery	15.6
Footwear	11.1	Telecoms equipment	14.2
Total incl. others	**325.6**	Total incl. others	**295.2**

Main export destinations		Main origins of imports	
	% of total		*% of total*
United States	21.5	Japan	18.1
Hong Kong	18.0	Taiwan	12.9
Japan	14.9	South Korea	9.7
South Korea	4.8	United States	9.2
Germany	3.5	Germany	5.6

Balance of payments, reserves and debt, $bn

Visible exports fob	325.7	Overall balance	75.2
Visible imports fob	-281.5	Change in reserves	77.7
Trade balance	44.2	Level of reserves	
Invisibles inflows	48.1	end Dec.	297.7
Invisibles outflows	-69.8	No. months of import cover	10.2
Net transfers	13.0	Foreign debt	168.3
Current account balance	35.4	– as % of GDP	15
– as % of GDP	2.8	– as % of total exports	52
Capital balance	32.3	Debt service ratio	9

Health and education

Health spending, % of GDP	5.5	Education spending, % of GDP	2.2
Doctors per 1,000 pop.	1.6	Enrolment, %: primary	106
Hospital beds per 1,000 pop.	2.5	secondary	63
Improved-water source access,		tertiary	7
% of pop.	75		

Society

No. of households	358.4m	Colour TVs per 100 households	45.5
Av. no. per household	3.6	Telephone lines per 100 pop.	16.7
Marriages per 1,000 pop.	6.4	Mobile telephone subscribers	
Divorces per 1,000 pop.	0.8	per 100 pop.	16.1
Cost of living, Dec. 2003		Computers per 100 pop.	2.8
New York = 100	90	Internet hosts per 1,000 pop.	0.1

Note: Data excludes Special Administrative Regions, ie Hong Kong and Macau.
a 2000

COLOMBIA

Area	1,141,748 sq km	Capital	Bogota
Arable as % of total land	2	Currency	Colombian peso (peso)

People

Population	43.5m	Life expectancy: men	69.2 yrs
Pop. per sq km	38.0	women	75.3 yrs
Av. ann. growth		Adult literacy	92.1%
in pop. 2000–05	1.59%	Fertility rate (per woman)	2.6
Pop. under 15	32.8%	Urban population	75.5%
Pop. over 60	6.9%		per 1,000 pop.
No. of men per 100 women	98	Crude birth rate	22.2
Human Development Index	77.9	Crude death rate	5.4

The economy

GDP	202,653bn pesos	GDP per head	$1,860
GDP	$80.9bn	GDP per head in purchasing	
Av. ann. growth in real		power parity (USA=100)	17.0
GDP 1992–2002	2.4%	Economic freedom index	3.13

Origins of GDP

	% of total
Agriculture	13.9
Industry, of which:	30.3
manufacturing	15.4
Services	55.8

Components of GDP

	% of total
Private consumption	65.4
Public consumption	20.7
Investment	14.7
Exports	19.5
Imports	-21.2

Structure of employment

	% of total		% of labour force
Agriculture	22	Unemployed 2002	15.9
Industry	18	Av. ann. rate 1995–2002	14.9
Services	59		

Energy

	m TOE		
Total output	73.9	Net energy imports as %	
Total consumption	29.2	of energy use	-153
Consumption per head,			
kg oil equivalent	680		

Inflation and finance

Consumer price		av. ann. increase 1997–2002	
inflation 2003	7.1%	Narrow money (M1)	14.6%
Av. ann. inflation 1998–2003	8.3%	Broad money	7.2%
Money market rate, 2003	6.95%		

Exchange rates

	end 2003		December 2003
Peso per $	2,781	Effective rates	1995 = 100
Peso per SDR	4,132	– nominal	38.9
Peso per €	3,504	– real	77.8

Trade

Principal exports		Principal imports	
	$bn fob		*$bn cif*
Oil	3.3	Intermediate goods &	
Coal	1.2	raw materials	5.8
Coffee	0.8	Capital goods	4.4
		Consumer goods	2.5
Total incl. others	**11.9**	Total	**12.7**

Main export destinations		Main origins of imports	
	% of total		*% of total*
United States	44.8	United States	31.1
Venezuela	9.4	Venezuela	6.6
Ecuador	6.8	Japan	5.1
Peru	2.9	Mexico	5.1

Balance of payments, reserves and debt, $bn

Visible exports fob	12.3	Overall balance	0.1
Visible imports fob	-12.1	Change in reserves	0.6
Trade balance	0.2	Level of reserves	
Invisibles inflows	2.6	end Dec.	10.8
Invisibles outflows	-6.8	No. months of import cover	6.9
Net transfers	2.5	Foreign debt	33.9
Current account balance	-1.6	– as % of GDP	43
– as % of GDP	-2.0	– as % of total exports	191
Capital balance	1.2	Debt service ratio	39

Health and education

Health spending, % of GDP	5.5	Education spending, % of GDP	4.1
Doctors per 1,000 pop.	...	Enrolment, %: primary	112
Hospital beds per 1,000 pop.	...	secondary	70
Improved-water source access,		tertiary	23
% of pop.	91		

Society

No. of households	9.5m	Colour TVs per 100 households	85.8
Av. no. per household	4.3	Telephone lines per 100 pop.	17.9
Marriages per 1,000 pop.	3.3	Mobile telephone subscribers	
Divorces per 1,000 pop.	0.2	per 100 pop.	10.6
Cost of living, Dec. 2003		Computers per 100 pop.	4.9
New York = 100	56	Internet hosts per 1,000 pop.	2.6

CÔTE D'IVOIRE

Area	322,463 sq km	Capital	Abidjan/Yamoussoukro
Arable as % of total land	10	Currency	CFA franc (CFAfr)

People

Population	16.7m	Life expectancy: men	40.8 yrs
Pop. per sq km	51.8	women	41.2 yrs
Av. ann. growth		Adult literacy[a]	47.6%
in pop. 2000–05	1.67%	Fertility rate (per woman)	4.7
Pop. under 15	42.7%	Urban population	44.0%
Pop. over 60	5.0%		per 1,000 pop.
No. of men per 100 women	104	Crude birth rate	35.5
Human Development Index	39.6	Crude death rate	20.0

The economy

GDP	CFAfr8,142bn	GDP per head	$700
GDP	$11.7bn	GDP per head in purchasing	
Av. ann. growth in real		power parity (USA=100)	4.0
GDP 1992–2002	2.7%	Economic freedom index	3.18

Origins of GDP

	% of total
Agriculture	26.2
Industry, of which:	20.4
manufacturing	13.0
Services	53.4

Components of GDP

	% of total
Private consumption	64.6
Public consumption	15.8
Investment	9.6
Exports	41.5
Imports	-31.6

Structure of employment

	% of total		% of labour force
Agriculture	...	Unemployed 2002	...
Industry	...	Av. ann. rate 1995–2002	...
Services	...		

Energy

	m TOE		
Total output	6.2	Net energy imports as %	
Total consumption	6.5	of energy use	5
Consumption per head,			
kg oil equivalent	402		

Inflation and finance

		av. ann. change 1996–2001	
Consumer price			
inflation 2003	3.4%	Narrow money (M1)	10.1%
Av. ann. inflation 1998–2003	2.8%	Broad money	8.3%
Money market rate, 2003	4.95%		

Exchange rates

	end 2003		December 2003
CFAfr per $	519.4	Effective rates	1995 = 100
CFAfr per SDR	771.8	– nominal	106.4
CFAfr per €	654.4	– real	110.5

Trade

Principal exports		Principal imports	
	$bn fob		$bn cif
Cocoa beans & products	2.3	Capital goods	0.8
Petroleum products	0.7	Food products	0.6
Timber	0.2	Fuel & lubricants	0.5
Coffee & products	0.1		
Total incl. others	**5.1**	Total incl. others	**2.5**

Main export destinations		Main origins of imports	
	% of total		% of total
France	14.5	France	23.1
Netherlands	12.9	Nigeria	16.9
United States	7.6	China	8.0
Germany	5.2	Italy	4.2
Mali	4.6	Germany	3.1

Balance of payments, reserves and debt, $bn

Visible exports fob	5.2	Overall balance	-0.4
Visible imports fob	-2.4	Change in reserves	0.8
Trade balance	2.7	Level of reserves	
Invisibles inflows	0.7	end Dec.	1.9
Invisibles outflows	-2.2	No. months of import cover	4.8
Net transfers	-0.5	Foreign debt	11.8
Current account balance	0.8	– as % of GDP	114
– as % of GDP	6.6	– as % of total exports	235
Capital balance	-1.1	Debt service ratio	17

Health and education

Health spending, % of GDP	6.2	Education spending, % of GDP	4.6
Doctors per 1,000 pop.	...	Enrolment, %: primary	81
Hospital beds per 1,000 pop.	...	secondary	23
Improved-water source access,		tertiary[c]	7
% of pop.	81		

Society

No. of households	3.5m	Colour TVs per 100 households	28.0
Av. no. per household	4.6	Telephone lines per 100 pop.	2.0
Marriages per 1,000 pop.	...	Mobile telephone subscribers	
Divorces per 1,000 pop.	...	per 100 pop.	6.2
Cost of living, Dec. 2003		Computers per 100 pop.	0.9
New York = 100	90	Internet hosts per 1,000 pop.	...

a 1999

CZECH REPUBLIC

Area	78,864 sq km	Capital	Prague
Arable as % of total land	40	Currency	Koruna (Kc)

People

Population	10.3m	Life expectancy: men	72.1 yrs
Pop. per sq km	130.6	women	78.7 yrs
Av. ann. growth		Adult literacy	99.0%
in pop. 2000–05	-0.10	Fertility rate (per woman)	1.2
Pop. under 15	16.4%	Urban population	74.5%
Pop. over 60	18.3%		per 1,000 pop.
No. of men per 100 women	95	Crude birth rate	8.8
Human Development Index	86.1	Crude death rate	10.8

The economy

GDP	Kc2,276bn	GDP per head	$6,750
GDP	$69.5bn	GDP per head in purchasing	
Av. ann. growth in real		power parity (USA=100)	41.3
GDP 1992–2002	2.1%	Economic freedom index	2.39

Origins of GDP		**Components of GDP**	
	% of total		% of total
Agriculture	3.4	Private consumption	52.8
Industry, of which:	35.6	Public consumption	21.4
manufacturing	...	Investment	28.1
Services	61.0	Exports	65.2
		Imports	-67.5

Structure of employment

	% of total		% of labour force
Agriculture	5	Unemployed 2002	7.3
Industry	40	Av. ann. rate 1995–2002	6.5
Services	55		

Energy

	m TOE		
Total output	30.5	Net energy imports as %	
Total consumption	41.4	of energy use	26
Consumption per head,			
kg oil equivalent	4,049		

Inflation and finance

Consumer price		av. ann. increase 1997–2002	
inflation 2003	0.1%	Narrow money (M1)	14.6%
Av. ann. inflation 1998–2003	2.5%	Broad money	7.9%
Money market rate, 2003	2.08%	Household saving rate, 2002	11.3%

Exchange rates

	end 2003		December 2003
Kc per $	25.65	Effective rates	1995 = 100
Kc per SDR	38.12	– nominal	116.9
Kc per €	33.32	– real	129.9

Trade

Principal exports		Principal imports	
	$bn fob		*$bn cif*
Machinery & transport		Machinery & transport	
equipment	19.0	equipment	17.1
Semi-manufactures	9.0	Semi-manufactures	8.3
Chemicals	2.3	Chemicals	4.5
Raw materials & fuels	2.2	Raw materials & fuels	4.2
Total incl. others	**38.2**	Total incl. others	**40.4**

Main export destinations		Main origins of imports	
	% of total		*% of total*
Germany	35.5	Germany	35.9
Slovakia	6.3	Slovakia	5.6
Austria	5.2	Austria	5.3
Poland	4.9	Italy	5.0
United Kingdom	4.5	France	4.8
EU15	68.4	EU15	60.2

Balance of payments, reserves and debt, $bn

Visible exports fob	38.5	Overall balance	6.6
Visible imports fob	-40.7	Change in reserves	9.2
Trade balance	-2.2	Level of reserves	
Invisibles inflows	9.3	end Dec.	23.7
Invisibles outflows	-12.4	No. months of import cover	5.4
Net transfers	0.9	Foreign debt	26.4
Current account balance	-4.5	– as % of GDP	46
– as % of GDP	-6.5	– as % of total exports	62
Capital balance	11.2	Debt service ratio	11

Health and education

Health spending, % of GDP	7.4	Education spending, % of GDP	4.4
Doctors per 1,000 pop.	3.4	Enrolment, %: primary	104
Hospital beds per 1,000 pop.	8.8	secondary	95
Improved-water source access,		tertiary	30
% of pop.	...		

Society

No. of households	3.7m	Colour TVs per 100 households	89.3
Av. no. per household	2.8	Telephone lines per 100 pop.	36.2
Marriages per 1,000 pop.	4.1	Mobile telephone subscribers	
Divorces per 1,000 pop.	3.2	per 100 pop.	84.9
Cost of living, Dec. 2003		Computers per 100 pop.	17.7
New York = 100	69	Internet hosts per 1,000 pop.	30.7

DENMARK

Area	43,075 sq km	Capital	Copenhagen
Arable as % of total land	54	Currency	Danish krone (DKr)

People

Population	5.3m	Life expectancy: men	74.2 yrs
Pop. per sq km	123.0	women	79.1 yrs
Av. ann. growth		Adult literacy	99.0%
in pop. 2000–05	0.24	Fertility rate (per woman)	1.8
Pop. under 15	18.3%	Urban population	85.1%
Pop. over 60	20.0%		*per 1,000 pop.*
No. of men per 100 women	98	Crude birth rate	11.8
Human Development Index	93.0	Crude death rate	11.3

The economy

GDP	DKr1,365bn	GDP per head	$32,630
GDP	$172.9bn	GDP per head in purchasing	
Av. ann. growth in real		power parity (USA=100)	84.7
GDP 1992–2002	2.4%	Economic freedom index	1.80

Origins of GDP		**Components of GDP**	
	% of total		*% of total*
Agriculture	2.6	Private consumption	48.2
Industry, of which:	26.3	Public consumption	26.1
manufacturing	...	Investment	19.8
Services	71.1	Exports	44.2
		Imports	-38.3

Structure of employment

	% of total		*% of labour force*
Agriculture	3	Unemployed 2002	4.7
Industry	26	Av. ann. rate 1995–2002	5.6
Services	71		

Energy

	m TOE		
Total output	27.2	Net energy imports as %	
Total consumption	19.8	of energy use	-37
Consumption per head,			
kg oil equivalent	3,692		

Inflation and finance

Consumer price		*av. ann. increase 1997–2002*	
inflation 2003	2.1%	Narrow money (M1)	4.6%
Av. ann. inflation 1998–2003	2.5%	Broad money	1.0%
Money market rate, 2003	2.38%	Household saving rate, 2002	7.2%

Exchange rates

	end 2003		*December 2003*
DKr per $	5.59	Effective rates	*1995 = 100*
DKr per SDR	8.85	– nominal	97.3
DKr per €	7.04	– real	102.3

Trade

Principal exports		**Principal imports**	
	$bn fob		*$bn cif*
Manufactured goods	42.6	Intermediate goods	21.0
Agric. products	5.5	Consumer goods	13.7
Energy & products	3.8	Capital goods	7.0
Ships	0.5	Transport equipment	0.3
Total incl. others	**56.0**	Total incl. others	**49.1**

Main export destinations		**Main origins of imports**	
	% of total		*% of total*
Germany	19.4	Germany	22.3
Sweden	11.8	Sweden	12.0
United Kingdom	9.8	United Kingdom	8.9
United States	6.4	Netherlands	6.8
Norway	6.0	France	6.1
France	4.7	Italy	4.2
EU15	65.0	EU15	71.5

Balance of payments, reserves and aid, $bn

Visible exports fob	55.6	Capital balance	2.6
Visible imports fob	-47.3	Overall balance	5.6
Trade balance	8.3	Change in reserves	10.0
Invisibles inflows	39.5	Level of reserves	
Invisibles outflows	-40.2	end Dec.	27.7
Net transfers	-2.6	No. months of import cover	3.8
Current account balance	5.0	Aid given	1.54
– as % of GDP	2.9	– as % of GDP	0.96

Health and education

Health spending, % of GDP	8.4	Education spending, % of GDP	8.3
Doctors per 1,000 pop.	3.4	Enrolment, %: primary	102
Hospital beds per 1,000 pop.	4.5	secondary	128
Improved-water source access,		tertiary	59
% of pop.	100		

Society

No. of households	2.5m	Colour TVs per 100 households	92.4
Av. no. per household	2.1	Telephone lines per 100 pop.	68.9
Marriages per 1,000 pop.	6.4	Mobile telephone subscribers	
Divorces per 1,000 pop.	2.7	per 100 pop.	83.3
Cost of living, Dec. 2003		Computers per 100 pop.	57.7
New York = 100	116	Internet hosts per 1,000 pop.	276.9

EGYPT

Area	1,000,250 sq km	Capital	Cairo
Arable as % of total land	3	Currency	Egyptian pound (£E)

People

Population	70.3m	Life expectancy: men	66.7 yrs
Pop. per sq km	70.3	women	71.0 yrs
Av. ann. growth		Adult literacy[a]	56.3%
in pop. 2000–05	1.99%	Fertility rate (per woman)	3.3
Pop. under 15	36.3%	Urban population	42.7%
Pop. over 60	6.8%		per 1,000 pop.
No. of men per 100 women	100	Crude birth rate	26.6
Human Development Index	64.8	Crude death rate	6.2

The economy

GDP	£E388bn	GDP per head	$1,280
GDP	$89.9bn	GDP per head in purchasing	
Av. ann. growth in real		power parity (USA=100)	10.6
GDP 1992–2002	4.4%	Economic freedom index	3.28

Origins of GDP[b]

	% of total
Agriculture	16.6
Industry, of which:	26.8
manufacturing	...
Services	56.6

Components of GDP[b]

	% of total
Private consumption	73.7
Public consumption	11.8
Investment	18.1
Exports	18.2
Imports	-21.8

Structure of employment

	% of total		% of labour force
Agriculture	30	Unemployed 2001	8.2
Industry	21	Av. ann. rate 1995–2001	9.2
Services	49		

Energy

	m TOE		
Total output	59.3	Net energy imports as %	
Total consumption	48.0	of energy use	-24
Consumption per head,			
kg oil equivalent	737		

Inflation and finance

Consumer price		av. ann. increase 1997–2002	
inflation 2003	4.3%	Narrow money (M1)	9.2%
Av. ann. inflation 1998–2003	3.0%	Broad money	10.7%
Treasury bill rate, 2003	6.9%		

Exchange rates

	end 2003		December 2003
£E per $	6.15	Effective rates	1995 = 100
£E per SDR	9.14	– nominal	...
£E per €	7.75	– real	...

Trade

Principal exports[c]		**Principal imports**[c]	
	$bn fob		*$bn fob*
Petroleum & products	3.2	Intermediate goods	4.4
Cotton yarn & textiles	0.7	Investment goods	3.2
Metals	0.4	Consumer goods	2.6
Agricultural products	0.1	Fuels	2.3
Total incl. others	**6.3**	Total incl. others	**13.3**

Main export destinations		**Main origins of imports**	
	% of total		*% of total*
United States	18.6	United States	17.1
Italy	13.8	Germany	7.6
United Kingdom	8.5	Italy	6.8
France	4.0	France	6.6

Balance of payments, reserves and debt, $bn

Visible exports fob	7.1	Overall balance	-0.8
Visible imports fob	-12.9	Change in reserves	0.5
Trade balance	-5.8	Level of reserves	
Invisibles inflows	10.0	end Dec.	14.1
Invisibles outflows	-7.6	No. months of import cover	8.3
Net transfers	4.0	Foreign debt	30.8
Current account balance	0.6	– as % of GDP	32
– as % of GDP	0.7	– as % of total exports	149
Capital balance	-3.3	Debt service ratio	10

Health and education

Health spending, % of GDP	3.9	Education spending, % of GDP	2.3
Doctors per 1,000 pop.	...	Enrolment, %: primary	100
Hospital beds per 1,000 pop.	...	secondary	86
Improved-water source access,		tertiary	39
% of pop.	97		

Society

No. of households	14.2m	Colour TVs per 100 households	48.4
Av. no. per household	4.5	Telephone lines per 100 pop.	11.0
Marriages per 1,000 pop.	10.6	Mobile telephone subscribers	
Divorces per 1,000 pop.	1.5	per 100 pop.	6.7
Cost of living, Dec. 2003		Computers per 100 pop.	1.7
New York = 100	51	Internet hosts per 1,000 pop.	0.3

a 2000 estimate.
b Year ending June 30, 2002.
c Year ending June 30, 2003.

ESTONIA

Area	45,200 sq km	Capital	Tallinn
Arable as % of total land	16	Currency	Kroon (EEK)

People

Population	1.4m	Life expectancy: men	66.5 yrs
Pop. per sq km	31.0	women	76.8 yrs
Av. ann. growth		Adult literacy[a]	99.8%
in pop. 2000–05	-1.10%	Fertility rate (per woman)	1.2
Pop. under 15	18%	Urban population	69.0%
Pop. over 60	21.2%		per 1,000 pop.
No. of men per 100 women	86	Crude birth rate	8.7
Human Development Index	83.3	Crude death rate	13.6

The economy

GDP	EEK108bn	GDP per head	$4,650
GDP	$6.5bn	GDP per head in purchasing	
Av. ann. growth in real		power parity (USA=100)	32.2
GDP 1992–2002	2.8%	Economic freedom index	1.76

Origins of GDP		Components of GDP	
	% of total		% of total
Agriculture	5.4	Private consumption	57.5
Industry, of which:	29.3	Public consumption	20.0
manufacturing	...	Investment	31.9
Services	65.3	Exports	85.1
		Imports	-94.8

Structure of employment

	% of total		% of labour force
Agriculture	7	Unemployed 2002	10.3
Industry	33	Av. ann. rate 1995–2002	11.0
Services	60		

Energy

	m TOE		
Total output	3.0	Net energy imports as %	
Total consumption	4.7	of energy use	36
Consumption per head,			
kg oil equivalent	3,444		

Inflation and finance

Consumer price		av. ann. increase 1997–2002	
inflation 2003	1.3%	Narrow money (M1)	14.3%
Av. ann. inflation 1998–2003	1.6%	Broad money	17.3%
Money market rate, 2003	2.92%		

Exchange rates

	end 2003		December 2003
EEK per $	12.41	Effective rates	1995 = 100
EEK per SDR	18.44	– nominal	...
EEK per €	15.64	– real	...

Trade

Principal exports		**Principal imports**	
	$bn fob		*$bn cif*
Machinery & equipment	0.8	Machinery & equipment	1.4
Wood & paper	0.6	Chemicals	0.6
Clothing & footwear	0.5	Clothing & footwear	0.5
Food	0.3	Transport equipment	0.5
Furniture	0.3		
Total incl. others	**3.4**	Total incl. others	**4.8**

Main export destinations		**Main origins of imports**	
	% of total		*% of total*
Finland	24.8	Finland	17.1
Sweden	15.3	Germany	11.2
Germany	9.9	Sweden	9.5
Latvia	7.4	Russia	7.4
United Kingdom	4.8	China	5.2

Balance of payments, reserves and debt, $bn

Visible exports fob	3.5	Overall balance	0.0
Visible imports fob	-4.6	Change in reserves	0.2
Trade balance	-1.1	Level of reserves	
Invisibles inflows	1.9	end Dec.	1.0
Invisibles outflows	-1.8	No. months of import cover	1.9
Net transfers	0.1	Foreign debt	4.7
Current account balance	-0.8	– as % of GDP	87
– as % of GDP	-12.3	– as % of total exports	90
Capital balance	0.8	Debt service ratio	15

Health and education

Health spending, % of GDP	5.5	Education spending, % of GDP	7.5
Doctors per 1,000 pop.	3.1	Enrolment, %: primary	103
Hospital beds per 1,000 pop.	6.7	secondary	92
Improved-water source access,		tertiary	48
% of pop.	...		

Society

No. of households	0.6m	Colour TVs per 100 households	85.1
Av. no. per household	2.4	Telephone lines per 100 pop.	35.1
Marriages per 1,000 pop.	4.0	Mobile telephone subscribers	
Divorces per 1,000 pop.	3.1	per 100 pop.	65.0
Cost of living, Dec. 2003		Computers per 100 pop.	21.0
New York = 100	...	Internet hosts per 1,000 pop.	80.8

a 2000

FINLAND

Area	338,145 sq km	Capital	Helsinki
Arable as % of total land	7	Currency	Euro (€)

People

Population	5.2m	Life expectancy: men	74.4 yrs
Pop. per sq km	15.4	women	81.5 yrs
Av. ann. growth		Adult literacy	99.0%
in pop. 2000–05	0.18%	Fertility rate (per woman)	1.7
Pop. under 15	18.1%	Urban population	58.5%
Pop. over 60	19.9%		per 1,000 pop.
No. of men per 100 women	95	Crude birth rate	10.8
Human Development Index	93.0	Crude death rate	9.8

The economy

GDP	€140bn	GDP per head	$25,290
GDP	$131.5bn	GDP per head in purchasing	
Av. ann. growth in real		power parity (USA=100)	72.4
GDP 1992–2002	3.4%	Economic freedom index	1.95

Origins of GDP

	% of total
Agriculture	3.1
Industry, of which:	29.4
manufacturing & mining	23.0
Services	67.5

Components of GDP

	% of total
Private consumption	50.2
Public consumption	21.3
Investment	18.5
Exports	43.3
Imports	-33.5

Structure of employment

	% of total		% of labour force
Agriculture	6	Unemployed 2002	9.1
Industry	27	Av. ann. rate 1995–2002	11.4
Services	67		

Energy

	m TOE		
Total output	15.2	Net energy imports as %	
Total consumption	33.8	of energy use	55
Consumption per head,			
kg oil equivalent	6,518		

Inflation and finance

Consumer price		av. ann. increase 1997–2002
inflation 2003	0.6%	Euro area:
Av. ann. inflation 1998–2003	1.7%	Narrow money (M1)	9.0%
Money market rate, 2003	2.33%	Broad money	6.4%
		Household saving rate, 2002	-1.4%

Exchange rates

	end 2003		December 2003
€ per $	0.79	Effective rates	1995 = 100
€ per SDR	1.18	– nominal	94.4
		– real	80.8

Trade

Principal exports		Principal imports	
	$bn fob		*$bn cif*
Electrical & optical equipment	13.0	Raw materials	13.9
Metals, machinery &		Consumer goods	9.5
transport equipment	12.7	Capital goods	7.8
Paper & products	9.8	Other goods	4.1
Chemicals	4.0		
Total incl. others	**44.5**	Total incl. others	**33.5**

Main export destinations		Main origins of imports	
	% of total		*% of total*
Germany	11.8	Germany	14.5
United Kingdom	9.6	Sweden	11.0
United States	8.9	Russia	10.1
Sweden	8.5	United States	6.6
Russia	6.6	United Kingdom	5.7
France	4.6	Japan	4.4

Balance of payments, reserves and aid, $bn

Visible exports fob	44.9	Capital balance	-8.5
Visible imports fob	-31.7	Overall balance	-0.1
Trade balance	13.1	Change in reserves	1.4
Invisibles inflows	15.2	Level of reserves	
Invisibles outflows	-17.5	end Dec.	9.8
Net transfers	-0.6	No. months of import cover	2.4
Current account balance	10.2	Aid given	0.43
– as % of GDP	7.8	– as % of GDP	0.38

Health and education

Health spending, % of GDP	7.0	Education spending, % of GDP	5.9
Doctors per 1,000 pop.	3.1	Enrolment, %: primary	102
Hospital beds per 1,000 pop.	7.5	secondary	126
Improved-water source access,		tertiary[a]	83
% of pop.	100		

Society

No. of households	2.3m	Colour TVs per 100 households	98.3
Av. no. per household	2.2	Telephone lines per 100 pop.	52.4
Marriages per 1,000 pop.	4.5	Mobile telephone subscribers	
Divorces per 1,000 pop.	2.7	per 100 pop.	86.7
Cost of living, Dec. 2003		Computers per 100 pop.	44.2
New York = 100	103	Internet hosts per 1,000 pop.	235.4

FRANCE

Area	543,965 sq km	Capital	Paris
Arable as % of total land	34	Currency	Euro (€)

People

Population	59.7m	Life expectancy: men	75.2 yrs
Pop. per sq km	109.8	women	82.8 yrs
Av. ann. growth		Adult literacy	99.0%
in pop. 2000–05	0.47%	Fertility rate (per woman)	1.9
Pop. under 15	18.8%	Urban population	75.5%
Pop. over 60	20.5%		per 1,000 pop.
No. of men per 100 women	95	Crude birth rate	12.8
Human Development Index	92.5	Crude death rate	9.3

The economy

GDP	€1,521bn	GDP per head	$23,970
GDP	$1,431bn	GDP per head in purchasing	
Av. ann. growth in real		power parity (USA=100)	74.9
GDP 1992–2002	1.9%	Economic freedom index	2.63

Origins of GDP

Components of GDP

	% of total		% of total
Agriculture	2.7	Private consumption	54.8
Industry, of which:	25.0	Public consumption	23.8
manufacturing	...	Investment	19.5
Services	72.3	Exports	27.1
		Imports	-25.0

Structure of employment

	% of total		% of labour force
Agriculture	2	Unemployed 2002	8.9
Industry	24	Av. ann. rate 1995–2002	10.9
Services	74		

Energy

	m TOE		
Total output	132.7	Net energy imports as %	
Total consumption	265.6	of energy use	50
Consumption per head, kg oil equivalent	4,487		

Inflation and finance

Consumer price			av. ann. increase 1997–2002
inflation 2003	2.1%	Euro area:	
Av. ann. inflation 1998–2003	1.6%	Narrow money (M1)	9.0%
Deposit rate, 2003	2.69%	Broad money	6.4%
		Household saving rate, 2002	12.0%

Exchange rates

	end 2003		December 2003
€ per $	0.79	Effective rates	1995 = 100
€ per SDR	1.18	– nominal	98.1
		– real	91.3

Trade

Principal exports		Principal imports	
	$bn fob		*$bn cif*
Intermediate goods	94.3	Intermediate goods	94.8
Capital goods	75.0	Capital goods	66.7
Consumer goods	47.4	Consumer goods	52.3
Motor vehicles & other		Motor vehicles & other	
transport equipment	45.9	transport equipment	35.2
Food & drink	27.7	Energy	21.3
Total incl. others	**311.1**	Total incl. others	**310.7**

Main export destinations		Main origins of imports	
	% of total		*% of total*
Germany	14.5	Germany	17.2
United Kingdom	10.3	Italy	9.0
Spain	9.7	United States	8.0
Italy	9.1	United Kingdom	7.3
United States	8.1	Spain	7.2
EU15	62.0	EU15	59.7

Balance of payments, reserves and aid, $bn

Visible exports fob	305.6	Capital balance	-33.2
Visible imports fob	-296.6	Overall balance	-4.0
Trade balance	9.0	Change in reserves	3.1
Invisibles inflows	167.5	Level of reserves	
Invisibles outflows	-136.9	end Dec.	61.7
Net transfers	-13.9	No. months of import cover	1.7
Current account balance	25.7	Aid given[a]	5.13
– as % of GDP	1.8	– as % of GDP	0.38

Health and education

Health spending, % of GDP	9.6	Education spending, % of GDP	5.8
Doctors per 1,000 pop.	3.3	Enrolment, %: primary	105
Hospital beds per 1,000 pop.	8.2	secondary	108
Improved-water source access,		tertiary	54
% of pop.	...		

Society

No. of households	24.5m	Colour TVs per 100 households	95.9
Av. no. per household	2.4	Telephone lines per 100 pop.	56.9
Marriages per 1,000 pop.	5.1	Mobile telephone subscribers	
Divorces per 1,000 pop.	1.9	per 100 pop.	64.7
Cost of living, Dec. 2003		Computers per 100 pop.	34.7
New York = 100	116	Internet hosts per 1,000 pop.	46.4

a Including aid to French overseas territories.

GERMANY

Area	357,868 sq km	Capital	Berlin
Arable as % of total land	34	Currency	Euro (€)

People

Population	82.0m	Life expectancy: men	75.2 yrs
Pop. per sq km	229.1	women	81.2 yrs
Av. ann. growth		Adult literacy	99.0%
in pop. 2000–05	0.07%	Fertility rate (per woman)	1.4
Pop. under 15	15.6%	Urban population	87.7%
Pop. over 60	23.2%		per 1,000 pop.
No. of men per 100 women	96	Crude birth rate	8.7
Human Development Index	92.1	Crude death rate	10.6

The economy

GDP	€2,108bn	GDP per head	$24,200
GDP	$1,984bn	GDP per head in purchasing	
Av. ann. growth in real		power parity (USA=100)	74.7
GDP 1992–2002	1.3%	Economic freedom index	2.03

Origins of GDP

	% of total
Agriculture	1.1
Industry, of which:	28.6
manufacturing	...
Services	70.3

Components of GDP

	% of total
Private consumption	58.9
Public consumption	19.1
Investment	18.1
Exports	35.5
Imports	-31.6

Structure of employment

	% of total		% of labour force
Agriculture	3	Unemployed 2002	8.7
Industry	33	Av. ann. rate 1995–2002	9.0
Services	65		

Energy

	m TOE		
Total output	133.7	Net energy imports as %	
Total consumption	351.1	of energy use	62
Consumption per head,			
kg oil equivalent	4,264		

Inflation and finance

Consumer price		av. ann. increase 1997–2002
inflation 2003	1.1%	Euro area:
Av. ann. inflation 1998–2003	1.5%	Narrow money (M1) 9.0%
Money market rate, 2003	2.32%	Broad money 6.4%
		Household saving rate, 2002 10.6%

Exchange rates

	end 2003		December 2003
€ per $	0.79	Effective rates	1995 = 100
€ per SDR	1.18	– nominal	93.8
		– real	85.2

Trade

Principal exports

	$bn fob
Road vehicles	117.7
Machinery	87.1
Chemicals	72.7
Telecoms technology	30.0
Electricity devices	29.6
Total incl. others	**610.1**

Principal imports

	$bn cif
Chemicals	52.4
Road vehicles	51.0
Machinery	34.4
Fuels	30.0
Telecoms technology	30.0
Total incl. others	**489.9**

Main export destinations

	% of total
France	10.8
United States	10.3
United Kingdom	8.4
Italy	7.3
Netherlands	6.1
Austria	5.1
Belgium	4.8

Main origins of imports

	% of total
France	9.0
Netherlands	7.8
United States	7.3
Italy	6.1
United Kingdom	6.1
Belgium	4.9
Austria	3.8

Balance of payments, reserves and aid, $bn

Visible exports fob	615.0	Capital balance	-76.9
Visible imports fob	-492.8	Overall balance	-2.0
Trade balance	122.2	Change in reserves	7.1
Invisibles inflows	209.3	Level of reserves	
Invisibles outflows	259.8	end Dec.	89.1
Net transfers	-25.1	No. months of import cover	1.4
Current account balance	46.6	Aid given	4.98
– as % of GDP	2.3	– as % of GDP	0.27

Health and education

Health spending, % of GDP	10.8	Education spending, % of GDP	4.6
Doctors per 1,000 pop.	3.3	Enrolment, %: primary	104
Hospital beds per 1,000 pop.	9.1	secondary	99
Improved-water source access, % of pop.	...	tertiary	46

Society

No. of households	38.3m	Colour TVs per 100 households	97.1
Av. no. per household	2.2	Telephone lines per 100 pop.	65.1
Marriages per 1,000 pop.	4.6	Mobile telephone subscribers	
Divorces per 1,000 pop.	2.3	per 100 pop.	72.8
Cost of living, Dec. 2003		Computers per 100 pop.	43.1
New York = 100	95	Internet hosts per 1,000 pop.	41.7

GREECE

Area	131,957 sq km	Capital	Athens
Arable as % of total land	21	Currency	Euro (€)

People

Population	10.6m	Life expectancy: men	75.7 yrs
Pop. per sq km	80.3	women	80.9 yrs
Av. ann. growth		Adult literacy	97.4%
in pop. 2000–05	0.14%	Fertility rate (per woman)	1.3
Pop. under 15	15.1%	Urban population	60.3%
Pop. over 60	23.4%		per 1,000 pop.
No. of men per 100 women	97	Crude birth rate	9.1
Human Development Index	89.2	Crude death rate	10.5

The economy

GDP	€141bn	GDP per head	$12,530
GDP	$132.8bn	GDP per head in purchasing	
Av. ann. growth in real		power parity (USA=100)	52.0
GDP 1992–2002	2.8%	Economic freedom index	2.80

Origins of GDP		**Components of GDP**	
	% of total		% of total
Agriculture	7.4	Private consumption	69.8
Industry, of which:	22.4	Public consumption	13.5
manufacturing	...	Investment	25.8
Services	70.3	Exports	23.8
		Imports	-33.0

Structure of employment

	% of total		% of labour force
Agriculture	16	Unemployed 2002	9.6
Industry	23	Av. ann. rate 1995–2002	10.5
Services	61		

Energy

	m TOE		
Total output	10.0	Net energy imports as %	
Total consumption	28.7	of energy use	65
Consumption per head,			
kg oil equivalent	2,710		

Inflation and finance

Consumer price		av. ann. increase 1997–2002	
inflation 2003	3.6%	Euro area:	
Av. ann. inflation 1998–2003	3.3%	Narrow money (M1)	9.0%
Treasury bill rate, 2003	2.30%	Broad money	6.4%

Exchange rates

	end 2003		December 2003
€ per $	0.79	Effective rates	1995 = 100
€ per SDR	1.18	– nominal	87.7
		– real	110.8

Trade

Principal exports[a]		Principal imports[a]	
	$bn fob		$bn cif
Food & beverages	1.5	Machinery	5.1
Petroleum products	0.9	Transport equipment	4.2
Chemicals	0.8	Chemicals	3.3
Non-ferrous metals	0.7	Fuels	1.4
Textiles	0.7	Iron & steel	1.0
Total incl. others	**11.6**	Total incl. others	**26.1**

Main export destinations[b]		Main origins of imports[b]	
	% of total		% of total
Germany	12.3	Italy	13.5
Italy	9.2	Germany	13.4
United Kingdom	6.4	France	7.1
United States	5.3	Netherlands	5.7
EU	46.7	EU	54.8

Balance of payments, reserves and debt, $bn

Visible exports fob	9.9	Overall balance	1.9
Visible imports fob	-31.3	Change in reserves	3.2
Trade balance	-21.5	Level of reserves	
Invisibles inflows	21.8	end Dec.	9.4
Invisibles outflows	-14.2	No. months of import cover	2.5
Net transfers	3.5	Aid given	0.25
Current account balance	-10.4	– as % of GDP	0.21
– as % of GDP	-7.8		
Capital balance	13.1		

Health and education

Health spending, % of GDP	9.4	Education spending, % of GDP	3.8
Doctors per 1,000 pop.	4.4	Enrolment, %: primary	99
Hospital beds per 1,000 pop.	4.9	secondary	98
Improved-water source access,		tertiary[a]	50
% of pop.	...		

Society

No. of households	3.5m	Colour TVs per 100 households	91.4
Av. no. per household	3.0	Telephone lines per 100 pop.	49.1
Marriages per 1,000 pop.	4.5	Mobile telephone subscribers	
Divorces per 1,000 pop.	0.9	per 100 pop.	84.5
Cost of living, Dec. 2003		Computers per 100 pop.	8.2
New York = 100	80	Internet hosts per 1,000 pop.	23.2

a 1999
b 2001

HONG KONG

Area	1,075 sq km	Capital	Victoria
Arable as % of total land	5	Currency	Hong Kong dollar (HK$)

People

Population	7.0m	Life expectancy: men	77.3 yrs
Pop. per sq km	6,511.6	women	82.8 yrs
Av. ann. growth		Adult literacy[a]	93.5%
in pop. 2000–05	1.07%	Fertility rate (per woman)	1.0
Pop. under 15	16.6%	Urban population	100.0%
Pop. over 60	14.4%		per 1,000 pop.
No. of men per 100 women	96	Crude birth rate	8.5
Human Development Index	88.9	Crude death rate	5.9

The economy

GDP	HK$1,260bn	GDP per head	$23,080
GDP	$161.5bn	GDP per head in purchasing	
Av. ann. growth in real		power parity (USA=100)	76.1
GDP 1992–2002	3.6%	Economic freedom index	1.34

Origins of GDP

	% of total
Agriculture	0.1
Industry, of which:	12.8
manufacturing	4.7
Services	87.1

Components of GDP

	% of total
Private consumption	57.8
Public consumption	10.4
Investment	23.4
Exports	150.8
Imports	-142.5

Structure of employment

	% of total		% of labour force
Agriculture	0	Unemployed 2002	7.3
Industry	20	Av. ann. rate 1995–2002	4.6
Services	80		

Energy

	m TOE		
Total output	0.04	Net energy imports as %	
Total consumption	16.3	of energy use	100
Consumption per head,			
kg oil equivalent	2,421		

Inflation and finance

Consumer price		av. ann. increase 1997–2002	
inflation 2003	-2.6%	Narrow money (M1)	7.5%
Av. ann. inflation 1998–2003	-3.0%	Broad money	5.7%
Money market rate, 2003	0.07%		

Exchange rates

	end 2003		December 2003
HK$ per $	7.76	Effective rates	1995 = 100
HK$ per SDR	11.53	– nominal	107.8
HK$ per €	9.75	– real	...

Trade

Principal exports[b]		Principal imports	
	$bn fob		$bn cif
Clothing	8.3	Raw materials &	
Electrical machinery		semi-manufactures	71.6
& apparatus	2.0	Consumer goods	69.7
Textiles	1.2	Capital goods	54.8
Jewellery	0.7	Food	7.6
Office machinery	0.4		
Total incl. others	**16.8**	Total incl. others	**207.6**

Main export destinations[b]		Main origins of imports	
	% of total		% of total
United States	32.0	China	44.3
China	31.6	Japan	11.3
United Kingdom	5.8	Taiwan	7.2
Taiwan	3.4	United States	5.6

Balance of payments, reserves and debt, $bn

Visible exports fob	200.3	Overall balance	-2.4
Visible imports cif	-205.4	Change in reserves	0.7
Trade balance	-5.1	Level of reserves	
Services inflows	86.6	end Dec.	111.9
Services outflows	-65.9	No. months of import cover	5.0
Net transfers	-1.9	Foreign debt	48.0
Current account balance	13.7	– as % of GDP	30
– as % of GDP	8.5	– as % of total exports	17
Capital balance	-21.8	Debt service ratio	2

Health and education

Health spending, % of GDP	...	Education spending, % of GDP	4.1
Doctors per 1,000 pop.	...	Enrolment, %: primary	109
Hospital beds per 1,000 pop.	...	secondary	78
Improved-water source access,		tertiary	25
% of pop.	98		

Society

No. of households	2.2m	Colour TVs per 100 households	99.1
Av. no. per household	3.3	Telephone lines per 100 pop.	56.5
Marriages per 1,000 pop.	4.0	Mobile telephone subscribers	
Divorces per 1,000 pop.	1.8	per 100 pop.	94.3
Cost of living, Dec. 2003		Computers per 100 pop.	42.2
New York = 100	113	Internet hosts per 1,000 pop.	84.6

a 2000
b Domestic, excluding re-exports.
Note: Hong Kong became a Special Administrative Region of China on July 1 1997.

HUNGARY

Area	93,030 sq km	Capital	Budapest
Arable as % of total land	50	Currency	Forint (Ft)

People

Population	9.9m	Life expectancy: men	67.7 yrs
Pop. per sq km	106.4	women	76.0 yrs
Av. ann. growth		Adult literacy	99.4%
in pop. 2000–05	-0.46%	Fertility rate (per woman)	1.2
Pop. under 15	17.0%	Urban population	64.8%
Pop. over 60	19.7%		per 1,000 pop.
No. of men per 100 women	91	Crude birth rate	8.8
Human Development Index	83.7	Crude death rate	13.5

The economy

GDP	Ft16,980bn	GDP per head	$6,650
GDP	$65.8bn	GDP per head in purchasing	
Av. ann. growth in real		power parity (USA=100)	36.2
GDP 1992–2002	3.1%	Economic freedom index	2.60

Origins of GDP		Components of GDP	
	% of total		% of total
Agriculture	3.8	Private consumption	66.2
Industry, of which:	30.6	Public consumption	12.0
manufacturing	...	Investment	24.0
Services	65.6	Exports	64.5
		Imports	-66.7

Structure of employment

	% of total		% of labour force
Agriculture	6	Unemployed 2002	5.8
Industry	35	Av. ann. rate 1995–2002	7.7
Services	59		

Energy

	m TOE		
Total output	10.8	Net energy imports as %	
Total consumption	25.3	of energy use	57
Consumption per head,			
kg oil equivalent	2,487		

Inflation and finance

Consumer price			av. ann. increase 1997–2002
inflation 2003	4.6%	Narrow money (M1)	16.5%
Av. ann. inflation 1998–2003	7.8%	Broad money	14.9%
Treasury bill rate, 2003	8.2%		

Exchange rates

	end 2003		December 2003
Ft per $	207.9	Effective rates	1995 = 100
Ft per SDR	309.0	– nominal	65.9
Ft per €	262.0	– real	131.0

Trade

Principal exports		Principal imports	
	$bn fob		*$bn cif*
Machinery & transport		Machinery & transport	
equipment	20.2	equipment	19.6
Other manufactures	10.6	Other manufactures	13.3
Food & beverages	2.3	Fuels	2.8
Raw materials	0.7	Food & food products	1.1
Total incl. others	**34.4**	Total incl. others	**37.6**

Main export destinations		Main origins of imports	
	% of total		*% of total*
Germany	33.7	Germany	23.9
Austria	8.2	Austria	7.7
Italy	5.4	Italy	7.5
Netherlands	5.2	Russia	6.0

Balance of payments, reserves and debt, $bn

Visible exports fob	34.8	Overall balance	-1.8
Visible imports fob	-36.9	Change in reserves	-0.4
Trade balance	-2.1	Level of reserves	
Invisibles inflows	9.0	end Dec.	10.4
Invisibles outflows	-10.0	No. months of import cover	2.7
Net transfers	0.4	Foreign debt	35.0
Current account balance	-2.6	– as % of GDP	66
– as % of GDP	-4.0	– as % of total exports	88
Capital balance	0.3	Debt service ratio	37

Health and education

Health spending, % of GDP	6.8	Education spending, % of GDP	5.2
Doctors per 1,000 pop.	2.9	Enrolment, %: primary	102
Hospital beds per 1,000 pop.	8.2	secondary	99
Improved-water source access,		tertiary	40
% of pop.	99		

Society

No. of households	3.7m	Colour TVs per 100 households	89.2
Av. no. per household	2.7	Telephone lines per 100 pop.	36.1
Marriages per 1,000 pop.	4.4	Mobile telephone subscribers	
Divorces per 1,000 pop.	2.5	per 100 pop.	67.6
Cost of living, Dec. 2003		Computers per 100 pop.	10.8
New York = 100	62	Internet hosts per 1,000 pop.	31.7

INDIA

Area	3,287,263 sq km	Capital	New Delhi
Arable as % of total land	54	Currency	Indian rupee (Rs)

People

Population	1,041.1m	Life expectancy: men	63.2 yrs
Pop. per sq km	316.7	women	64.6 yrs
Av. ann. growth		Adult literacy[a]	61.3%
in pop. 2000–05	1.51%	Fertility rate (per woman)	3.0
Pop. under 15	34.1%	Urban population	27.9%
Pop. over 60	7.5%		per 1,000 pop.
No. of men per 100 women	106	Crude birth rate	23.8
Human Development Index	59.0	Crude death rate	8.5

The economy

GDP	Rs24,696bn	GDP per head	$490
GDP	$510.2bn	GDP per head in purchasing	
Av. ann. growth in real		power parity (USA=100)	7.3
GDP 1992–2002	5.9%	Economic freedom index	3.53

Origins of GDP[b]

Components of GDP[b]

	% of total		% of total
Agriculture	23.3	Private consumption	64.4
Industry, of which:	26.2	Public consumption	12.5
manufacturing	15.4	Investment	22.8
Services	50.5	Exports	14.8
		Imports	-15.2

Structure of employment

	% of total		% of labour force
Agriculture	67	Unemployed 2002	11.6
Industry	12	Av. ann. rate 1995–2002	11.6
Services	21		

Energy

	m TOE		
Total output	438.1	Net energy imports as %	
Total consumption	531.5	of energy use	18
Consumption per head,			
kg oil equivalent	515		

Inflation and finance

Consumer price		*av. ann. increase 1997–2002*	
inflation 2003	3.8%	Narrow money (M1)	12.3%
Av. ann. inflation 1998–2003	4.1%	Broad money	16.3%
Bank rate, 2003	6.25%		

Exchange rates

	end 2003		December 2003
Rs per $	45.61	Effective rates	1995 = 100
Rs per SDR	67.78	– nominal	...
Rs per €	57.47	– real	...

Trade

Principal exports[b]

	$bn fob
Gems & jewellery	8.8
Engineering goods	8.4
Textiles	5.8
Ready made garments	5.4
Chemicals	5.0
Total incl. others	**49.3**

Principal imports[b]

	$bn cif
Petroleum & products	17.7
Capital goods	7.7
Gems	6.1
Electronic goods	5.4
Total incl. others	**56.5**

Main export destinations

	% of total
United States	22.9
United Arab Emirates	5.2
United Kingdom	5.2
Hong Kong	4.6
Germany	4.3

Main origins of imports

	% of total
United States	8.0
Belgium	7.5
China	5.2
Singapore	5.2
United Kingdom	5.2

Balance of payments, reserves and debt, $bn

Visible exports fob	52.7	Overall balance	16.9
Visible imports fob	-65.2	Change in reserves	22.6
Trade balance	-12.4	Level of reserves	
Invisibles inflows	27.2	end Dec.	71.6
Invisibles outflows	-24.9	No. months of import cover	9.5
Net transfers	14.8	Foreign debt	104.4
Current account balance	4.7	– as % of GDP	22
– as % of GDP	0.9	– as % of total exports	130
Capital balance	11.5	Debt service ratio	16

Health and education

Health spending, % of GDP	5.1	Education spending, % of GDP	4.1
Doctors per 1,000 pop.	...	Enrolment, %: primary	102
Hospital beds per 1,000 pop.	...	secondary	49
Improved-water source access,		tertiary	11
% of pop.	84		

Society

No. of households	174.9m	Colour TVs per 100 households	32.4
Av. no. per household	5.9	Telephone lines per 100 pop.	4.0
Marriages per 1,000 pop.	...	Mobile telephone subscribers	
Divorces per 1,000 pop.	...	per 100 pop.	1.2
Cost of living, Dec. 2003		Computers per 100 pop.	0.7
New York = 100	45	Internet hosts per 1,000 pop.	0.1

a 2001
b Year ending March 31, 2003.

INDONESIA

Area	1,904,443 sq km	Capital	Jakarta
Arable as % of total land	11	Currency	Rupiah (Rp)

People

Population	217.5m	Life expectancy: men	64.8 yrs
Pop. per sq km	114.2	women	68.8 yrs
Av. ann. growth		Adult literacy	87.9%
in pop. 2000–05	1.26%	Fertility rate (per woman)	2.4
Pop. under 15	30.9%	Urban population	42.1%
Pop. over 60	7.6%		per 1,000 pop.
No. of men per 100 women	100	Crude birth rate	20.7
Human Development Index	68.2	Crude death rate	7.3

The economy

GDP	Rp1,610trn	GDP per head	$790
GDP	$172.9bn	GDP per head in purchasing	
Av. ann. growth in real		power parity (USA=100)	8.5
GDP 1992–2002	3.3%	Economic freedom index	3.76

Origins of GDP

	% of total
Agriculture	15.9
Industry, of which:	43.9
manufacturing	26.6
Services	40.2

Components of GDP

	% of total
Private consumption	70.7
Public consumption	8.2
Investment	14.3
Exports	35.4
Imports	-28.5

Structure of employment

	% of total		% of total
Agriculture	44	Unemployed 2002	9.1
Industry	17	Av. ann. rate 1995–2002	5.9
Services	39		

Energy

	m TOE		
Total output	234.3	Net energy imports as %	
Total consumption	152.3	of energy use	-54
Consumption per head,			
kg oil equivalent	729		

Inflation and finance

Consumer price		*av. ann. increase 1997–2002*	
inflation 2003	5.8%	Narrow money (M1)	19.6%
Av. ann. inflation 1998–2003	10.7%	Broad money	20.0%
Money market rate, 2003	7.76%		

Exchange rates

	end 2003		December 2003
Rp per $	8,465	Effective rates	1995 = 100
Rp per SDR	12,579	– nominal	...
Rp per €	10,666	– real	...

Trade

Principal exports		Principal imports	
	$bn fob		*$bn cif*
Garments & textiles	6.8	Raw materials	24.2
Petroleum & products	6.3	Capital goods	4.4
Natural gas	6.0	Consumer goods	2.7
Total incl. others	**58.1**	**Total incl. others**	**25.4**

Main export destinations		Main origins of imports	
	% of total		*% of total*
Japan	22.6	Japan	22.0
United States	16.6	Singapore	12.5
Singapore	13.2	China	12.1
South Korea	7.5	South Korea	11.1

Balance of payments, reserves and debt, $bn

Visible exports fob	59.2	Overall balance	5.0
Visible imports fob	-35.7	Change in reserves	3.9
Trade balance	23.5	Level of reserves	
Invisibles inflows	8.0	end Dec.	32.0
Invisibles outflows	-25.4	No. months of import cover	6.3
Net transfers	1.8	Foreign debt	132.2
Current account balance	7.8	– as % of GDP	90
– as % of GDP	4.5	– as % of total exports	191
Capital balance	-1.2	Debt service ratio	24

Health and education

Health spending, % of GDP	2.4	Education spending, % of GDP	1.3
Doctors per 1,000 pop.	...	Enrolment, %: primary	110
Hospital beds per 1,000 pop.	...	secondary	57
Improved-water source access,		tertiary	15
% of pop.	78		

Society

No. of households	54.6m	Colour TVs per 100 households	48.5
Av. no. per household	4.0	Telephone lines per 100 pop.	3.7
Marriages per 1,000 pop.	6.7	Mobile telephone subscribers	
Divorces per 1,000 pop.	...	per 100 pop.	5.5
Cost of living, Dec. 2003		Computers per 100 pop.	1.2
New York = 100	73	Internet hosts per 1,000 pop.	0.3

IRAN

Area	1,648,000 sq km	Capital	Tehran
Arable as % of total land	9	Currency	Rial (IR)

People

Population	72.4m	Life expectancy: men	68.9 yrs
Pop. per sq km	43.9	women	71.9 yrs
Av. ann. growth		Adult literacy[a]	77.1%
in pop. 2000–05	1.24%	Fertility rate (per woman)	2.3
Pop. under 15	35.2%	Urban population	64.7%
Pop. over 60	6.4%		per 1,000 pop.
No. of men per 100 women	103	Crude birth rate	20.3
Human Development Index	71.9	Crude death rate	5.4

The economy

GDP	IR861trn	GDP per head	$1,500
GDP	$108.2bn	GDP per head in purchasing	
Av. ann. growth in real		power parity (USA=100)	18.5
GDP 1992–2002	3.6%	Economic freedom index	4.26

Origins of GDP		**Components of GDP**	
	% of total		% of total
Agriculture	12.1	Private consumption	56.3
Industry, of which:	39.0	Public consumption	9.7
manufacturing	13.7	Investment	26.6
Services	48.9	Net exports	2.6

Structure of employment

	% of total		% of labour force
Agriculture	...	Unemployed 2002	12.3
Industry	...	Av. ann. rate 2000–2002	12.4
Services	...		

Energy

	m TOE		
Total output	246.6	Net energy imports as %	
Total consumption	120.0	of energy use	-106
Consumption per head,			
kg oil equivalent	1,860		

Inflation and finance

Consumer price		*av. ann. increase 1997–2002*	
inflation 2003	16.5%	Narrow money (M1)	24.2%
Av. ann. inflation 1998–2003	15.3%	Broad money	23.9%

Exchange rates

	end 2003		December 2003
IR per $	8,272	Effective rates	1995 = 100
IR per SDR	12,292	– nominal	65.6
IR per €	10,423	– real	179.2

Trade

Principal exports[b]		**Principal imports**[b]	
	$bn fob		*$bn cif*
Oil & gas	24.3	Transport, machinery & tools	5.2
Industrial goods	2.3	Chemicals & pharmaceuticals	2.0
Agricultural goods	1.5	Food & animals	2.0
Total incl. others	**28.5**	Total incl. others	**14.3**

Main export destinations		**Main origins of imports**	
	% of total		*% of total*
Japan	17.3	Germany	10.6
China	8.6	Italy	9.1
United Arab Emirates	7.5	France	7.9
Italy	6.5	China	7.4
South Korea	4.9	South Korea	6.5

Balance of payments[c], reserves and debt, $bn

Visible exports fob	28.2	Overall balance[d]	1.1
Visible imports fob	-23.8	Change in reserves	...
Trade balance	4.4	Level of reserves	
Invisibles inflows[d]	1.9	end Dec.	...
Invisibles outflows[d]	-2.9	No. months of import cover	...
Net transfers[d]	0.6	Foreign debt	9.2
Current account balance	3.7	– as % of GDP	9
– as % of GDP	3.4	– as % of total exports	29
Capital balance[d]	-10.2	Debt service ratio	5

Health and education

Health spending, % of GDP	6.6	Education spending, % of GDP	5.0
Doctors per 1,000 pop.	...	Enrolment, %: primary	86
Hospital beds per 1,000 pop.	...	secondary	7
Improved-water source access,		tertiary	10
% of pop.	92		

Society

No. of households	12.5m	Colour TVs per 100 households	9.5
Av. no. per household	5.5	Telephone lines per 100 pop.	18.7
Marriages per 1,000 pop.	8.4	Mobile telephone subscribers	
Divorces per 1,000 pop.	0.8	per 100 pop.	3.4
Cost of living, Dec. 2003		Computers per 100 pop.	7.5
New York = 100	32	Internet hosts per 1,000 pop.	...

a 2001
b 2000
c Iranian year ending March 20, 2003.
d Iranian year ending March 20, 2001.

IRELAND

Area	70,282 sq km	Capital	Dublin
Arable as % of total land	15	Currency	Euro (€)

People

Population	3.9m	Life expectancy:	men	74.4 yrs
Pop. per sq km	55.5		women	79.6 yrs
Av. ann. growth		Adult literacy		99.0%
in pop. 2000–05	1.12%	Fertility rate (per woman)		1.9
Pop. under 15	21.5%	Urban population		59.3%
Pop. over 60	15.2%			per 1,000 pop.
No. of men per 100 women	99	Crude birth rate		14.4
Human Development Index	93.0	Crude death rate		8.3

The economy

GDP	€129bn	GDP per head	$31,140
GDP	$121.4bn	GDP per head in purchasing	
Av. ann. growth in real		power parity (USA=100)	81.9
GDP 1992–2002	7.7%	Economic freedom index	1.74

Origins of GDP[a]		Components of GDP	
	% of total		% of total
Agriculture	5.0	Private consumption	46.5
Industry, of which:	46.1	Public consumption	13.6
manufacturing	...	Investment	22.2
Services	48.9	Exports	93.7
		Imports	-75.0

Structure of employment

	% of total		% of labour force
Agriculture	7	Unemployed 2001	3.7
Industry	29	Av. ann. rate 1995–2001	8.0
Services	64		

Energy

	m TOE		
Total output	1.7	Net energy imports as %	
Total consumption	15.0	of energy use	88
Consumption per head, kg oil equivalent	3,876		

Inflation and finance

Consumer price			av. ann. increase 1997–2002
inflation 2003	3.5%	Euro area:	
Av. ann. inflation 1998–2003	4.0%	Narrow money (M1)	9.0%
Money market rate, 2003	2.08%	Broad money	6.4%

Exchange rates

	end 2003		December 2003
€ per $	0.79	Effective rates	1995 = 100
€ per SDR	1.18	– nominal	98.4
		– real	...

Trade

Principal exports		Principal imports	
	$bn fob		*$bn cif*
Chemicals	37.0	Machinery & transport	
Machinery & transport		equipment	26.3
equipment	31.8	Chemicals	6.6
Foodstuffs & tobacco	6.3	Manufactured materials	4.0
Manufactured materials	1.7	Food	2.9
		Fuels	1.6
Total incl. others	**87.4**	Total incl. others	**51.6**

Main export destinations		Main origins of imports	
	% of total		*% of total*
United Kingdom	23.9	United Kingdom	35.9
United States	18.1	United States	15.8
Germany	7.2	Belgium	14.4
France	5.0	Germany	6.4
Japan	3.6	France	4.1
Netherlands	3.3	Italy	3.8
EU15	59.4	EU15	63.7

Balance of payments, reserves and aid, $bn

Visible exports fob	85.8	Capital balance	0.4
Visible imports fob	-50.9	Overall balance	-0.3
Trade balance	34.9	Change in reserves	-0.2
Invisibles inflows	54.6	Level of reserves	
Invisibles outflows	-91.4	end Dec.	5.5
Net transfers	0.8	No. months of import cover	0.5
Current account balance	-0.9	Aid given	0.36
– as % of GDP	-0.8	– as % of GDP	0.40

Health and education

Health spending, % of GDP	6.5	Education spending, % of GDP	4.3
Doctors per 1,000 pop.	2.4	Enrolment, %: primary	119
Hospital beds per 1,000 pop.	9.7	secondary	109
Improved-water source access,		tertiary	48
% of pop.	...		

Society

No. of households	1.2m	Colour TVs per 100 households	99.3
Av. no. per household	3.2	Telephone lines per 100 pop.	50.2
Marriages per 1,000 pop.	5.1	Mobile telephone subscribers	
Divorces per 1,000 pop.	...	per 100 pop.	76.3
Cost of living, Dec. 2003		Computers per 100 pop.	42.1
New York = 100	94	Internet hosts per 1,000 pop.	28.6

a 2001

ISRAEL

Area	20,770 sq km	Capital	Jerusalem
Arable as % of total land	16	Currency	New Shekel (NIS)

People

Population	6.3m	Life expectancy: men	77.1 yrs
Pop. per sq km	303.3	women	81.0 yrs
Av. ann. growth		Adult literacy	95.3%
in pop. 2000–05	2.02%	Fertility rate (per woman)	2.7
Pop. under 15	28.3%	Urban population	91.8%
Pop. over 60	13.1%		per 1,000 pop.
No. of men per 100 women	98	Crude birth rate	19.8
Human Development Index	90.5	Crude death rate	6.0

The economy

GDP	NIS491bn	GDP per head	$16,460
GDP	$103.7bn	GDP per head in purchasing	
Av. ann. growth in real		power parity (USA=100)	52.6
GDP 1992–2002	3.9%	Economic freedom index	2.36

Origins of GDPa		Components of GDP	
	% of total		% of total
Agriculture	2.8	Private consumption	59.4
Industry, of which:	37.6	Public consumption	31.2
manufacturing	26.7	Investment	17.8
Services	61.9	Exports	37.0
		Imports	-45.8

Structure of employment

	% of total		% of labour force
Agriculture	19	Unemployed 2002	10.3
Industry	24	Av. ann. rate 1995–2002	8.4
Services	57		

Energy

	m TOE		
Total output	0.7	Net energy imports as %	
Total consumption	21.2	of energy use	98
Consumption per head,			
kg oil equivalent	3,291		

Inflation and finance

Consumer price		av. ann. increase 1997–2002	
inflation 2003	-0.6%	Narrow money (M1)	11.4%
Av. ann. inflation 1998–2003	2.5%	Broad money	11.8%
Treasury bill rate, 2003	7.0%		

Exchange rates

	end 2003		December 2003
NIS per $	4.38	Effective rates	1995 = 100
NIS per SDR	6.51	– nominal	72.1
NIS per €	5.52	– real	89.6

Trade

Principal exports		Principal imports	
	$bn fob		*$bn cif*
Diamonds	8.5	Diamonds	7.2
Communications, medical &		Investment goods	5.9
scientific equipment	4.3	Machinery & equipment	4.5
Chemicals	4.0	Fuel	3.1
Electronics	2.5	Chemicals	2.1
Total incl. others	**25.8**	Total incl. others	**32.6**

Main export destinations		Main origins of imports	
	% of total		*% of total*
United States	44.8	United States	23.8
Belgium	6.3	Belgium	8.3
Germany	5.0	Germany	7.4
United Kingdom	4.8	United Kingdom	7.3
Hong Kong	4.5	Switzerland	5.4

Balance of payments, reserves and debt, $bn

Visible exports fob	27.7	Overall balance	-0.9
Visible imports fob	-31.2	Change in reserves	0.7
Trade balance	-3.6	Level of reserves	
Invisibles inflows	13.7	end Dec.	24.1
Invisibles outflows	-17.9	No. months of import cover	5.9
Net transfers	6.5	Foreign debt	66.0
Current account balance	-1.2	– as % of GDP	64.0
– as % of GDP	-1.2	– as % of total exports	153
Capital balance	-1.8	Debt service ratio	17

Health and education

Health spending, % of GDP	8.7	Education spending, % of GDP	7.3
Doctors per 1,000 pop.	3.7	Enrolment, %: primary	114
Hospital beds per 1,000 pop.	6.2	secondary	93
Improved-water source access,		tertiary	53
% of pop.	...		

Society

No. of households	1.8m	Colour TVs per 100 households	96.5
Av. no. per household	3.6	Telephone lines per 100 pop.	46.7
Marriages per 1,000 pop.	4.5	Mobile telephone subscribers	
Divorces per 1,000 pop.	2.0	per 100 pop.	95.5
Cost of living, Dec. 2003		Computers per 100 pop.	24.3
New York = 100	89	Internet hosts per 1,000 pop.	100.6

a 2001

ITALY

Area	301,245 sq km	Capital	Rome
Arable as % of total land	28	Currency	Euro (€)

People

Population	57.4m	Life expectancy: men	75.5 yrs
Pop. per sq km	190.5	women	81.9 yrs
Av. ann. growth		Adult literacy	98.5%
in pop. 2000–05	-0.10%	Fertility rate (per woman)	1.2
Pop. under 15	14.3%	Urban population	67.1%
Pop. over 60	24.1%		per 1,000 pop.
No. of men per 100 women	94	Crude birth rate	8.8
Human Development Index	91.6	Crude death rate	10.9

The economy

GDP	€1,258trn	GDP per head	$20,630
GDP	$1,184bn	GDP per head in purchasing	
Av. ann. growth in real		power parity (USA=100)	72.5
GDP 1992–2002	1.6%	Economic freedom index	2.26

Origins of GDP

Components of GDP

	% of total		% of total
Agriculture	2.3	Private consumption	59.8
Industry, of which:	29.4	Public consumption	19.2
manufacturing	...	Investment	19.7
Services	68.3	Exports	26.9
		Imports	-25.8

Structure of employment

	% of total		% of labour force
Agriculture	5	Unemployed 2002	9.0
Industry	32	Av. ann. rate 1995–2002	10.8
Services	63		

Energy

	m TOE		
Total output	26.3	Net energy imports as %	
Total consumption	172.0	of energy use	85
Consumption per head,			
kg oil equivalent	2,981		

Inflation and finance

Consumer price			av. ann. increase 1999–2002
inflation 2003	2.7%	Euro area:	
Av. ann. inflation 1998–2003	2.4%	Narrow money (M1)	9.0%
Money market rate, 2003	2.33%	Broad money	6.4%
		Household saving rate, 2002	15.9%

Exchange rates

	end 2003		December 2003
€ per $	0.79	Effective rates	1995 = 100
€ per SDR	1.18	– nominal	72.1
		– real	89.6

Trade

Principal exports
	$bn fob
Engineering products	93.3
Textiles & clothing	38.6
Transport equipment	28.7
Chemicals	25.4
Food, drink & tobacco	14.0
Total incl. others	**252.1**

Principal imports
	$bn cif
Engineering products	74.0
Transport equipment	36.8
Chemicals	33.1
Energy products	24.9
Textiles & clothing	19.0
Total incl. others	**243.3**

Main export destinations
	% of total
Germany	13.7
France	12.2
United States	9.7
United Kingdom	6.9
Spain	6.3
EU15	53.1

Main origins of imports
	% of total
Germany	17.8
France	11.3
Netherlands	5.9
United Kingdom	5.0
United States	4.9
EU15	56.9

Balance of payments, reserves and aid, $bn
Visible exports fob	253.7	Capital balance	11.9
Visible imports fob	-237.1	Overall balance	3.2
Trade balance	16.5	Change in reserves	9.4
Invisibles inflows	103.6	Level of reserves	
Invisibles outflows	-121.4	end Dec.	55.6
Net transfers	-5.4	No. months of import cover	1.9
Current account balance	-6.7	Aid given	2.16
– as % of GDP	-0.6	– as % of GDP	0.20

Health and education
Health spending, % of GDP	8.4	Education spending, % of GDP	4.7
Doctors per 1,000 pop.	4.3	Enrolment, %: primary	101
Hospital beds per 1,000 pop.	4.9	secondary	96
Improved-water source access, % of pop.	...	tertiary	50

Society
No. of households	22.5m	Colour TVs per 100 households	94.2
Av. no. per household	2.6	Telephone lines per 100 pop.	48.1
Marriages per 1,000 pop.	4.5	Mobile telephone subscribers	
Divorces per 1,000 pop.	0.8	per 100 pop.	93.4
Cost of living, Dec. 2003		Computers per 100 pop.	23.1
New York = 100	88	Internet hosts per 1,000 pop.	95.3

JAPAN

Area	377,727 sq km	Capital	Tokyo
Arable as % of total land	12	Currency	Yen (¥)

People

Population	127.5m	Life expectancy: men	77.9 yrs
Pop. per sq km	337.5	women	85.1 yrs
Av. ann. growth		Adult literacy	99.0%
in pop. 2000–05	0.14%	Fertility rate (per woman)	1.3
Pop. under 15	14.6%	Urban population	78.9%
Pop. over 60	23.3%		per 1,000 pop.
No. of men per 100 women	96	Crude birth rate	9.2
Human Development Index	93.2	Crude death rate	8.2

The economy

GDP	¥501trn	GDP per head	$31,320
GDP	$3,993bn	GDP per head in purchasing	
Av. ann. growth in real		power parity (USA=100)	75.8
GDP 1992–2002	0.9%	Economic freedom index	2.53

Origins of GDP

	% of total
Agriculture	1.3
Industry, of which:	30.2
manufacturing	20.5
Services	68.5

Components of GDP

	% of total
Private consumption	57.2
Public consumption	17.9
Investment	23.7
Exports	11.2
Imports	-9.9

Structure of employment

	% of total		% of labour force
Agriculture	5	Unemployed 2002	5.4
Industry	31	Av. ann. rate 1995–2002	4.2
Services	64		

Energy

	m TOE		
Total output	104.0	Net energy imports as %	
Total consumption	520.7	of energy use	80
Consumption per head,			
kg oil equivalent	4,099		

Inflation and finance

Consumer price		*av. ann. increase 1997–2002*	
inflation 2003	-0.3%	Narrow money (M1)	11.2%
Av. ann. inflation 1998–2003	-0.6%	Broad money	2.8%
Money market rate, 2003	0.00%	Household saving rate, 2002	5.9%

Exchange rates

	end 2003		December 2003
¥ per $	107.1	Effective rates	1995 = 100
¥ per SDR	159.2	– nominal	88.3
¥ per €	134.9	– real	75.1

Trade

Principal exports		Principal imports	
	$bn fob		*$bn cif*
Transport equipment	104.0	Machinery & equipment	107.3
Electrical machinery	95.4	Mineral fuels	66.9
Non-electrical machinery	84.8	Food	42.2
Chemicals	33.4	Chemicals	25.9
Metals	25.8	Raw materials	20.1
Total incl. others	**415.6**	Total incl. others	**336.4**

Main export destinations		Main origins of imports	
	% of total		*% of total*
United States	28.5	China	18.3
China	9.6	United States	17.1
South Korea	6.9	South Korea	4.6
Taiwan	6.3	Indonesia	4.2
Hong Kong	6.1	Australia	4.1

Balance of payments, reserves and aid, $bn

Visible exports fob	395.6	Capital balance	-66.7
Visible imports fob	-301.8	Overall balance	46.1
Trade balance	93.8	Change in reserves	67.7
Invisibles inflows	157.2	Level of reserves	
Invisibles outflows	-133.7	end Dec.	469.6
Net transfers	-4.9	No. months of import cover	12.9
Current account balance	112.5	Aid given	9.73
– as % of GDP	2.8	– as % of GDP	0.23

Health and education

Health spending, % of GDP	8.0	Education spending, % of GDP	3.6
Doctors per 1,000 pop.	1.9	Enrolment, %: primary	101
Hospital beds per 1,000 pop.	16.5	secondary	102
Improved-water source access,		tertiary	48
% of pop.	97		

Society

No. of households	48.2m	Colour TVs per 100 households	99.1
Av. no. per household	2.6	Telephone lines per 100 pop.	55.8
Marriages per 1,000 pop.	5.9	Mobile telephone subscribers	
Divorces per 1,000 pop.	1.9	per 100 pop.	63.7
Cost of living, Dec. 2003		Computers per 100 pop.	38.2
New York = 100	138	Internet hosts per 1,000 pop.	101.7

KENYA

Area	582,646 sq km	Capital	Nairobi
Arable as % of total land	8	Currency	Kenyan shilling (KSh)

People

Population	31.9m	Life expectancy: men	43.5 yrs
Pop. per sq km	54.8	women	45.6 yrs
Av. ann. growth		Adult literacy	83.4%
in pop. 2000–05	1.45%	Fertility rate (per woman)	4.0%
Pop. under 15	43.4%	Urban population	34.4%
Pop. over 60	4.2%		per 1,000 pop.
No. of men per 100 women	98	Crude birth rate	32.5
Human Development Index	48.9	Crude death rate	16.7

The economy

GDP	KSh969bn	GDP per head	$390
GDP	$12.3bn	GDP per head in purchasing	
Av. ann. growth in real		power parity (USA=100)	2.8
GDP 1992–2002	1.9%	Economic freedom index	3.26

Origins of GDP		**Components of GDP**	
	% of total		% of total
Agriculture	24.3	Private consumption	71.5
Industry, of which:	...	Public consumption	19.0
manufacturing	13.0	Investment	13.1
Other	62.7	Exports	26.2
		Imports	-30.6

Structure of employment

	% of total		% of labour force
Agriculture	19	Unemployed 2002	...
Industry	20	Av. ann. rate 1995–2002	...
Services	61		

Energy

	m TOE		
Total output	12.6	Net energy imports as %	
Total consumption	15.4	of energy use	18
Consumption per head,			
kg oil equivalent	500		

Inflation and finance

Consumer price			av. ann. increase 1997–2002
inflation 2003	9.8%	Narrow money (M1)	10.5%
Av. ann. inflation 1998–2003	6.6%	Broad money	5.4%
Treasury bill rate, 2003	3.51%		

Exchange rates

	end 2003		December 2003
KSh per $	76.1	Effective rates	1995 = 100
KSh per SDR	113.1	– nominal	...
KSh per €	95.9	– real	...

Trade

Principal exports		Principal imports	
	$m fob		*$m cif*
Tea	439	Industrial machinery	484
Horticultural products	253	Crude petroleum	397
Petroleum products	157	Refined petroleum products	331
Coffee	95	Motor vehicles & chassis	185
Total incl. others	**2,116**	Total incl. others	**3,245**

Main export destinations		Main origins of imports	
	% of total		*% of total*
United Kingdom	13.5	United Kingdom	12.0
Tanzania	12.5	United Arab Emirates	9.8
Uganda	12.0	Japan	6.5
Netherlands	6.5	India	4.4

Balance of payments, reserves and debt, $bn

Visible exports fob	2.2	Overall balance	-0.0
Visible imports fob	-3.2	Change in reserves	0.0
Trade balance	-1.0	Level of reserves	
Invisibles inflows	1.1	end Dec.	1.1
Invisibles outflows	-0.8	No. months of import cover	3.2
Net transfers	0.6	Foreign debt	6.0
Current account balance	-0.1	– as % of GDP	54
– as % of GDP	-1.1	– as % of total exports	197
Capital balance	-0.1	Debt service ratio	15

Health and education

Health spending, % of GDP	7.8	Education spending, % of GDP	6.2
Doctors per 1,000 pop.	...	Enrolment, %: primary	94
Hospital beds per 1,000 pop.	...	secondary	31
Improved-water source access,		tertiary	3
% of pop.	57		

Society

No. of households	7.1m	Colour TVs per 100 households	11.9
Av. no. per household	4.6	Telephone lines per 100 pop.	1.0
Marriages per 1,000 pop.	...	Mobile telephone subscribers	
Divorces per 1,000 pop.	...	per 100 pop.	4.2
Cost of living, Dec. 2003		Computers per 100 pop.	0.6
New York = 100	62	Internet hosts per 1,000 pop.	0.3

LATVIA

Area	63,700 sq km	Capital	Riga
Arable as % of total land	30	Currency	Lats (LVL)

People

Population	2.4m	Life expectancy: men	65.6 yrs
Pop. per sq km	37.7	women	76.2 yrs
Av. ann. growth		Adult literacy[a]	99.7%
in pop. 2000–05	-0.93%	Fertility rate (per woman)	1.1
Pop. under 15	18.0%	Urban population	60.0%
Pop. over 60	21.2%		per 1,000 pop.
No. of men per 100 women	85	Crude birth rate	7.8
Human Development Index	81.1	Crude death rate	13.6

The economy

GDP	LVL5.2bn	GDP per head	$3,500
GDP	$8.4bn	GDP per head in purchasing	
Av. ann. growth in real		power parity (USA=100)	25.5
GDP 1992–2002	2.3%	Economic freedom index	2.36

Origins of GDP		Components of GDP	
	% of total		% of total
Agriculture	4.7	Private consumption	62.7
Industry, of which:	24.5	Public consumption	20.5
manufacturing	14.8	Investment	27.3
Services	70.8	Exports	45.5
		Imports	-56.1

Structure of employment

	% of total		% of labour force
Agriculture	15	Unemployed 2002	12.0
Industry	26	Av. ann. rate 1996–2002	14.8
Services	59		

Energy

	m TOE		
Total output	1.7	Net energy imports as %	
Total consumption	4.3	of energy use	60
Consumption per head,			
kg oil equivalent	182.2		

Inflation and finance

Consumer price		av. ann. increase 1997–2002	
inflation 2003	2.9%	Narrow money (M1)	13.1%
Av. ann. inflation 1998–2003	2.5%	Broad money	16.1%
Money market rate, 2003	2.86%		

Exchange rates

	end 2003		December 2003
LVL per $	0.54	Effective rates	1995 = 100
LVL per SDR	0.80	– nominal	...
LVL per €	0.68	– real	...

Trade

Principal exports		Principal imports	
	$bn fob		*$bn cif*
Wood & wood products	0.8	Machinery & equipment	0.9
Metals	0.3	Chemicals	0.4
Textiles	0.3	Mineral products	0.4
		Transport equipment	0.4
Total incl. others	**2.3**	Total incl. others	**4.0**

Main export destinations		Main origins of imports	
	% of total		*% of total*
Germany	15.5	Germany	17.2
United Kingdom	14.6	Lithuania	9.8
Sweden	10.5	Russia	8.8
Lithuania	8.4	Finland	8.0
Estonia	6.0	Sweden	6.4
EU15	60.4	EU15	53.0

Balance of payments, reserves and debt, $bn

Visible exports fob	2.6	Overall balance	0.0
Visible imports fob	-4.0	Change in reserves	0.1
Trade balance	-1.4	Level of reserves	
Invisibles inflows	1.5	end Dec.	1.3
Invisibles outflows	-1.0	No. months of import cover	3.2
Net transfers	0.3	Foreign debt	6.7
Current account balance	-0.6	– as % of GDP	86
– as % of GDP	-7.7	– as % of total exports	175
Capital balance	0.7	Debt service ratio	17

Health and education

Health spending, % of GDP	6.4	Education spending, % of GDP	5.9
Doctors per 1,000 pop.	2.9	Enrolment, %: primary	100
Hospital beds per 1,000 pop.	8.2	secondary	91
Improved-water source access,		tertiary	50
% of pop.	...		

Society

No. of households	1.0m	Colour TVs per 100 households	68.4
Av. no. per household	2.4	Telephone lines per 100 pop.	30.1
Marriages per 1,000 pop.	3.1	Mobile telephone subscribers	
Divorces per 1,000 pop.	2.4	per 100 pop.	39.4
Cost of living, Dec. 2003		Computers per 100 pop.	17.2
New York = 100	...	Internet hosts per 1,000 pop.	12.3

a 2000

LITHUANIA

Area	65,200 sq km	Capital	Vilnius
Arable as % of total land	45	Currency	Litas (LTL)

People

Population	3.7m	Life expectancy: men	67.5 yrs
Pop. per sq km	56.7	women	77.6 yrs
Av. ann. growth		Adult literacy[a]	99.6%
in pop. 2000–05	-0.58%	Fertility rate (per woman)	1.3
Pop. under 15	20.1%	Urban population	69.0%
Pop. over 60	19.3%		per 1,000 pop.
No. of men per 100 women	88	Crude birth rate	8.8
Human Development Index	82.4	Crude death rate	11.6

The economy

GDP	LTL50.7bn	GDP per head	$3,730
GDP	$13.8bn	GDP per head in purchasing	
Av. ann. growth in real		power parity (USA=100)	28.2
GDP 1992–2002	1.1%	Economic freedom index	2.19

Origins of GDP

Components of GDP

	% of total		% of total
Agriculture	7.1	Private consumption	62.2
Industry, of which:	30.8	Public consumption	20.4
manufacturing and mining	20.1	Investment	22.4
Services	62.1	Exports	54.0
		Imports	-59.1

Structure of employment

	% of total		% of labour force
Agriculture	16	Unemployed 2002	13.8
Industry	28	Av. ann. rate 1995–2002	15.3
Services	56		

Energy

	m TOE		
Total output	4.1	Net energy imports as %	
Total consumption	8.0	of energy use	48
Consumption per head,			
kg oil equivalent	2,304		

Inflation and finance

Consumer price		av. ann. increase 1997–2002	
inflation 2003	-1.7%	Narrow money (M1)	10.3%
Av. ann. inflation 1998–2003	0.3%	Broad money	15.3%
Money market rate, 2003	1.79%		

Exchange rates

	end 2003		December 2003
LTL per $	2.76	Effective rates	1995 = 100
LTL per SDR	4.10	– nominal	...
LTL per €	3.48	– real	...

Trade

Principal exports		Principal imports	
	$bn fob		*$bn cif*
Mineral products	1.0	Mineral products	1.4
Transport equipment	0.9	Machinery & equipment	1.3
Textiles	0.8	Transport equipment	1.3
Machinery & equipment	0.6	Chemicals	0.7
Total incl. others	**5.5**	Total incl. others	**7.8**

Main export destinations		Main origins of imports	
	% of total		*% of total*
United Kingdom	13.4	Russia	21.3
Russia	12.2	Germany	17.0
Germany	10.4	Italy	4.9
Latvia	9.6	Poland	4.8
Denmark	8.1	United Kingdom	3.3
EU15	48.4	EU15	44.5

Balance of payments, reserves and debt, $bn

Visible exports fob	6.0	Overall balance	0.5
Visible imports fob	-7.3	Change in reserves	0.7
Trade balance	-1.3	Level of reserves	
Invisibles inflows	1.7	end Dec.	2.4
Invisibles outflows	-1.3	No. months of import cover	3.4
Net transfers	0.2	Foreign debt	6.2
Current account balance	-0.7	– as % of GDP	51
– as % of GDP	-5.2	– as % of total exports	97
Capital balance	1.1	Debt service ratio	20

Health and education

Health spending, % of GDP	6.0	Education spending, % of GDP	2.9
Doctors per 1,000 pop.	4.0	Enrolment, %: primary	101
Hospital beds per 1,000 pop.	9.2	secondary	95
Improved-water source access, % of pop.	...	tertiary	40

Society

No. of households	1.4m	Colour TVs per 100 households	72.6
Av. no. per household	2.6	Telephone lines per 100 pop.	27.0
Marriages per 1,000 pop.	4.8	Mobile telephone subscribers	
Divorces per 1,000 pop.	3.2	per 100 pop.	47.5
Cost of living, Dec. 2003		Computers per 100 pop.	11.0
New York = 100	...	Internet hosts per 1,000 pop.	12.1

a 2001

MALAYSIA

Area	332,665 sq km	Capital	Kuala Lumpur
Arable as % of total land	6	Currency	Malaysian dollar/ringgit (M$)

People

Population	23.0m	Life expectancy: men	70.8 yrs
Pop. per sq km	69.1	women	75.7 yrs
Av. ann. growth		Adult literacy[a]	88.7%
in pop. 2000–05	1.93%	Fertility rate (per woman)	2.9
Pop. under 15	33.7%	Urban population	58.1%
Pop. over 60	6.5%		per 1,000 pop.
No. of men per 100 women	103	Crude birth rate	22.6
Human Development Index	79.0	Crude death rate	4.6

The economy

GDP	M$361bn	GDP per head	$4,130
GDP	$94.9bn	GDP per head in purchasing	
Av. ann. growth in real		power parity (USA=100)	23.5
GDP 1992–2002	5.7%	Economic freedom index	3.16

Origins of GDP

	% of total
Agriculture	8.4
Industry, of which:	45.3
manufacturing	30.1
Services	46.3

Components of GDP

	% of total
Private consumption	44.2
Public consumption	13.9
Investment	24.4
Exports	114.1
Imports	-96.6

Structure of employment

	% of total		% of labour force
Agriculture	18	Unemployed 2002	3.8
Industry	32	Av. ann. rate 1995–2002	3.2
Services	50		

Energy

	m TOE		
Total output	77.6	Net energy imports as %	
Total consumption	51.6	of energy use	-50
Consumption per head,			
kg oil equivalent	2,168		

Inflation and finance

		av. ann. increase 1997–2002	
Consumer price inflation 2003	1.1%	Narrow money (M1)	2.1%
Av. ann. inflation 1998–2003	1.7%	Broad money	6.0%
Money market rate, 2003	2.74%		

Exchange rates

	end 2003		December 2003
M$ per $	3.80	Effective rates	1995 = 100
M$ per SDR	5.65	– nominal	74.8
M$ per €	4.79	– real	79.5

Trade

Principal exports		Principal imports	
	$bn fob		*$bn cif*
Electronics	40.6	Intermediate goods	57.0
Electrical machinery	14.4	Capital goods & transport	
Consumption goods	5.1	equipment	12.0
Chemicals & products	4.5		
Palm oil	3.9		
Textiles, clothing & footwear	2.3		
Total incl. others	**93.3**	Total incl. others	**79.9**

Main export destinations		Main origins of imports	
	% of total		*% of total*
United States	20.2	Japan	17.8
Singapore	17.1	United States	16.4
Japan	11.2	Singapore	12.0
Hong Kong	5.7	China	7.7
China	5.6	South Korea	5.3
Netherlands	3.7	Thailand	4.0

Balance of payments, reserves and debt, $bn

Visible exports fob	93.4	Overall balance	3.7
Visible imports fob	-75.2	Change in reserves	3.8
Trade balance	18.1	Level of reserves	
Invisibles inflows	17.0	end Dec.	34.6
Invisibles outflows	-25.2	No. months of import cover	4.1
Net transfers	-2.8	Foreign debt	48.6
Current account balance	7.2	as % of GDP	58
– as % of GDP	7.6	– as % of total exports	44
Capital balance	-3.1	Debt service ratio	7

Health and education

Health spending, % of GDP	3.8	Education spending, % of GDP	7.9
Doctors per 1,000 pop.	...	Enrolment, %: primary	99
Hospital beds per 1,000 pop.	...	secondary	70
Improved-water source access,		tertiary	28
% of pop.	...		

Society

No. of households	5.1m	Colour TVs per 100 households	90.2
Av. no. per household	4.6	Telephone lines per 100 pop.	19.0
Marriages per 1,000 pop.	3.1	Mobile telephone subscribers	
Divorces per 1,000 pop.	...	per 100 pop.	37.7
Cost of living, Dec. 2003		Computers per 100 pop.	14.7
New York = 100	62	Internet hosts per 1,000 pop.	4.7

a 2000

MEXICO

Area	1,972,545 sq km	Capital	Mexico city
Arable as % of total land	13	Currency	Mexican peso (PS)

People

Population	101.8m	Life expectancy: men	70.4 yrs
Pop. per sq km	51.6	women	76.4 yrs
Av. ann. growth		Adult literacy[a]	90.5%
in pop. 2000–05	1.45%	Fertility rate (per woman)	2.5
Pop. under 15	33.8%	Urban population	74.6%
Pop. over 60	6.9%		per 1,000 pop.
No. of men per 100 women	96	Crude birth rate	22.4
Human Development Index	80.0	Crude death rate	5.0

The economy

GDP	6,153bn pesos	GDP per head	$6,260
GDP	$637.2bn	GDP per head in purchasing	
Av. ann. growth in real		power parity (USA=100)	24.4
GDP 1992–2002	2.7%	Economic freedom index	2.90

Origins of GDP

	% of total
Agriculture	4.0
Industry, of which:	26.6
manufacturing & mining	20.3
Services	69.4

Components of GDP

	% of total
Private consumption	70.0
Public consumption	11.8
Investment	20.3
Exports	27.2
Imports	-29.2

Structure of employment

	% of total		% of labour force
Agriculture	18	Unemployed 2002	1.9
Industry	26	Av. ann. rate 1995–2002	2.5
Services	56		

Energy

	m TOE		
Total output	230.2	Net energy imports as %	
Total consumption	152.3	of energy use	-51
Consumption per head,			
kg oil equivalent	1,532		

Inflation and finance

Consumer price			av. ann. increase 1997–2002
inflation 2003	4.6%	Narrow money (M1)	18.7%
Av. ann. inflation 1998–2003	8.3%	Broad money	18.7%
Money market rate, 2003	6.83%		

Exchange rates

	end 2003		December 2003
			1995 = 100
PS per $	11.24	Effective rates	
PS per SDR	16.70	– nominal	...
PS per €	14.16	– real	...

Trade

Principal exports		Principal imports	
	$bn fob		*$bn fob*
Manufactured products	143.2	Intermediate goods	126.5
Maquiladora	78.1	Maquiladora	59.3
Crude oil & products	13.1	Consumer goods	21.2
Agricultural products	3.5	Capital goods	21.0
Total incl. others	**160.7**	Total	**168.7**

Main export destinations		Main origins of imports	
	% of total		*% of total*
United States	77.0	United States	63.6
Canada	5.0	Germany	3.3
Japan	1.0	Japan	2.5
Spain	0.8	Canada	1.9

Balance of payments, reserves and debt, $bn

Visible exports fob	160.8	Overall balance	7.4
Visible imports fob	-168.7	Change in reserves	5.9
Trade balance	-7.9	Level of reserves	
Invisibles inflows	16.8	end Dec.	50.7
Invisibles outflows	-33.1	No. months of import cover	3.0
Net transfers	10.3	Foreign debt	141.3
Current account balance	-14.0	– as % of GDP	24
– as % of gdp	-2.2	– as % of total exports	75
Capital balance	22.2	Debt service ratio	23

Health and education

Health spending, % of GDP	6.1	Education spending, % of GDP	5.1
Doctors per 1,000 pop.	1.5	Enrolment, %: primary	113
Hospital beds per 1,000 pop.	1.1	secondary	75
Improved-water source access,		tertiary	21
% of pop.	88		

Society

No. of households	23.3m	Colour TVs per 100 households	89.7
Av. no. per household	4.4	Telephone lines per 100 pop.	14.7
Marriages per 1,000 pop.	6.7	Mobile telephone subscribers	
Divorces per 1,000 pop.	0.5	per 100 pop.	25.5
Cost of living, Dec. 2003		Computers per 100 pop.	8.2
New York = 100	82	Internet hosts per 1,000 pop.	13.1

MOROCCO

Area	446,550 sq km	Capital	Rabat
Arable as % of total land	20	Currency	Dirham (Dh)

People

Population	31.0m	Life expectancy: men	66.8 yrs
Pop. per sq km	69.4	women	70.5 yrs
Av. ann. growth		Adult literacy	50.7%
in pop. 2000–05	1.62%	Fertility rate (per woman)	2.3
Pop. under 15	32.9%	Urban population	56.1%
Pop. over 60	6.5%		per 1,000 pop.
No. of men per 100 women	100	Crude birth rate	23.2
Human Development Index	60.6	Crude death rate	6.0

The economy

GDP	Dh398bn	GDP per head	$1,160
GDP	$36.1bn	GDP per head in purchasing	
Av. ann. growth in real		power parity (USA=100)	10.3
GDP 1992–2002	3.1%	Economic freedom index	2.93

Origins of GDP

	% of total
Agriculture	16.1
Industry, of which:	30.3
manufacturing	16.8
Services	53.6

Components of GDP

	% of total
Private consumption	66.4
Public consumption	20.1
Investment	22.5
Exports	29.2
Imports	-32.2

Structure of employment

	% of total		% of labour force
Agriculture	6	Unemployed 2002	11.6
Industry	33	Av. ann. rate 1995–2002	16.1
Services	61		

Energy

	m TOE		
Total output	0.6	Net energy imports as %	
Total consumption	11.0	of energy use	95
Consumption per head,			
kg oil equivalent	377		

Inflation and finance

Consumer price		*av. ann. increase 1997–2002*	
inflation 2002	2.8%	Narrow money (M1)	10.3%
Av. ann. inflation 1998–2002	1.5%	Broad money	9.0%
Money market rate, 2003	3.22%		

Exchange rates

	end 2003		December 2003
Dh per $	8.75	Effective rates	1995 = 100
Dh per SDR	13.00	– nominal	102.1
Dh per €	11.03	– real	98.7

Trade

Principal exports	$bn fob	Principal imports	$bn cif
Consumer goods	3.4	Consumer goods	2.8
Semi-finished goods	1.8	Semi-finished goods	2.6
Food, drink & tobacco	1.6	Machinery & equipment	2.3
Minerals	0.7	Energy & lubricants	1.8
Energy & lubricants	0.2	Food, drink & tobacco	1.4
Total incl. others	**7.8**	Total incl. others	**11.8**

Main export destinations	% of total	Main origins of imports	% of total
France	26.7	France	21.0
Spain	14.4	Spain	12.7
United Kingdom	8.0	Italy	6.4
Italy	5.6	Germany	5.3

Balance of payments, reserves and debt, $bn

Visible exports fob	7.8	Overall balance	-0.1
Visible imports fob	-10.9	Change in reserves	1.7
Trade balance	-3.1	Level of reserves	
Invisibles inflows	4.7	end Dec.	10.4
Invisibles outflows	-3.5	No. months of import cover	8.6
Net transfers	3.3	Foreign debt	18.6
Current account balance	1.5	– as % of GDP	55
– as % of GDP	4.1	– as % of total exports	129
Capital balance	-1.3	Debt service ratio	26

Health and education

Health spending, % of GDP	5.1	Education spending, % of GDP	5.1
Doctors per 1,000 pop.	...	Enrolment, %: primary	94
Hospital beds per 1,000 pop.	...	secondary	39
Improved-water source access,		tertiary	10
% of pop.	80		

Society

No. of households	5.5m	Colour TVs per 100 households	45.3
Av. no. per household	5.3	Telephone lines per 100 pop.	3.8
Marriages per 1,000 pop.	...	Mobile telephone subscribers	
Divorces per 1,000 pop.	...	per 100 pop.	20.9
Cost of living, Dec. 2003		Computers per 100 pop.	2.4
New York = 100	...	Internet hosts per 1,000 pop.	0.2

NETHERLANDS

Area[a]	41,526 sq km	Capital	Amsterdam
Arable as % of total land	27	Currency	Euro (€)

People

Population	16.0m	Life expectancy: men	75.6 yrs
Pop. per sq km	385.3	women	81.0 yrs
Av. ann. growth		Adult literacy	99.0%
in pop. 2000–05	0.50%	Fertility rate (per woman)	1.7
Pop. under 15	18.5%	Urban population	89.6%
Pop. over 60	18.2%		per 1,000 pop.
No. of men per 100 women	98	Crude birth rate	12.1
Human Development Index	93.8	Crude death rate	8.9

The economy

GDP	€444bn	GDP per head	$26,120
GDP	$417.9bn	GDP per head in purchasing	
Av. ann. growth in real		power parity (USA=100)	78.5
GDP 1992–2002	2.6%	Economic freedom index	2.04

Origins of GDP		Components of GDP	
	% of total		% of total
Agriculture	2.5	Private consumption	49.9
Industry, of which:	24.9	Public consumption	24.5
manufacturing	...	Investment	20.7
Services	72.7	Exports	62.6
		Imports	-57.5

Structure of employment

	% of total		% of labour force
Agriculture	3	Unemployed 2002	2.7
Industry	21	Av. ann. rate 1995–2002	4.7
Services	76		

Energy

	m TOE		
Total output	60.4	Net energy imports as %	
Total consumption	77.2	of energy use	22
Consumption per head,			
kg oil equivalent	4,814		

Inflation and finance

Consumer price			av. ann. increase 1997–2002
inflation 2003	2.1%	Euro area:	
Av. ann. inflation 1998–2003	3.0%	Narrow money (M1)	9.0%
Lending rate, 2003	3.00%	Broad money	6.4%
		Household saving rate, 2002	8.6%

Exchange rates

	end 2003		December 2003
€ per $	0.79	Effective rates	1995 = 100
€ per SDR	1.18	– nominal	94.4
		– real	99.8

Trade

Principal exports		Principal imports	
	$bn fob		*$bn cif*
Machinery & transport equipment	72.7	Machinery & transport equipment	72.6
Chemicals	36.1	Chemicals	23.6
Food, drink & tobacco	33.7	Food, drink & tobacco	19.3
Fuels	17.7	Fuels	19.1
Total incl. others	**221.5**	Total incl. others	**193.1**

Main export destinations		Main origins of imports	
	% of total		*% of total*
Germany	24.4	Germany	19.4
Belgium	11.9	Belgium	9.8
United Kingdom	10.9	United States	8.7
France	10.0	United Kingdom	8.0
Italy	6.1	France	5.9
EU15	75.8	EU15	56.8

Balance of payments, reserves and aid, $bn

Visible exports fob	206.9	Capital balance	-13.1
Visible imports fob	-186.9	Overall balance	-0.1
Trade balance	19.9	Change in reserves	2.0
Invisibles inflows	96.1	Level of reserves	
Invisibles outflows	-99.7	end Dec.	18.9
Net transfers	-6.2	No. months of import cover	0.8
Current account balance	10.1	Aid given	3.07
– as % of GDP	2.4	– as % of GDP	0.81

Health and education

Health spending, % of GDP	8.9	Education spending, % of GDP	4.8
Doctors per 1,000 pop.	3.3	Enrolment, %: primary	108
Hospital beds per 1,000 pop.	10.8	secondary	124
Improved-water source access, % of pop.	100	tertiary	55

Society

No. of households	6.9m	Colour TVs per 100 households	98.5
Av. no. per household	2.3	Telephone lines per 100 pop.	61.8
Marriages per 1,000 pop.	5.1	Mobile telephone subscribers	
Divorces per 1,000 pop.	1.9	per 100 pop.	74.5
Cost of living, Dec. 2003		Computers per 100 pop.	46.7
New York = 100	100	Internet hosts per 1,000 pop.	213.7

a Includes water.

NEW ZEALAND

Area	270,534 sq km	Capital	Wellington
Arable as % of total land	6	Currency	New Zealand dollar (NZ$)

People

Population	3.8m	Life expectancy: men		75.8 yrs
Pop. per sq km	14.0		women	80.7 yrs
Av. ann. growth		Adult literacy		99.0%
in pop. 2000–05	0.77%	Fertility rate (per woman)		2.0
Pop. under 15	22.9%	Urban population		85.9%
Pop. over 60	15.7%			per 1,000 pop.
No. of men per 100 women	97	Crude birth rate		14.0
Human Development Index	91.7	Crude death rate		7.6

The economy

GDP	NZ$126bn	GDP per head	$15,420
GDP	$58.6bn	GDP per head in purchasing	
Av. ann. growth in real		power parity (USA=100)	56.9
GDP 1992–2002	3.5%	Economic freedom index	1.70

Origins of GDP		**Components of GDP**	
	% of total		% of total
Agriculture & mining	8.1	Private consumption	58.7
Manufacturing	15.3	Public consumption	17.6
Other	76.6	Investment	22.2
		Exports	33.2
		Imports	-31.6

Structure of employment

	% of total		% of labour force
Agriculture	9	Unemployed 2002	5.2
Industry	23	Av. ann. rate 1995–2002	6.2
Services	68		

Energy

	m TOE		
Total output	14.9	Net energy imports as %	
Total consumption	18.3	of energy use	18
Consumption per head,			
kg oil equivalent	4,714		

Inflation and finance

		av. ann. increase 1997–2002	
Consumer price			
inflation 2003	1.8%	Narrow money (M1)	11.9%
Av. ann. inflation 1998–2003	1.9%	Broad money	4.7%
Money market rate, 2003	5.33%	Household saving rate, 2002	-5.2%

Exchange rates

	end 2003		December 2003
NZ$ per $	1.53	Effective rates	1995 = 100
NZ$ per SDR	2.27	– nominal	103.3
NZ$ per €	1.93	– real	103.7

Trade

Principal exports		Principal imports	
	$bn fob		*$bn cif*
Dairy produce	2.5	Machinery & electrical	
Meat	1.9	equipment	3.7
Forestry products	1.7	Transport equipment	2.9
Fish	0.7	Mineral fuels	1.5
Total incl. others	**14.4**	**Total incl. others**	**15.0**

Main export destinations		Main origins of imports	
	% of total		*% of total*
Australia	20.0	Australia	23.0
United States	15.4	United States	13.7
Japan	11.5	Japan	11.7
United Kingdom	4.8	United Kingdom	4.5

Balance of payments, reserves and aid, $bn

Visible exports fob	14.5	Capital balance	2.0
Visible imports fob	-14.0	Overall balance	1.1
Trade balance	0.5	Change in reserves	0.7
Invisibles inflows	6.2	Level of reserves	
Invisibles outflows	-9.0	end Dec.	3.7
Net transfers	0.1	No. months of import cover	1.9
Current account balance	-2.3	Aid given	0.11
– as % of GDP	-3.9	– as % of GDP	0.22

Health and education

Health spending, % of GDP	8.3	Education spending, % of GDP	6.6
Doctors per 1,000 pop.	2.2	Enrolment, %: primary	100
Hospital beds per 1,000 pop.	6.2	secondary	112
Improved-water source access,		tertiary	69
% of pop.	95		

Society

No. of households	1.4m	Colour TVs per 100 households	97.4
Av. no. per household	2.8	Telephone lines per 100 pop.	44.8
Marriages per 1,000 pop.	5.3	Mobile telephone subscribers	
Divorces per 1,000 pop.	3.3	per 100 pop.	62.2
Cost of living, Dec. 2003		Computers per 100 pop.	41.4
New York = 100	82	Internet hosts per 1,000 pop.	124.8

NIGERIA

Area	923,768 sq km	Capital	Abuja
Arable as % of total land	31	Currency	Naira (N)

People

Population	120.0m	Life expectancy: men	51.1 yrs
Pop. per sq km	129.9	women	51.8 yrs
Av. ann. growth		Adult literacy	66.8%
in pop. 2000–05	2.53%	Fertility rate (per woman)	5.4
Pop. under 15	45.0%	Urban population	44.9%
Pop. over 60	4.8%		per 1,000 pop.
No. of men per 100 women	101	Crude birth rate	39.1
Human Development Index	46.3	Crude death rate	13.7

The economy

GDP	N5,250bn	GDP per head	$360
GDP	$43.5bn	GDP per head in purchasing	
Av. ann. growth in real		power parity (USA=100)	2.2
GDP 1992–2002	2.1%	Economic freedom index	3.95

Origins of GDP

	% of total
Agriculture	41.2
Manufacturing	6.0
Other	52.8

Components of GDP

	% of total
Private consumption	59.8
Public consumption	14.2
Investment	7.0
Exports	25.5
Imports	-6.7

Structure of employment

	% of total		% of labour force
Agriculture	...	Unemployed 2001	3.9
Industry	...	Av. ann. rate 1995–2001	3.7
Services	...		

Energy

	m TOE		
Total output	207.0	Net energy imports as %	
Total consumption	95.4	of energy use	-117
Consumption per head, kg oil equivalent	735		

Inflation and finance

		av. ann. increase 1997–2002	
Consumer price inflation 2003	14.0%	Narrow money (M1)	28.0%
Av. ann. inflation 1998–2003	11.8%	Broad money	30.1%
Treasury bill rate 2003	14.79%		

Exchange rates

	end 2003		December 2003
N per $	136.5	Effective rates	1995 = 100
N per SDR	202.8	– nominal	31.8
N per €	172.0	– real	85.8

Trade

Principal exports		Principal imports	
	$bn fob		*$bn cif*
Oil	13.7	Manufactured goods	3.0
Gas	1.1	Machinery & transport equipment	2.5
		Chemicals	2.3
		Agric products & foodstuffs	1.2
Total incl. others	**15.5**	Total incl. others	**10.4**

Main export destinations[a]		Main origins of imports[a]	
	% of total		*% of total*
United States	33.4	United Kingdom	9.8
Brazil	8.4	United States	9.6
Spain	7.4	China	9.2
France	5.8	France	8.9

Balance of payments[b], reserves and debt, $bn

Visible exports fob	21.4	Overall balance[c]	-3.5
Visible imports fob	-11.1	Change in reserves	-3.1
Trade balance	10.3	Level of reserves	
Invisibles inflows	1.1	end Dec.	7.6
Invisibles outflows	-8.8	No. months of import cover[a]	6.2
Net transfers	1.6	Foreign debt	30.5
Current account balance	4.3	– as % of GDP	78
– as % of GDP	2.3	– as % of total exports	138
Capital balance[c]	-4.1	Debt service ratio	7

Health and education

Health spending, % of GDP	3.4	Education spending, % of GDP	...
Doctors per 1,000 pop.	...	Enrolment, %: primary	...
Hospital beds per 1,000 pop.	...	secondary	...
Improved-water source access, % of pop.[b]	62	tertiary	...

Society

No. of households	23.8m	Colour TVs per 100 households	50.0
Av. no. per household	5.2	Telephone lines per 100 pop.	0.6
Marriages per 1,000 pop.	...	Mobile telephone subscribers	
Divorces per 1,000 pop.	...	per 100 pop.	1.3
Cost of living, Dec. 2003		Computers per 100 pop.	0.7
New York = 100	80	Internet hosts per 1,000 pop.	...

a Estimate.
b 2000
c 1999

NORWAY

Area	323,878 sq km	Capital	Oslo
Arable as % of total land	3	Currency	Norwegian krone (Nkr)

People

Population	4.5m	Life expectancy: men	76.0 yrs
Pop. per sq km	13.9	women	81.9 yrs
Av. ann. growth		Adult literacy	99.0%
in pop. 2000–05	0.43%	Fertility rate (per woman)	1.8
Pop. under 15	19.8%	Urban p0pulation	75.0%
rop. over 60	19.	%	
per 1,000 po1.			
No. of men per 100 women	98	Crude birth rate	12.0
Human Development Index	94.4	Crude death rate	9.9

The economy

GDP	Nkr1,521bn	GDP per head	$42,330
GDP	$190.5bn	GDP per head in purchasing	
Av. ann. growth in real		power parity (USA=100)	101.6
GDP 1992–2002	3.1%	Economic freedom index	2.35

Origins of GDP		Components of GDP	
	% of total		% of total
Agriculture	1.7	Private consumption	44.6
Industry, of which:	34.0	Public consumption	22.0
manufacturing	...	Investment	18.7
Services	64.3	Exports	41.8
		Imports	-27.1

Structure of employment

	% of total		% of labour force
Agriculture	4	Unemployed 2002	3.9
Industry	22	Av. ann. rate 1995–2002	3.9
Services	74		

Energy

	m TOE		
Total output	226.6	Net energy imports as %	
Total consumption	26.6	of energy use	-752
Consumption per head,			
kg oil equivalent	5,896		

Inflation and finance

Consumer price		av. ann. increase 1997–2002	
inflation 2003	2.5%	Narrow money (M1)	11.3%
Av. ann. inflation 1998–2003	2.4%	Broad money	8.3%
Interbank rate, 2003	4.10%	Household saving rate, 2002	6.9%

Exchange rates

	end 2003		December 2003
Nkr per $	6.68	Effective rates	1995 = 100
Nkr per SDR	9.93	– nominal	98.8
Nkr per €	8.42	– real	135.0

Trade

Principal exports		Principal imports	
	$bn fob		*$bn cif*
Oil, gas & products	37.2	Machinery & equipment	14.0
Machinery & equipment	6.9	Misc. manufactures	5.7
Manufactured materials	6.3	Manufactured materials	5.4
Food, drink & tobacco	3.8	Chemicals	3.4
Total incl. others	**59.3**	Total incl. others	**34.6**

Main export destinations		Main origins of imports	
	% of total		*% of total*
United Kingdom	19.3	Sweden	15.4
Germany	12.3	Germany	13.1
France	11.6	Denmark	7.9
Netherlands	9.3	United Kingdom	7.3
Sweden	7.3	United States	6.1
EU15	75.4	EU15	66.7

Balance of payments, reserves and aid, $bn

Visible exports fob	60.1	Capital balance	-7.6
Visible imports fob	-35.7	Overall balance	4.0
Trade balance	24.4	Change in reserves	5.3
Invisibles inflows	28.6	Level of reserves	
Invisibles outflows	-25.4	end Dec.	21.1
Net transfers	-2.4	No. months of import cover	4.1
Current account balance	25.1	Aid given	1.52
– as % of GDP	13.2	– as % of GDP	0.89

Health and education

Health spending, % of GDP	8.0	Education spending, % of GDP	6.9
Doctors per 1,000 pop.	3.0	Enrolment, %: primary	101
Hospital beds per 1,000 pop.	14.6	secondary	115
Improved-water source access,		tertiary	70
% of pop.	100		

Society

No. of households	2.1m	Colour TVs per 100 households	92.7
Av. no. per household	2.2	Telephone lines per 100 pop.	73.4
Marriages per 1,000 pop.	5.5	Mobile telephone subscribers	
Divorces per 1,000 pop.	2.4	per 100 pop.	84.4
Cost of living, Dec. 2003		Computers per 100 pop.	52.8
New York = 100	123	Internet hosts per 1,000 pop.	225.1

PAKISTAN

Area	803,940 sq km	Capital	Islamabad
Arable as % of total land	28	Currency	Pakistan rupee (PRs)

People

Population	148.7m	Life expectancy:	men	61.2 yrs
Pop. per sq km	185.0		women	60.9 yrs
Av. ann. growth		Adult literacy[a]		44.4%
in pop. 2000–05	2.44%	Fertility rate (per woman)		5.1
Pop. under 15	42.0%	Urban population		33.4%
Pop. over 60	5.7%			per 1,000 pop.
No. of men per 100 women	105	Crude birth rate		35.9
Human Development Index	49.9	Crude death rate		9.6

The economy

GDP	PRs3,629bn	GDP per head	$400
GDP	$59.1bn	GDP per head in purchasing	
Av. ann. growth in real		power parity (USA=100)	5.4
GDP 1992–2002	3.4%	Economic freedom index	3.40

Origins of GDP[b]		Components of GDP[b]	
	% of total		% of total
Agriculture	23.6	Private consumption	75.2
Industry, of which:	25.1	Public consumption	11.2
manufacturing	18.4	Investment	12.9
Other	51.2	Exports	18.1
		Imports	-18.9

Structure of employment

	% of total		% of labour force
Agriculture	48	Unemployed 2000	7.8
Industry	18	Av. ann. rate 1995–2000	6.1
Services	34		

Energy

	m TOE		
Total output	48.6	Net energy imports as %	
Total consumption	64.5	of energy use	25
Consumption per head,			
kg oil equivalent	456		

Inflation and finance

Consumer price		av. ann. increase 1997–2002	
inflation 2003	2.9%	Narrow money (M1)	9.8%
Av. ann. inflation 1998–2003	3.6%	Broad money	10.5%
Money market rate, 2003	2.14%		

Exchange rates

	end 2003		December 2003
PRs per $	57.22	Effective rates	1995 = 100
PRs per SDR	82.02	– nominal	59.52
PRs per €	72.10	– real	82.78

Trade

Principal exports[c]		**Principal imports**[c]	
	$bn fob		*$bn fob*
Textile yarn & fabrics	2.4	Fuels etc	2.8
Apparel & clothing accessories	1.7	Machinery	1.6
Rice	0.4	Chemicals	1.3
		Transport equipment	0.5
Total incl. others	**9.1**	Total incl. others	**10.3**

Main export destinations		**Main origins of imports**	
	% of total		*% of total*
United States	24.3	United Arab Emirates	11.7
United Arab Emirates	8.3	Saudi Arabia	11.5
United Kingdom	7.2	China	6.8
Germany	4.7	Kuwait	6.6

Balance of payments, reserves and debt, $bn

Visible exports fob	9.8	Overall balance	4.1
Visible imports fob	-10.4	Change in reserves	4.6
Trade balance	-0.6	Level of reserves	
Invisibles inflows	2.6	end Dec.	8.8
Invisibles outflows	-4.7	No. months of import cover	7.1
Net transfers	6.5	Foreign debt	33.7
Current account balance	3.9	– as % of GDP	57
– as % of GDP	6.6	– as % of total exports	256
Capital balance	-0.7	Debt service ratio	22

Health and education

Health spending, % of GDP	3.9	Education spending, % of GDP	1.8
Doctors per 1,000 pop.	...	Enrolment, %: primary	74
Hospital beds per 1,000 pop.	...	secondary	24
Improved-water source access,		tertiary	4
% of pop.	90		

Society

No. of households	21.6m	Colour TVs per 100 households	36.0
Av. no. per household	7.6	Telephone lines per 100 pop.	2.5
Marriages per 1,000 pop.	...	Mobile telephone subscribers	
Divorces per 1,000 pop.	...	per 100 pop.	0.9
Cost of living, Dec. 2003		Computers per 100 pop.	0.4
New York = 100	44	Internet hosts per 1,000 pop.	0.1

a 2000 estimate.
b Fiscal year ending June 30, 2003.
c Fiscal year ending June 30, 2002.

PERU

Area	1,285,216 sq km	Capital	Lima
Arable as % of total land	3	Currency	Nuevo Sol (New Sol)

People

Population	26.5m	Life expectancy: men	67.3 yrs
Pop. per sq km	20.6	women	72.4 yrs
Av. ann. growth		Adult literacy	85%
in pop. 2000–05	1.50%	Fertility rate (per woman)	2.3
Pop. under 15	34.5%	Urban population	73.1%
Pop. over 60	7.1%		per 1,000 pop.
No. of men per 100 women	101	Crude birth rate	23.3
Human Development Index	75.2	Crude death rate	6.1

The economy

GDP	New Soles 198bn	GDP per head	$2,130
GDP	$56.5bn	GDP per head in purchasing	
Av. ann. growth in real		power parity (USA=100)	13.5
GDP 1992–2002	4.4%	Economic freedom index	2.83

Origins of GDP		**Components of GDP**	
	% of total		% of total
Agriculture	9.6	Private consumption	72.0
Industry, of which:	26.0	Public consumption	10.4
manufacturing	14.7	Investment	18.4
Services	64.4	Exports	16.4
		Imports	-17.3

Structure of employment

	% of total		% of labour force
Agriculture	9	Unemployed 2002	7.9
Industry	18	Av. ann. rate 1996–2002	7.6
Services	73		

Energy

	m TOE		
Total output	9.4	Net energy imports as %	
Total consumption	12.1	of energy use	23
Consumption per head,			
kg oil equivalent	460		

Inflation and finance

Consumer price		av. ann. increase 1997–2002	
inflation 2003	2.3%	Narrow money (M1)	4.9%
Av. ann. inflation 1998–2003	2.3%	Broad money	4.9%
Deposit rate, 2003	3.83%		

Exchange rates

	end 2003		December 2003
New Soles per $	3.46	Effective rates	1995 = 100
New Soles per SDR	5.15	– nominal	...
New Soles per €	4.36	– real	...

Trade

Principal exports

	$bn fob
Gold	1.5
Copper	1.2
Fishmeal	0.9
Zinc	0.4
Total incl. others	**7.6**

Principal imports

	$bn fob
Intermediate goods	3.7
Capital goods	1.8
Consumer goods	1.8
Other goods	0.8
Total incl. others	**7.4**

Main export destinations

	% of total
United States	26.0
China	9.1
United Kingdom	6.4
Switzerland	5.6

Main origins of imports

	% of total
United States	25.3
Chile	7.7
Spain	5.0
Colombia	4.9

Balance of payments, reserves and debt, $bn

Visible exports fob	7.6	Overall balance	1.0
Visible imports fob	-7.4	Change in reserves	0.7
Trade balance	0.2	Level of reserves	
Invisibles inflows	1.9	end Dec.	9.7
Invisibles outflows	-4.3	No. months of import cover	9.9
Net transfers	1.0	Foreign debt	28.2
Current account balance	-1.2	– as % of GDP	53
– as % of GDP	-2.1	– as % of total exports	280
Capital balance	2.1	Debt service ratio	33

Health and education

Health spending, % of GDP	4.7	Education spending, % of GDP	3.3
Doctors per 1,000 pop.	...	Enrolment, %: primary	128
Hospital beds per 1,000 pop.	...	secondary[c]	81
Improved-water source access,		tertiary[c]	29
% of pop.	80		

Society

No. of households	5.6m	Colour TVs per 100 households	47.6
Av. no. per household	4.7	Telephone lines per 100 pop.	6.6
Marriages per 1,000 pop.	4.1	Mobile telephone subscribers	
Divorces per 1,000 pop.	...	per 100 pop.	8.6
Cost of living, Dec. 2003		Computers per 100 pop.	4.3
New York = 100	61	Internet hosts per 1,000 pop.	2.5

PHILIPPINES

Area	300,000 sq km	Capital	Manila
Arable as % of total land	19	Currency	Philippine peso (P)

People

Population	78.6m	Life expectancy: men	68.0 yrs
Pop. per sq km	262.0	women	72.0 yrs
Av. ann. growth		Adult literacy[a]	92.6%
in pop. 2000–05	1.79%	Fertility rate (per woman)	3.2
Pop. under 15	37.5%	Urban population	59.4%
Pop. over 60	5.5%		per 1,000 pop.
No. of men per 100 women	101	Crude birth rate	25.3
Human Development Index	75.1	Crude death rate	5.1

The economy

GDP	P4,023bn	GDP per head	$990
GDP	$78.0bn	GDP per head in purchasing	
Av. ann. growth in real		power parity (USA=100)	12.3
GDP 1992–2002	3.7%	Economic freedom index	3.05

Origins of GDP

Components of GDP

	% of total		% of total
Agriculture	14.7	Private consumption	68.4
Industry, of which:	32.5	Public consumption	12.1
manufacturing	22.8	Investment	19.3
Services	52.8	Exports	48.9
		Imports	-49.4

Structure of employment

	% of total		% of labour force
Agriculture	37	Unemployed 2002	9.8
Industry	16	Av. ann. rate 1995–2002	9.0
Services	47		

Energy

	m TOE		
Total output	20.0	Net energy imports as %	
Total consumption	42.2	of energy use	53
Consumption per head,			
kg oil equivalent	538		

Inflation and finance

		av. ann. increase 1997–2002	
Consumer price			
inflation 2003	3.1%	Narrow money (M1)	12.4%
Av. ann. inflation 1998–2003	4.6%	Broad money	9.4%
Treasury bill rate, 2003	5.87%		

Exchange rates

	end 2003		December 2003
			1995 = 100
P per $	55.57	Effective rates	
P per SDR	82.57	– nominal	51.6
P per €	70.02	– real	72.2

Trade

Principal exports		Principal imports	
	$bn fob		*$bn fob*
Electrical & electronic equipment	18.7	Semi-processed raw materials	11.8
Machinery & transport equipment	7.1	Telecom & electrical machinery	7.2
Clothing	2.4	Electrical equipment parts	5.4
Coconut products	0.5	Chemicals	2.5
Chemicals	0.4	Crude petroleum	2.3
Total incl. others	**36.5**	Total incl. others	**35.4**

Main export destinations		Main origins of imports	
	% of total		*% of total*
United States	29.6	Japan	25.7
Japan	16.8	United States	22.1
China	6.9	Singapore	9.2
Singapore	6.5	South Korea	9.0
Netherlands	6.3	China	6.2
Hong Kong	6.0	Hong Kong	5.2

Balance of payments, reserves and debt, $bn

Visible exports fob	34.4	Overall balance	0.0
Visible imports fob	-34.0	Change in reserves	0.5
Trade balance	0.4	Level of reserves	
Invisibles inflows	11.0	end Dec.	16.1
Invisibles outflows	-7.7	No. months of import cover	4.6
Net transfers	0.5	Foreign debt	59.3
Current account balance	4.2	– as % of GDP	75
– as % of GDP	5.4	– as % of total exports	130
Capital balance	-2.7	Debt service ratio	20

Health and education

Health spending, % of GDP	3.3	Education spending, % of GDP	3.2
Doctors per 1,000 pop.	...	Enrolment, %: primary	113
Hospital beds per 1,000 pop.	...	secondary	77
Improved-water source access, % of pop.	86	tertiary	31

Society

No. of households	16.1m	Colour TVs per 100 households	65.2
Av. no. per household	4.9	Telephone lines per 100 pop.	4.2
Marriages per 1,000 pop.	6.7	Mobile telephone subscribers	
Divorces per 1,000 pop.	...	per 100 pop.	19.1
Cost of living, Dec. 2003		Computers per 100 pop.	2.8
New York = 100	39	Internet hosts per 1,000 pop.	0.4

a 2001

POLAND

Area	312,683 sq km	Capital	Warsaw
Arable as % of total land	46	Currency	Zloty (Zl)

People

Population	38.5m	Life expectancy: men	69.8 yrs
Pop. per sq km	123.1	women	78.0 yrs
Av. ann. growth		Adult literacy	99.7%
in pop. 2000–05	-0.08%	Fertility rate (per woman)	1.3
Pop. under 15	19.2%	Urban population	62.5%
Pop. over 60	16.6%		per 1,000 pop.
No. of men per 100 women	94	Crude birth rate	9.6
Human Development Index	84.1	Crude death rate	10.0

The economy

GDP	Zl771bn	GDP per head	$4,910
GDP	$189.0bn	GDP per head in purchasing	
Av. ann. growth in real		power parity (USA=100)	28.9
GDP 1992–2002	4.4%	Economic freedom index	2.81

Origins of GDP

	% of total
Agriculture	3.2
Industry, of which:	30.5
manufacturing	17.6
Services	66.4

Components of GDP

	% of total
Private consumption	66.4
Public consumption	17.9
Investment	19.3
Exports	30.0
Imports	-33.4

Structure of employment

	% of total		% of labour force
Agriculture	19	Unemployed 2002	19.9
Industry	31	Av. ann. rate 1995–2002	14.4
Services	50		

Energy

	m TOE		
Total output	79.9	Net energy imports as %	
Total consumption	90.6	of energy use	12
Consumption per head,			
kg oil equivalent	2,344		

Inflation and finance

		av. ann. increase 1997–2002	
Consumer price			
inflation 2003	0.7%	Narrow money (M1)	12.8%
Av. ann. inflation 1998–2003	5.1%	Broad money	13.3%
Money market rate, 2003	5.8%		

Exchange rates

	end 2003		December 2003
			1995 = 100
Zl per $	3.74	Effective rates	
Zl per SDR	5.56	– nominal	71.1
Zl per €	4.71	– real	113.9

Trade

Principal exports		Principal imports	
	$bn fob		*$bn cif*
Machinery & transport equipment	15.4	Machinery & transport equipment	20.7
Semi-manufactured goods	9.8	Semi-manufactured goods	11.4
Other manufactured goods	7.1	Chemicals	8.2
Agric. products & foodstuffs	3.0	Mineral fuels	5.0
Total incl. others	**41.0**	Total incl. others	**55.1**

Main export destinations		Main origins of imports	
	% of total		*% of total*
Germany	32.3	Germany	24.3
France	6.0	Italy	8.4
Italy	5.5	Russia	8.0
United Kingdom	5.2	France	7.0

Balance of payments, reserves and debt, $bn

Visible exports fob	46.7	Overall balance	0.6
Visible imports fob	-54.0	Change in reserves	3.2
Trade balance	-7.2	Level of reserves	
Invisibles inflows	12.0	end Dec.	29.8
Invisibles outflows	-13.0	No. months of import cover	5.3
Net transfers	3.3	Foreign debt	69.5
Current account balance	-5.0	– as % of GDP	39
– as % of GDP	-2.6	– as % of total exports	127
Capital balance	6.9	Debt service ratio	25

Health and education

Health spending, % of GDP	6.1	Education spending, % of GDP	5.4
Doctors per 1,000 pop.	2.2	Enrolment, %: primary	100
Hospital beds per 1,000 pop.	4.9	secondary	101
Improved-water source access, % of pop.	...	tertiary	56

Society

No. of households	13.7m	Colour TVs per 100 households	82.8
Av. no. per household	2.8	Telephone lines per 100 pop.	45.1
Marriages per 1,000 pop.	5.5	Mobile telephone subscribers	
Divorces per 1,000 pop.	1.1	per 100 pop.	36.3
Cost of living, Dec. 2003		Computers per 100 pop.	10.6
New York = 100	66	Internet hosts per 1,000 pop.	33.7

PORTUGAL

Area	88,940 sq km	Capital	Lisbon
Arable as % of total land	22	Currency	Euro (€)

People

Population	10.0m	Life expectancy: men	72.6 yrs
Pop. per sq km	112.4	women	79.6 yrs
Av. ann. growth		Adult literacy	92.9%
in pop. 2000–05	0.13%	Fertility rate (per woman)	1.5
Pop. under 15	16.7%	Urban population	65.8%
Pop. over 60	20.8%		per 1,000 pop.
No. of men per 100 women	93	Crude birth rate	11.0
Human Development Index	89.6	Crude death rate	10.8

The economy

GDP	€129bn	GDP per head	$12,160
GDP	$121.6bn	GDP per head in purchasing	
Av. ann. growth in real		power parity (USA=100)	49.3
GDP 1992–2002	2.4%	Economic freedom index	2.38

Origins of GDP		Components of GDP	
	% of total		% of total
Agriculture	3.7	Private consumption	60.5
Industry, of which:	29.3	Public consumption	21.3
manufacturing	...	Investment	25.8
Services	67.0	Exports	30.1
		Imports	-37.7

Structure of employment

	% of total		% of labour force
Agriculture	13	Unemployed 2002	5.1
Industry	35	Av. ann. rate 1995–2002	5.5
Services	52		

Energy

	m TOE		
Total output	3.4	Net energy imports as %	
Total consumption	24.7	of energy use	86
Consumption per head,			
kg oil equivalent	2,435		

Inflation and finance

Consumer price		*av. ann. increase 1997–2002*	
inflation 2003	3.3%	Euro area:	
Av. ann. inflation 1998–2003	3.3%	Narrow money (M1)	9.0%
Interbank rate, 2003	2.34%	Broad money	6.4%
		Household saving rate, 2002	12.1%

Exchange rates

	end 2003		December 2003
€ per $	0.79	Effective rates	1995 = 100
€ per SDR	1.18	– nominal	98.3
		– real	106.8

Trade

Principal exports

	$bn fob
Consumer goods	9.2
Capital goods	8.1
Raw materials & semi-manufactures	7.7
Energy products	0.4
Total incl. others	**25.5**

Principal imports

	$bn cif
Capital goods	12.9
Raw materials & semi-manufactures	12.2
Consumer goods	9.5
Energy products	3.7
Total incl. others	**38.3**

Main export destinations

	% of total
Spain	20.2
Germany	18.4
France	12.6
United Kingdom	10.5
United States	5.8
EU15	79.6

Main origins of imports

	% of total
Spain	28.1
Germany	15.0
France	10.2
Italy	6.5
United Kingdom	5.2
EU15	76.9

Balance of payments, reserves and debt, $bn

Visible exports fob	27.0	Overall balance	1.0
Visible imports fob	-39.1	Change in reserves	2.6
Trade balance	-12.1	Level of reserves	
Invisibles inflows	15.3	end Dec.	17.7
Invisibles outflows	-15.3	No. months of import cover	3.9
Net transfers	3.3	Aid given	0.29
Current account balance	-8.8	– as % of GDP	0.27
– as % of GDP	-7.2		
Capital balance	11.1		

Health and education

Health spending, % of GDP	9.2	Education spending, % of GDP	5.8
Doctors per 1,000 pop.	3.2	Enrolment, %: primary	121
Hospital beds per 1,000 pop.	4.0	secondary[a]	114
Improved-water source access, % of pop.	...	tertiary	45

Society

No. of households	3.7m	Colour TVs per 100 households	97.7
Av. no. per household	2.9	Telephone lines per 100 pop.	42.1
Marriages per 1,000 pop.	6.6	Mobile telephone subscribers	
Divorces per 1,000 pop.	1.6	per 100 pop.	82.5
Cost of living, Dec. 2003		Computers per 100 pop.	13.5
New York = 100	77	Internet hosts per 1,000 pop.	30.0

a Includes training for unemployed.

ROMANIA

Area	237,500 sq km	Capital	Bucharest
Arable as % of total land	41	Currency	Leu (L)

People

Population	22.3m	Life expectancy: men	67.0 yrs
Pop. per sq km	93.9	women	74.2 yrs
Av. ann. growth		Adult literacy	97.3%
in pop. 2000–05	-0.23%	Fertility rate (per woman)	1.3
Pop. under 15	18.2%	Urban population	55.2%
Pop. over 60	18.9%		per 1,000 pop.
No. of men per 100 women	95	Crude birth rate	10.4
Human Development Index	77.3	Crude death rate	12.5

The economy

GDP	L1,512trn	GDP per head	$2,050
GDP	$45.7bn	GDP per head in purchasing	
Av. ann. growth in real		power parity (USA=100)	18.0
GDP 1992–2002	1.4%	Economic freedom index	3.66

Origins of GDP

	% of total
Agriculture	13.1
Industry, of which:	38.1
manufacturing	...
Services	48.8

Components of GDP

	% of total
Private consumption	76.0
Public consumption	6.6
Investment	23.1
Exports	35.4
Imports	-41.2

Structure of employment

	% of total		% of labour force
Agriculture	42	Unemployed 2002	8.4
Industry	26	Av. ann. rate 1995–2002	7.0
Services	32		

Energy

	m TOE		
Total output	28.2	Net energy imports as %	
Total consumption	36.8	of energy use	23
Consumption per head,			
kg oil equivalent	1,644		

Inflation and finance

		av. ann. increase 1997–2002	
Consumer price			
inflation 2003	15.3%	Narrow money (M1)	36.1%
Av. ann. inflation 1998–2003	32.2%	Broad money	43.2%
Treasury bill rate, 2002	27.0%		

Exchange rates

	end 2003		December 2003
			1995 = 100
L per $	32,595	Effective rates	
L per SDR	48,435	– nominal	0.09
L per €	41,070	– real	109.47

Trade

Principal exports		Principal imports	
	$bn fob		*$bn cif*
Textiles	3.5	Machinery & equipment	4.1
Machinery & equipment	2.2	Textiles & footwear	2.9
Basic metals & products	1.8	Fuels & minerals	2.3
Minerals & fuels	1.2	Chemicals	1.5
Total incl. others	**13.9**	Total incl. others	**17.9**

Main export destinations		Main origins of imports	
	% of total		*% of total*
Italy	24.9	Italy	20.7
Germany	15.6	Germany	14.8
France	7.6	Russia	7.2
EU15	67.0	EU15	58.4

Balance of payments, reserves and debt, $bn

Visible exports fob	13.9	Overall balance	1.8
Visible imports fob	-16.5	Change in reserves	2.0
Trade balance	-2.6	Level of reserves	
Invisibles inflows	2.8	end Dec.	8.4
Invisibles outflows	-3.2	No. months of import cover	5.1
Net transfers	1.5	Foreign debt	14.7
Current account balance	-1.5	– as % of GDP	36
– as % of GDP	-3.3	– as % of total exports	103
Capital balance	4.2	Debt service ratio	22

Health and education

Health spending, % of GDP	6.5	Education spending, % of GDP	3.5
Doctors per 1,000 pop.	1.9	Enrolment, %: primary	99
Hospital beds per 1,000 pop.	7.5	secondary	82
Improved-water source access,		tertiary	27
% of pop.	58		

Society

No. of households	7.6m	Colour TVs per 100 households	52.7
Av. no. per household	2.9	Telephone lines per 100 pop.	19.4
Marriages per 1,000 pop.	5.6	Mobile telephone subscribers	
Divorces per 1,000 pop.	2.0	per 100 pop.	23.6
Cost of living, Dec. 2003		Computers per 100 pop.	8.3
New York = 100	53	Internet hosts per 1,000 pop.	6.3

RUSSIA

Area	17,075,400 sq km	Capital	Moscow
Arable as % of total land	7	Currency	Rouble (Rb)

People

Population	143.8m	Life expectancy: men		60.8 yrs
Pop. per sq km	8.4	women		73.1 yrs
Av. ann. growth		Adult literacy		99.6%
in pop. 2000–05	-0.57%	Fertility rate (per woman)		1.1
Pop. under 15	18.0%	Urban population		72.9%
Pop. over 60	18.5%			per 1,000 pop.
No. of men per 100 women	88	Crude birth rate		8.6
Human Development Index	77.9	Crude death rate		14.6

The economy

GDP	Rb10,863bn	GDP per head	$2,410
GDP	$346.5bn	GDP per head in purchasing	
Av. ann. growth in real		power parity (USA=100)	22.4
GDP 1992–2002	-1.1%	Economic freedom index	3.46

Origins of GDP		**Components of GDP**	
	% of total		% of total
Agriculture	5.8	Private consumption	50.5
Industry, of which:	34.6	Public consumption	16.9
manufacturing	...	Investment	20.6
Services	59.7	Net exports	11.2

Structure of employment

	% of total		% of labour force
Agriculture	12	Unemployed 2002	10.2
Industry	29	Av. ann. rate 1995–2002	11.2
Services	59		

Energy

	m TOE		
Total output	996.1	Net energy imports as %	
Total consumption	621.3	of energy use	-60
Consumption per head,			
kg oil equivalent	4,293		

Inflation and finance

		av. ann. increase 1997–2002	
Consumer price			
inflation 2003	13.7%	Narrow money (M1)	38.1%
Av. ann. inflation 1998–2003	29.1%	Broad money	44.1%
Money market rate, 2003	3.77%		

Exchange rates

	end 2003		December 2003
			1995 = 100
Rb per $	29.45	Effective rates	
Rb per SDR	43.77	– nominal	32.47
Rb per €	37.11	– real	116.64

Trade

Principal exports		Principal imports	
	$bn fob		$bn fob
Mineral products	57.7	Machinery & equipment	16.7
Metals	14.9	Food products	10.3
Machinery & equipment	10.0	Chemicals	7.7
Chemicals	7.4	Metals	2.9
Total incl. others	**105.8**	Total incl. others	**46.0**

Main export destinations		Main origins of imports	
	% of total		% of total
Germany	7.7	Germany	10.7
Netherlands	6.5	Belarus	6.5
Italy	6.3	Ukraine	5.9
China	6.2	China	4.4
Ukraine	5.2	Kazakhstan	3.9

Balance of payments, reserves and debt, $bn

Visible exports fob	107.3	Overall balance	11.6
Visible imports fob	-61.0	Change in reserves	12.0
Trade balance	46.3	Level of reserves	
Invisibles inflows	19.3	end Dec.	48.3
Invisibles outflows	-35.7	No. months of import cover	7.2
Net transfers	-0.4	Foreign debt	147.5
Current account balance	29.5	– as % of GDP	49
– as % of GDP	8.5	– as % of total exports	121
Capital balance	-11.5	Debt service ratio	12

Health and education

Health spending, % of GDP	5.4	Education spending, % of GDP	3.1
Doctors per 1,000 pop.	4.2	Enrolment, %: primary	107
Hospital beds per 1,000 pop.	10.8	secondary	83
Improved-water source access,		tertiary	64
% of pop.	99		

Society

No. of households	51.6m	Colour TVs per 100 households	76.3
Av. no. per household	2.8	Telephone lines per 100 pop.	24.2
Marriages per 1,000 pop.	4.8	Mobile telephone subscribers	
Divorces per 1,000 pop.	2.9	per 100 pop.	12.0
Cost of living, Dec. 2003		Computers per 100 pop.	8.9
New York = 100	92	Internet hosts per 1,000 pop.	4.4

SAUDI ARABIA

Area	2,200,000 sq km	Capital	Riyadh
Arable as % of total land	2	Currency	Riyal (SR)

People

Population	21.7m	Life expectancy: men	71.1 yrs
Pop. per sq km	9.9	women	73.7 yrs
Av. ann. growth		Adult literacy	77.9%
in pop. 2000–05	2.92%	Fertility rate (per woman)	4.5
Pop. under 15	39.7%	Urban population	86.7%
Pop. over 60	4.1%		per 1,000 pop.
No. of men per 100 women	116	Crude birth rate	31.5
Human Development Index	76.9	Crude death rate	3.7

The economy

GDP	SR706bn	GDP per head	$8,690
GDP	$188.5bn	GDP per head in purchasing	
Av. ann. growth in real		power parity (USA=100)	35.1
GDP 1992–2002	1.6%	Economic freedom index	3.05

Origins of GDP

Components of GDP

	% of total		% of total
Agriculture	5.2	Private consumption	37.0
Industry, of which:	50.6	Public consumption	25.7
manufacturing	10.5	Investment	18.4
Services	44.2	Exports	40.8
		Imports	-23.0

Structure of employment

	% of total		% of labour force
Agriculture	5	Unemployed 2001	4.6
Industry	26	Av. ann. rate 1995–2001	4.2
Services	69		

Energy

	m TOE		
Total output	476.8	Net energy imports as %	
Total consumption	110.6	of energy use	-331
Consumption per head,			
kg oil equivalent	5,195		

Inflation and finance

		av. ann. increase 1997–2002	
Consumer price			
inflation 2003	0.6%	Narrow money (M1)	7.5%
Av. ann. inflation 1998–2003	-0.6%	Broad money	7.0%
Deposit rate, 2003	1.63%		

Exchange rates

	end 2003		December 2003
			1995 = 100
SR per $	3.75	Effective rates	107.6
SR pe0 SDR	5.57	– 3ominal	107.6
SREper €	4.73	–1real	90.6

Trade

Principal exports		Principal imports[a]	
	$bn fob		*$bn cif*
Crude oil & refined		Machinery & transport	
petroleum	48.6	equipment	13.1
Oil products	11.3	Foodstuffs	4.6
Total incl. others	**72.6**	Total incl. others	**32.3**

Main export destinations		Main origins of imports	
	% of total		*% of total*
United States	18.6	United States	11.3
Japan	15.6	Japan	8.9
South Korea	10.1	Germany	7.4
Singapore	5.1	United Kingdom	4.9

Balance of payments, reserves and aid, $bn

Visible exports fob	72.6	Overall balance	2.7
Visible imports fob	-29.7	Change in reserves	3.3
Trade balance	42.9	Level of reserves	
Invisibles inflows	8.9	end Dec.	22.2
Invisibles outflows	-23.9	No. months of import cover	5.0
Net transfers	-16.0	Aid given	2.48
Current account balance	11.9	– as % of GDP	1.31
– as % of GDP	6.3		
Capital balance	-9.2		

Health and education

Health spending, % of GDP	4.6	Education spending, % of GDP	9.5
Doctors per 1,000 pop.	...	Enrolment, %: primary	68
Hospital beds per 1,000 pop.	...	secondary	68
Improved-water source access,		tertiary	22
% of pop.	95		

Society

No. of households	2.8m	Colour TVs per 100 households	99.1
Av. no. per household	8.2	Telephone lines per 100 pop.	14.4
Marriages per 1,000 pop.	3.0	Mobile telephone subscribers	
Divorces per 1,000 pop.	0.8	per 100 pop.	21.7
Cost of living, Dec. 2003		Computers per 100 pop.	13.7
New York = 100	72	Internet hosts per 1,000 pop.	0.7

a 2001 estimates.

SINGAPORE

Area	639 sq km	Capital	Singapore
Arable as % of total land	2	Currency	Singapore dollar (S$)

People

Population	4.2m	Life expectancy: men		75.9 yrs
Pop. per sq km	6,572.8	women		80.3 yrs
Av. ann. growth		Adult literacy[a]		92.5%
in pop. 2000–05	1.69%	Fertility rate (per woman)		1.4
Pop. under 15	21.8%	Urban population		100.0%
Pop. over 60	10.5%			per 1,000 pop.
No. of men per 100 women	101	Crude birth rate		10.2
Human Development Index	88.4	Crude death rate		5.2

The economy

GDP	S$156bn	GDP per head	$20,710
GDP	$87.0bn	GDP per head in purchasing	
Av. ann. growth in real		power parity (USA=100)	65.7
GDP 1992–2002	6.2%	Economic freedom index	1.61

Origins of GDP		**Components of GDP**	
	% of total		% of total
Agriculture	0.1	Private consumption	43.0
Industry, of which:	35.7	Public consumption	13.2
manufacturing	28.1	Investment	20.6
Services	64.2	Exports	181.8
		Imports	-157.7

Structure of employment

	% of total		% of labour force
Agriculture	0	Unemployed 2002	5.2
Industry	26	Av. ann. rate 1995–2002	3.6
Services	74		

Energy

	m TOE		
Total output	0.06	Net energy imports as %	
Total consumption	29.2	of energy use	100
Consumption per head,			
kg oil equivalent	7,058		

Inflation and finance

Consumer price		*av. ann. increase 1997–2002*	
inflation 2003	0.5%	Narrow money (M1)	5.4%
Av. ann. inflation 1998–2003	0.5%	Broad money	7.9%
Money market rate, 2003	0.74%		

Exchange rates

	end 2003		December 2003
S$ per $	1.70	Effective rates	1995 = 100
S$ per SDR	2.53	– nominal	95.8
S$ per €	2.14	– real	87.2

Trade

Principal exports

	$bn fob
Machinery & equipment	79.5
Mineral fuels	12.7
Chemicals	11.6
Manufactured products	4.9
Food	1.6
Total incl. others	**125.0**

Principal imports

	$bn cif
Machinery & equipment	68.5
Mineral fuels	15.2
Manufactured products	8.6
Chemicals	7.3
Food	3.0
Total incl. others	**116.3**

Main export destinations

	% of total
Malaysia	17.4
United States	14.7
Hong Kong	9.2
Japan	7.1
China	5.5
Taiwan	5.0
Thailand	4.6

Main origins of imports

	% of total
Malaysia	18.2
United States	14.2
Japan	12.5
China	7.6
Thailand	4.7
Taiwan	4.6
Saudi Arabia	3.3

Balance of payments, reserves and debt, $bn

Visible exports fob	128.4	Overall balance	1.3
Visible imports fob	-109.8	Change in reserves	6.6
Trade balance	18.5	Level of reserves	
Invisibles inflows	44.1	end Dec.	82.0
Invisibles outflows	-42.8	No. months of import cover	6.4
Net transfers	-1.1	Foreign debt	14.2
Current account balance	18.7	– as % of GDP	1.6
– as % of GDP	21.5	– as % of total exports	8
Capital balance	-15.8	Debt service ratio	2

Health and education

Health spending, % of GDP	3.9	Education spending, % of GDP	3.7
Doctors per 1,000 pop.	1.6	Enrolment, %: primary	92
Hospital beds per 1,000 pop.	...	secondary	67
Improved-water source access,		tertiary	39
% of pop.	100		

Society

No. of households	1.0m	Colour TVs per 100 households	98.6
Av. no. per household	3.4	Telephone lines per 100 pop.	46.3
Marriages per 1,000 pop.	6.4	Mobile telephone subscribers	
Divorces per 1,000 pop.	1.8	per 100 pop.	79.6
Cost of living, Dec. 2003		Computers per 100 pop.	62.2
New York = 100	98	Internet hosts per 1,000 pop.	115.4

a 2001

SLOVAKIA

Area	49,035 sq km	Capital	Bratislava
Arable as % of total land	30	Currency	Koruna (Kc)

People

Population	5.4m	Life expectancy: men		69.8 yrs
Pop. per sq km	110.1	women		77.6 yrs
Av. ann. growth		Adult literacy[a]		99.7%
in pop. 2000–05	0.08%	Fertility rate (per woman)		1.3
Pop. under 15	19.5%	Urban population		57.6%
Pop. over 60	15.4%			per 1,000 pop.
No. of men per 100 women	94	Crude birth rate		10.2
Human Development Index	83.6	Crude death rate		9.8

The economy

GDP	Kc1,074bn	GDP per head	$4,390
GDP	$23.7bn	GDP per head in purchasing	
Av. ann. growth in real		power parity (USA=100)	34.9
GDP 1992–2002	3.4%	Economic freedom index	2.44

Origins of GDP		Components of GDP	
	% of total		% of total
Agriculture	4.2	Private consumption	57.7
Industry, of which:	29.2	Public consumption	20.1
manufacturing	20.5	Investment	29.3
Services	66.7	Exports	71.8
		Imports	-78.9

Structure of employment

	% of total		% of labour force
Agriculture	6	Unemployed 2002	18.5
Industry	38	Av. ann. rate 1995–2002	15.2
Services	56		

Energy

	m TOE		
Total output	6.6	Net energy imports as %	
Total consumption	18.7	of energy use	65
Consumption per head,			
kg oil equivalent	3,480		

Inflation and finance

Consumer price		av. ann. increase 1997–2002	
inflation 2003	8.6%	Narrow money (M1)	8.1%
Av. ann. inflation 1998–2003	8.3%	Broad money	9.5%
Money market rate, 2003	6.08%		

Exchange rates

	end 2003		December 2003
Kc per $	32.98	Effective rates	1995 = 100
Kc per SDR	49.00	– nominal	76.37
Kc per €	41.55	– real	101.83

Trade

Principal exports		Principal imports	
	$bn fob		$bn fob
Machinery & transport equipment	5.7	Machinery & transport equipment	6.3
Intermediate manufactured goods	3.9	Intermediate manufactured goods	3.2
Other manufactured goods	1.8	Fuels	2.2
Chemicals	1.0	Chemicals	1.8
Fuels	0.9	Other manufactured goods	1.6
Total incl. others	14.4	Total incl. others	16.5

Main export destinations		Main origins of imports	
	% of total		% of total
Germany	26.0	Germany	22.6
Czech Republic	15.2	Czech Republic	15.2
Italy	10.7	Russia	12.5
Austria	7.7	Italy	6.9
EU15	60.5	EU15	50.3

Balance of payments, reserves and debt, $bn

Visible exports fob	14.3	Overall balance	3.6
Visible imports fob	-16.5	Change in reserves	4.7
Trade balance	-2.1	Level of reserves	
Invisibles inflows	3.1	end Dec.	9.2
Invisibles outflows	-3.1	No. months of import cover	5.6
Net transfers	0.2	Foreign debt	13.0
Current account balance	-1.9	– as % of GDP	62
– as % of GDP	-8.0	– as % of total exports	84
Capital balance	5.2	Debt service ratio	22

Health and education

Health spending, % of GDP	5.7	Education spending, % of GDP	4.1
Doctors per 1,000 pop.	3.6	Enrolment, %: primary	103
Hospital beds per 1,000 pop.	7.8	secondary	87
Improved-water source access, % of pop.	100	tertiary	30

Society

No. of households	2.1m	Colour TVs per 100 households	86.1
Av. no. per household	2.7	Telephone lines per 100 pop.	26.8
Marriages per 1,000 pop.	4.9	Mobile telephone subscribers	
Divorces per 1,000 pop.	1.7	per 100 pop.	54.4
Cost of living, Dec. 2003		Computers per 100 pop.	18.0
New York = 100	...	Internet hosts per 1,000 pop.	18.3

a 2000

SLOVENIA

Area	20,253 sq km	Capital	Ljubljana
Arable as % of total land	9	Currency	Tolars (SIT)

People

Population	2.0m	Life expectancy: men	72.6 yrs
Pop. per sq km	98.8	women	79.8 yrs
Av. ann. growth		Adult literacy	99.7%
in pop. 2000–05	-0.11%	Fertility rate (per woman)	1.1
Pop. under 15	15.9%	Urban population	49.1%
Pop. over 60	19.2%		per 1,000 pop.
No. of men per 100 women	95	Crude birth rate	8.3
Human Development Index	88.1	Crude death rate	9.8

The economy

GDP	SIT5,276bn	GDP per head	$10,980
GDP	$22.0bn	GDP per head in purchasing	
Av. ann. growth in real		power parity (USA=100)	51.2
GDP 1992–2002	4.0%	Economic freedom index	2.75

Origins of GDP		Components of GDP	
	% of total		% of total
Agriculture	3.1	Private consumption	54.6
Industry, of which:	36.1	Public consumption	20.5
manufacturing	27.0	Investment	23.4
Services	60.7	Exports	57.9
		Imports	-56.5

Structure of employment

	% of total		% of labour force
Agriculture	10	Unemployed 2002	5.9
Industry	38	Av. ann. rate 1995–2002	7.0
Services	52		

Energy

	m TOE		
Total output	3.2	Net energy imports as %	
Total consumption	6.8	of energy use	54
Consumption per head,			
kg oil equivalent	3,459		

Inflation and finance

Consumer price			av. ann. increase 1997–2002
inflation 2003	5.6%	Narrow money (M1)	24.3%
Av. ann. inflation 1998–2003	7.3%	Broad money	18.9%
Money market rate, 2003	5.59%		

Exchange rates

	end 2003		December 2003
SIT per $	189.4	Effective rates	1995 = 100
SIT per SDR	281.4	– nominal	...
SIT per €	238.6	– real	...

Trade

Principal exports		Principal imports	
	$bn fob		*$bn fob*
Manufactures	4.6	Manufactures	3.8
Machinery & transport		Machinery & transport	
equipment	3.8	equipment	3.7
Chemicals	1.3	Chemicals	1.5
Food & live animals	0.2	Mineral fuels	0.8
Total incl. others	**9.5**	Total incl. others	**10.9**

Main export destinations		Main origins of imports	
	% of total		*% of total*
Germany	24.8	Germany	19.2
Italy	11.2	Italy	17.9
Croatia	8.7	France	10.2
Austria	7.1	Austria	8.3
France	6.7	Croatia	3.6
EU15	59.4	EU15	68.0

Balance of payments, reserves and debt, $bn

Visible exports fob	10.5	Overall balance	1.9
Visible imports fob	-10.7	Change in reserves	2.7
Trade balance	-0.2	Level of reserves	
Invisibles inflows	2.8	end Dec.	7.1
Invisibles outflows	-2.3	No. months of import cover	6.5
Net transfers	0.1	Foreign debt	9.0
Current account balance	0.4	– as % of GDP	40.1
– as % of GDP	1.7	– as % of total exports	66.3
Capital balance	1.5	Debt service ratio	14

Health and education

Health spending, % of GDP	8.4	Education spending, % of GDP	5.8
Doctors per 1,000 pop.	2.2	Enrolment, %: primary	100
Hospital beds per 1,000 pop.	5.2	secondary	99
Improved-water source access,		tertiary	61
% of pop.	100		

Society

No. of households	0.6m	Colour TVs per 100 households	88.6
Av. no. per household	3.1	Telephone lines per 100 pop.	50.6
Marriages per 1,000 pop.	3.6	Mobile telephone subscribers	
Divorces per 1,000 pop.	1.0	per 100 pop.	83.5
Cost of living, Dec. 2003		Computers per 100 pop.	30.1
New York = 100	...	Internet hosts per 1,000 pop.	17.4

SOUTH AFRICA

Area	1,225,815 sq km	Capital	Pretoria
Arable as % of total land	12	Currency	Rand (R)

People

Population	44.2m	Life expectancy: men	45.1 yrs
Pop. per sq km	36.0	women	50.7 yrs
Av. ann. growth		Adult literacy	86%
in pop. 2000–05	0.59%	Fertility rate (per woman)	2.6
Pop. under 15	34.0%	Urban population	57.7%
Pop. over 60	5.9%		per 1,000 pop.
No. of men per 100 women	96	Crude birth rate	22.6
Human Development Index	68.4	Crude death rate	16.9

The economy

GDP	R1,099bn	GDP per head	$2,360
GDP	$104.2bn	GDP per head in purchasing	
Av. ann. growth in real		power parity (USA=100)	27.2
GDP 1992–2002	2.7%	Economic freedom index	2.79

Origins of GDP

	% of total
Agriculture	4.3
Industry, of which:	32.1
manufacturing	20.2
Services	63.6

Components of GDP

	% of total
Private consumption	63.4
Public consumption	17.4
Investment	17.4
Exports	24.9
Imports	-23.1

Structure of employment

	% of total		% of labour force
Agriculture	11	Unemployed 2002	29.5
Industry	25	Av. ann. rate 1995–2002	23.1
Services	64		

Energy

	m TOE		
Total output	145.3	Net energy imports as %	
Total consumption	107.7	of energy use	-35
Consumption per head,			
kg oil equivalent	2,404		

Inflation and finance

		av. ann. increase 1997–2002	
Consumer price inflation 2003	6.0%	Narrow money (M1)	15.2%
Av. ann. inflation 1998–2003	6.0%	Broad money	12.3%
Money market rate, 2003	10.93%		

Exchange rates

	end 2003		December 2003
			1995 = 100
R per $	6.64	Effective rates	
R per SDR	9.87	– nominal	57.5
R per €	8.37	– real	83.7

Trade

Principal exports		Principal imports	
	$bn fob		*$bn cif*
Gold	4.1	Manufactures	25.6
		Non-fuel primary products	2.7
		Fuels	0.3
Total incl. others	**29.8**	Total incl. others	**28.8**

Main export destinations		Main origins of imports	
	% of total		*% of total*
United States	11.8	Germany	15.6
United Kingdom	11.3	United States	11.7
Germany	8.6	United Kingdom	8.9
Japan	6.8	Japan	6.1

Balance of payments, reserves and debt, $bn

Visible exports fob	31.1	Overall balance	1.6
Visible imports fob	-26.7	Change in reserves	0.2
Trade balance	4.4	Level of reserves	
Invisibles inflows	6.3	end Dec.	7.8
Invisibles outflows	-9.8	No. months of import cover	2.6
Net transfers	-0.6	Foreign debt	25.0
Current account balance	0.3	– as % of GDP	22
– as % of GDP	0.3	– as % of total exports	66
Capital balance	-0.1	Debt service ratio	12

Health and education

Health spending, % of GDP	8.6	Education spending, % of GDP	5.7
Doctors per 1,000 pop.	...	Enrolment, %: primary	111
Hospital beds per 1,000 pop.	...	secondary	87
Improved-water source access,		tertiary	15
% of pop.	86		

Society

No. of households	10.2m	Colour TVs per 100 households	64.4
Av. no. per household	4.3	Telephone lines per 100 pop.	10.7
Marriages per 1,000 pop.	4.2	Mobile telephone subscribers	
Divorces per 1,000 pop.	0.9	per 100 pop.	30.4
Cost of living, Dec. 2003		Computers per 100 pop.	7.3
New York = 100	65	Internet hosts per 1,000 pop.	6.5

SOUTH KOREA

Area	99,274 sq km	Capital	Seoul
Arable as % of total land	17	Currency	Won (W)

People

Population	47.4m	Life expectancy: men		71.8 yrs
Pop. per sq km	477.5	women		79.3 yrs
Av. ann. growth		Adult literacy[a]		97.8%
in pop. 2000–05	0.57%	Fertility rate (per woman)		2.0
Pop. under 15	20.9%	Urban population		82.5%
Pop. over 60	11.0%			per 1,000 pop.
No. of men per 100 women	101	Crude birth rate		11.9
Human Development Index	87.9	Crude death rate		5.9

The economy

GDP	W596trn	GDP per head	$10,060
GDP	$476.7bn	GDP per head in purchasing	
Av. ann. growth in real		power parity (USA=100)	47.0
GDP 1992–2002	5.6%	Economic freedom index	2.69

Origins of GDP		**Components of GDP**	
	% of total		% of total
Agriculture	4.0	Private consumption	59.1
Industry, of which:	40.9	Public consumption	10.6
manufacturing	29.2	Investment	29.6
Services	55.1	Exports	40.0
		Imports	-38.6

Structure of employment

	% of total		% of labour force
Agriculture	10	Unemployed 2002	3.1
Industry	28	Av. ann. rate 1995–2002	3.9
Services	62		

Energy

	m TOE		
Total output	34.2	Net energy imports as %	
Total consumption	194.8	of energy use	82
Consumption per head,			
kg oil equivalent	4,114		

Inflation and finance

Consumer price		av. ann. increase 1997–2002	
inflation 2003	3.6%	Narrow money (M1)	12.5%
Av. ann. inflation 1998–2003	2.7%	Broad money	20.6%
Money market rate, 2003	4.0%	Household saving rate, 2002	7.6%

Exchange rates

	end 2003		December 2003
W per $	1,193	Effective rates	1995 = 100
W per SDR	1,772	– nominal	...
W per €	1,503	– real	...

Trade

Principal exports		Principal imports	
	$bn fob		*$bn cif*
Electronic products	56.1	Electrical machinery	36.0
Motor vehicles	13.3	Crude petroleum	19.2
Machinery	12.8	Machinery & equipment	18.0
Chemicals	11.8	Chemicals	12.3
Metal goods	10.3	Iron & steel products	6.3
Total incl. others	**162.5**	**Total incl. others**	**152.1**

Main export destinations		Main origins of imports	
	% of total		*% of total*
United States	20.2	Japan	19.6
China	14.6	United States	15.1
Japan	9.3	China	11.4
Hong Kong	6.2	Saudi Arabia	5.0
Taiwan	4.1	Australia	3.9

Balance of payments, reserves and debt, $bn

Visible exports fob	162.6	Overall balance	11.8
Visible imports fob	-148.4	Change in reserves	18.6
Trade balance	14.2	Level of reserves	
Invisibles inflows	34.9	end Dec.	121.5
Invisibles outflows	-42.0	No. months of import cover	7.7
Net transfers	-1.1	Foreign debt	122
Current account balance	6.1	– as % of GDP	26
– as % of GDP	1.3	– as % of total exports	62
Capital balance	1.5	Debt service ratio	8

Health and education

Health spending, % of GDP	6.0	Education spending, % of GDP	3.6
Doctors per 1,000 pop.	1.4	Enrolment, %: primary	101
Hospital beds per 1,000 pop.	6.1	secondary	94
Improved-water source access,		tertiary	78
% of pop.	92		

Society

No. of households	14.6m	Colour TVs per 100 households	93.1
Av. no. per household	3.3	Telephone lines per 100 pop.	48.9
Marriages per 1,000 pop.	6.5	Mobile telephone subscribers	
Divorces per 1,000 pop.	1.8	per 100 pop.	68.0
Cost of living, Dec. 2003		Computers per 100 pop.	55.6
New York = 100	97	Internet hosts per 1,000 pop.	5.3

a 2000 estimate.

SPAIN

Area	504,782 sq km	Capital	Madrid
Arable as % of total land	26	Currency	Euro (€)

People

Population	39.9m	Life expectancy: men	75.9 yrs
Pop. per sq km	79.0	women	82.8 yrs
Av. ann. growth		Adult literacy	97.8%
in pop. 2000–05	0.21%	Fertility rate (per woman)	1.2
Pop. under 15	14.6%	Urban population	77.8%
Pop. over 60	21.2%		per 1,000 pop.
No. of men per 100 women	96	Crude birth rate	9.3
Human Development Index	91.8	Crude death rate	9.1

The economy

GDP	€694bn	GDP per head	$16,370
GDP	$653.1bn	GDP per head in purchasing	
Av. ann. growth in real		power parity (USA=100)	58.7
GDP 1992–2002	2.8%	Economic freedom index	2.31

Origins of GDP		**Components of GDP**	
	% of total		% of total
Agriculture	3.7	Private consumption	58.2
Industry, of which:	28.9	Public consumption	17.8
manufacturing	...	Investment	25.7
Services	67.4	Exports	28.4
		Imports	-29.9

Structure of employment

	% of total		% of labour force
Agriculture	6	Unemployed 2002	11.4
Industry	32	Av. ann. rate 1995–2002	17.4
Services	62		

Energy

	m TOE		
Total output	34.6	Net energy imports as %	
Total consumption	127.4	of energy use	74
Consumption per head,			
kg oil equivalent	3,127		

Inflation and finance

Consumer price			av. ann. increase 1997–2002
inflation 2003	3.0%	Euro area:	
Av. ann. inflation 1998–2003	3.1%	Narrow money (M1)	9.0%
Money market rate, 2003	2.31%	Broad money	6.4%
		Household saving rate, 2002	10.6%

Exchange rates

	end 2003		December 2003
€ per $	0.79	Effective rates	1995 = 100
€ per SDR	1.18	– nominal	96.4
		– real	112.5

Trade

Principal exports

	$bn fob
Raw materials & intermediate products	54.9
Consumer goods	50.4
Capital goods	15.0
Energy products	2.9
Total incl. others	**123.1**

Principal imports

	$bn cif
Raw materials & intermediate products (excl. fuels)	74.9
Consumer goods	44.5
Capital goods	25.7
Energy products	17.6
Total incl. others	**162.6**

Main export destinations

	% of total
France	19.2
Germany	11.6
United Kingdom	9.7
Italy	9.4
Portugal	9.3
EU15	71.3

Main origins of imports

	% of total
France	16.5
Germany	16.4
Italy	8.9
United Kingdom	6.4
United States	4.1
EU15	64.0

Balance of payments, reserves and aid, $bn

Visible exports fob	125.8	Capital balance	25.9
Visible imports fob	-158.9	Overall balance	3.7
Trade balance	-33.1	Change in reserves	6.1
Invisibles inflows	82.9	Level of reserves	
Invisibles outflows	-68.0	end Dec.	40.3
Net transfers	2.2	No. months of import cover	2.1
Current account balance	-15.9	Aid given	1.56
– as % of GDP	-2.4	– as % of GDP	0.26

Health and education

Health spending, % of GDP	7.5	Education spending, % of GDP	4.4
Doctors per 1,000 pop.	3.3	Enrolment, %: primary	105
Hospital beds per 1,000 pop.	4.1	secondary	116
Improved-water source access, % of pop.	...	tertiary	59

Society

No. of households	12.6m	Colour TVs per 100 households	98.4
Av. no. per household	3.2	Telephone lines per 100 pop.	50.6
Marriages per 1,000 pop.	5.2	Mobile telephone subscribers	
Divorces per 1,000 pop.	0.8	per 100 pop.	82.4
Cost of living, Dec. 2003		Computers per 100 pop.	19.6
New York = 100	85	Internet hosts per 1,000 pop.	28.3

SWEDEN

Area	449,964 sq km	Capital	Stockholm
Arable as % of total land	7	Currency	Swedish krona (Skr)

People

Population	8.8m	Life expectancy: men	77.6 yrs
Pop. per sq km	19.6	women	82.6 yrs
Av. ann. growth		Adult literacy	99.0%
in pop. 2000–05	0.09%	Fertility rate (per woman)	1.6
Pop. under 15	18.3%	Urban population	83.3%
Pop. over 60	22.3%		per 1,000 pop.
No. of men per 100 women	98	Crude birth rate	10.3
Human Development Index	94.1	Crude death rate	10.6

The economy

GDP	Skr2,340bn	GDP per head	$27,310
GDP	$240.3bn	GDP per head in purchasing	
Av. ann. growth in real		power parity (USA=100)	71.5
GDP 1992–2002	2.4%	Economic freedom index	1.90

Origins of GDP

	% of total
Agriculture	2.0
Industry, of which:	29.0
manufacturing	...
Services	69.0

Components of GDP

	% of total
Private consumption	48.7
Public consumption	28.0
Investment	17.2
Exports	43.3
Imports	-37.2

Structure of employment

	% of total		% of labour force
Agriculture	2	Unemployed 2002	4.0
Industry	24	Av. ann. rate 1995–2002	6.1
Services	74		

Energy

	m TOE		
Total output	34.4	Net energy imports as %	
Total consumption	51.1	of energy use	33
Consumption per head,			
kg oil equivalent	5,740		

Inflation and finance

Consumer price		av. ann. increase 1997–2002	
inflation 2003	1.9%	Narrow money (M0)	5.2%
Av. ann. inflation 1998–2003	1.6%	Broad money	5.6%
Repurchase rate, 2003	2.75%	Household saving rate, 2002	8.2%

Exchange rates

	end 2003		December 2003
Skr per $	7.19	Effective rates	1995 = 100
Skr per SDR	10.68	– nominal	101.9
Skr per €	9.06	– real	105.4

Trade

Principal exports

	$bn fob
Machinery & transport equipment	41.1
Wood & paper products	11.3
Chemicals	9.7
Manufactured goods	9.4
Total incl. others	**81.1**

Principal imports

	$bn cif
Machinery & transport equipment	30.5
Miscellaneous manufactures	14.1
Chemicals	7.9
Mineral fuels	5.9
Total incl. others	**66.5**

Main export destinations

	% of total
United States	11.5
Germany	10.1
Norway	8.8
United Kingdom	8.2
Denmark	6.2
EU15	53.9

Main origins of imports

	% of total
Germany	18.6
Denmark	9.2
United Kingdom	8.7
Norway	7.9
Netherlands	6.8
EU15	66.9

Balance of payments, reserves and aid, $bn

Visible exports fob	81.5	Capital balance	-9.6
Visible imports fob	-66.1	Overall balance	0.7
Trade balance	15.5	Change in reserves	3.5
Invisibles inflows	40.9	Level of reserves	
Invisibles outflows	-42.9	end Dec.	19.2
Net transfers	-2.9	No. months of import cover	2.1
Current account balance	10.6	Aid given	1.85
– as % of GDP	4.4	– as % of GDP	0.83

Health and education

Health spending, % of GDP	8.7	Education spending, % of GDP	7.7
Doctors per 1,000 pop.	3.0	Enrolment, %: primary	110
Hospital beds per 1,000 pop.	3.6	secondary	149
Improved-water source access, % of pop.	100	tertiary	70

Society

No. of households	4.4m	Colour TVs per 100 households	97.2
Av. no. per household	2.0	Telephone lines per 100 pop.	73.6
Marriages per 1,000 pop.	4.3	Mobile telephone subscribers	
Divorces per 1,000 pop.	2.1	per 100 pop.	89.0
Cost of living, Dec. 2003		Computers per 100 pop.	62.1
New York = 100	99	Internet hosts per 1,000 pop.	175.0

SWITZERLAND

Area	41,293 sq km	Capital	Berne
Arable as % of total land	10	Currency	Swiss franc (SFr)

People

Population	7.2m	Life expectancy: men		75.9 yrs
Pop. per sq km	174.4	women		82.3 yrs
Av. ann. growth		Adult literacy		99.0%
in pop. 2000–05	-0.05%	Fertility rate (per woman)		1.4
Pop. under 15	16.7%	Urban population		67.3%
Pop. over 60	21.3%			per 1,000 pop.
No. of men per 100 women	98	Crude birth rate		8.7
Human Development Index	93.8	Crude death rate		9.8

The economy

GDP	SFr417bn	GDP per head	$37,150
GDP	$267.4bn	GDP per head in purchasing	
Av. ann. growth in real		power parity (USA=100)	88.2
GDP 1992–2002	1.1%	Economic freedom index	1.84

Origins of GDPa

	% of total
Agriculture	1.2
Industry, of which:	26.7
manufacturing	...
Services	72.1

Components of GDP

	% of total
Private consumption	60.8
Public consumption	15.2
Investment	16.3
Exports	42.7
Imports	36.0

Structure of employment

	% of total		% of labour force
Agriculture	4	Unemployed 2002	2.9
Industry	26	Av. ann. rate 1995–2002	3.2
Services	70		

Energy

	m TOE		
Total output	12.4	Net energy imports as %	
Total consumption	28.0	of energy use	56
Consumption per head, kg oil equivalent	3,875		

Inflation and finance

Consumer price inflation 2003	0.6%	av. ann. increase 1997–2002	
		Narrow money (M1)	6.5%
Av. ann. inflation 1998–2003	0.9%	Broad money	1.7%
Money market rate, 2003	0.09%	Household saving rate, 2002	9.7%

Exchange rates

	end 2003		December 2003
SFr per $	1.24	Effective rates	1995 = 100
SFr per SDR	1.84	– nominal	98.7
SFr per €	1.56	– real	114.1

Trade

Principal exports	$bn	Principal imports	$bn
Chemicals	28.7	Chemicals	17.5
Machinery	20.3	Machinery	16.6
Watches & jewellery	6.8	Motor vehicles	8.2
Metals & metal manufactures	6.2	Textiles	5.5
Precision instruments	5.7	Precision instruments	5.2
Total incl. others	**83.9**	Total incl. others	**79.1**

Main export destinations	% of total	Main origins of imports	% of total
Germany	20.8	Germany	32.3
United States	11.0	Italy	10.8
France	9.2	France	10.4
Italy	8.3	Netherlands	5.4
United Kingdom	4.9	United States	5.3
Japan	3.8	United Kingdom	4.7
EU15	60.0	EU15	80.4

Balance of payments, reserves and aid, $bn

Visible exports fob	100.5	Capital balance	-34.5
Visible imports fob	-94.0	Overall balance	2.4
Trade balance	6.4	Change in reserves	9.7
Invisibles inflows	70.8	Level of reserves	
Invisibles outflows	-47.1	end Dec.	61.3
Net transfers	-4.2	No. months of import cover	5.2
Current account balance	26.0	Aid given	0.86
– as % of GDP	9.7	– as % of GDP	0.32

Health and education

Health spending, % of GDP	11.0	Education spending, % of GDP	5.5
Doctors per 1,000 pop.	3.5	Enrolment, %: primary	107
Hospital beds per 1,000 pop.	17.9	secondary	100
Improved-water source access,		tertiary	42
% of pop.	100		

Society

No. of households	3.2m	Colour TVs per 100 households	96.8
Av. no. per household	2.3	Telephone lines per 100 pop.	74.4
Marriages per 1,000 pop.	4.9	Mobile telephone subscribers	
Divorces per 1,000 pop.	2.7	per 100 pop.	78.9
Cost of living, Dec. 2003		Computers per 100 pop.	70.9
New York = 100	109	Internet hosts per 1,000 pop.	141.5

a 2000

TAIWAN

Area	36,179 sq km	Capital	Taipei
Arable as % of total land	25	Currency	Taiwan dollar (T$)

People

Population	22.5m	Life expectancy:[a] men	74.1 yrs
Pop. per sq km	621.9	women	79.9 yrs
Av. ann. growth		Adult literacy	96.1
in pop. 2000–05	0.55%	Fertility rate (per woman)	1.6
Pop. under 15	21.0%	Urban population	...
Pop. over 60	12.1%		per 1,000 pop.
No. of men per 100 women	104	Crude birth rate	13
Human Development Index	...	Crude death rate[a]	6.2

The economy

GDP	T$9,734bn	GDP per head	$12,520
GDP	$281.6bn	GDP per head in purchasing	
Av. ann. growth in real		power parity (USA=100)	49.8
GDP 1992–2002	5.0%	Economic freedom index	2.43

Origins of GDP		Components of GDP	
	% of total		% of total
Agriculture	1.9	Private consumption	63.1
Industry, of which:	30.6	Public consumption	12.6
manufacturing	25.7	Investment	16.8
Services	67.5	Exports	53.8
		Imports	-46.4

Structure of employment

	% of total		% of labour force
Agriculture	8	Unemployed 2002	4.6
Industry	36	Av. ann. rate 1995–2002	2.9
Services	56		

Energy

	m TOE		
Total output	...	Net energy imports as %	
Total consumption	...	of energy use	...
Consumption per head,			
kg oil equivalent	...		

Inflation and finance

		av. ann. increase 1997–2002	
Consumer price			
inflation 2003	-0.3%	Narrow money (M1)	8.1%
Av. ann. inflation 1998–2003	0.2%	Broad money	6.1%
Rediscount rate, 2003	1.38%		

Exchange rates

	end 2003		December 2003
T$ per $	34.1	Effective rates	1995 = 100
T$ per SDR	50.8	– nominal	...
T$ per €	42.8	– real	...

Trade

Principal exports	$bn fob	Principal imports	$bn cif
Machinery & electrical equipment	70.7	Machinery & electrical equipment	50.1
Base metals & manufactures	12.5	Minerals	12.6
Textiles & clothing	12.2	Chemicals	11.3
Plastics and rubber products	8.8	Metals	9.2
Vehicles, aircraft & ships	4.8	Precision instruments, clocks & watches	6.6
Total incl. others	130.6	Total incl. others	112.5

Main export destinations	% of total	Main origins of imports	% of total
Hong Kong	23.6	Japan	24.2
United States	20.5	United States	16.1
Japan	9.2	South Korea	6.9
Netherlands	2.9	Malaysia	3.9

Balance of payments, reserves and debt, $bn

Visible exports fob	129.9	Overall balance	33.7
Visible imports fob	-105.2	Change in reserves	39.5
Trade balance	24.7	Level of reserves	
Invisibles inflows	31.7	end Dec.	161.7
Invisibles outflows	-28.2	No. months of import cover	14.5
Net transfers	-2.5	Foreign debt	45.1
Current account balance	25.7	– as % of GDP	16
– as % of GDP	9.1	– as % of total exports	28
Capital balance	-8.2	Debt service ratio	3

Health and education

Health spending, % of GDP	...	Education spending, % of GDP	...
Doctors per 1,000 pop.	1.6	Enrolment, %: primary	100
Hospital beds per 1,000 pop.	5.9	secondary[b]	59
Improved-water source access, % of pop.	...	tertiary[b]	21

Society

No. of households	6.9m	Colour TVs per 100 households	99.4
Av. no. per household	3.3	Telephone lines per 100 pop.	58.2
Marriages per 1,000 pop.	7.5	Mobile telephone subscribers	
Divorces per 1,000 pop.	1.9	per 100 pop.	106.2
Cost of living, Dec. 2003		Computers per 100 pop.	39.5
New York = 100	89	Internet hosts per 1,000 pop.	123.4

a 2002 estimate.
b 1997

THAILAND

Area	513,115 sq km	Capital	Bangkok
Arable as % of total land	29	Currency	Baht (Bt)

People

Population	64.3m	Life expectancy: men	65.3 yrs
Pop. per sq km	125.3	women	73.5 yrs
Av. ann. growth		Adult literacy[a]	92.6%
in pop. 2000–05	1.01%	Fertility rate (per woman)	1.9
Pop. under 15	26.3%	Urban population	20.0%
Pop. over 60	8.4%		per 1,000 pop.
No. of men per 100 women	96	Crude birth rate	17.3
Human Development Index	76.8	Crude death rate	7.1

The economy

GDP	Bt5,452bn	GDP per head	$1,970
GDP	$126.9bn	GDP per head in purchasing	
Av. ann. growth in real		power parity (USA=100)	19.1
GDP 1992–2002	3.5%	Economic freedom index	2.86

Origins of GDP

	% of total
Agriculture	9.4
Industry, of which:	42.7
manufacturing	33.8
Services	48.0

Components of GDP

	% of total
Private consumption	56.5
Public consumption	11.2
Investment	24.0
Exports	64.7
Imports	-57.5

Structure of employment

	% of total		% of labour force
Agriculture	46	Unemployed 2001	2.6
Industry	21	Av. ann. rate 1995–2001	2.1
Services	33		

Energy

	m TOE		
Total output	40.1	Net energy imports as %	
Total consumption	75.5	of energy use	47
Consumption per head,			
kg oil equivalent	1,235		

Inflation and finance

Consumer price		av. ann. increase 1997–2002	
inflation 2003	1.8%	Narrow money (M1)	9.4%
Av. ann. inflation 1998–2003	1.2%	Broad money	4.4%
Money market rate, 2003	1.31%		

Exchange rates

	end 2003		December 2003
Bt per $	39.59	Effective rates	1995 = 100
Bt per SDR	58.83	– nominal	...
Bt per €	49.88	– real	...

Trade

Principal exports		Principal imports	
	$bn fob		*$bn cif*
Machinery & mech. appliances	9.2	Capital goods	29.6
Integrated circuits	8.9	Raw materials & intermediates	17.0
Computer parts	7.3	Petroleum & products	7.4
Electrical appliances	5.7	Consumer goods	6.8
Total incl. others	**68.8**	Total incl. others	**64.7**

Main export destinations		Main origins of imports	
	% of total		*% of total*
United States	19.7	Japan	23.0
Japan	14.5	United States	9.6
Singapore	8.1	China	7.6
Hong Kong	5.4	Malaysia	5.6
China	5.2	Singapore	4.5

Balance of payments, reserves and debt, $bn

Visible exports fob	66.8	Overall balance	5.5
Visible imports fob	-57.0	Change in reserves	5.9
Trade balance	9.8	Level of reserves	
Invisibles inflows	18.7	end Dec.	38.9
Invisibles outflows	-21.4	No. months of import cover	6.0
Net transfers	0.6	Foreign debt	59.2
Current account balance	7.7	– as % of GDP	50
– as % of GDP	6.0	– as % of total exports	71
Capital balance	-2.7	Debt service ratio	24

Health and education

Health spending, % of GDP	3.7	Education spending, % of GDP	5.0
Doctors per 1,000 pop.	...	Enrolment, %: primary	95
Hospital beds per 1,000 pop.	...	secondary	82
Improved-water source access,		tertiary	35
% of pop.	84		

Society

No. of households	15.9m	Colour TVs per 100 households	88.3
Av. no. per household	3.9	Telephone lines per 100 pop.	10.5
Marriages per 1,000 pop.	6.7	Mobile telephone subscribers	
Divorces per 1,000 pop.	1.0	per 100 pop.	26.0
Cost of living, Dec. 2003		Computers per 100 pop.	4.0
New York = 100	61	Internet hosts per 1,000 pop.	1.6

a 2000

TURKEY

Area	779,452 sq km	Capital	Ankara
Arable as % of total land	31	Currency	Turkish Lira (L)

People

Population	68.6m	Life expectancy: men	68.0 yrs
Pop. per sq km	88.0	women	73.2 yrs
Av. ann. growth		Adult literacy[a]	86.5%
in pop. 2000–05	1.42%	Fertility rate (per woman)	2.4
Pop. under 15	31.7%	Urban population	66.2%
Pop. over 60	8.0%		per 1,000 pop.
No. of men per 100 women	102	Crude birth rate	20.9
Human Development Index	73.4	Crude death rate	6.0

The economy

GDP	L276,469trn	GDP per head	$2,680
GDP	$183.7bn	GDP per head in purchasing	
Av. ann. growth in real		power parity (USA=100)	17.4
GDP 1992–2002	2.9%	Economic freedom index	3.39

Origins of GDP

	% of total
Agriculture	11.9
Industry, of which:	29.6
manufacturing	...
Services	58.5

Components of GDP

	% of total
Private consumption	66.7
Public consumption	14.0
Investment	21.4
Exports	28.8
Imports	-30.5

Structure of employment

	% of total		% of labour force
Agriculture	33	Unemployed 2002	10.6
Industry	24	Av. ann. rate 1995–2002	7.6
Services	43		

Energy

	m TOE		
Total output	26.2	Net energy imports as %	
Total consumption	72.5	of energy use	64
Consumption per head,			
kg oil equivalent	1,057		

Inflation and finance

Consumer price			av. ann. increase 1997–2002
inflation 2003	25.3%	Narrow money (M1)	58.3%
Av. ann. inflation 1998–2003	48.3%	Broad money	66.6%
Money market rate, 2003	36.2%		

Exchange rates

	end 2003		December 2003
L per $	1,396,638	Effective rates	1995 = 100
L per SDR	2,075,362	– nominal	...
L per €	1,759,764	– real	...

Trade

Principal exports		Principal imports	
	$bn fob		*$bn cif*
Chemicals & manufactured goods	21.3	Chemicals & manufactured goods	22.1
Machinery & transport equip.	15.6	Machinery & transport equip.	8.6
Fuels	9.0	Fuels	6.8
Crude materials	4.1	Food, animals & tobacco	3.5
Total incl. others	**34.6**	Total incl. others	**49.7**

Main export destinations		Main origins of imports	
	% of total		*% of total*
Germany	16.6	Germany	13.7
United States	9.2	Italy	8.1
United Kingdom	8.5	Russia	7.6
Italy	6.4	United States	6.0
France	6.0	France	5.9
EU15	51.5	EU15	45.5

Balance of payments, reserves and debt, $bn

Visible exports fob	40.1	Overall balance	-0.2
Visible imports fob	-48.5	Change in reserves	8.4
Trade balance	-8.3	Level of reserves	
Invisibles inflows	17.3	end Dec.	28.3
Invisibles outflows	-13.9	No. months of import cover	5.5
Net transfers	3.5	Foreign debt	131.6
Current account balance	-1.5	– as % of GDP	75
– as % of GDP	-0.8	– as % of total exports	227
Capital balance	1.3	Debt service ratio	48

Health and education

Health spending, % of GDP	6.9	Education spending, % of GDP	3.7
Doctors per 1,000 pop.	1.3	Enrolment, %: primary	101
Hospital beds per 1,000 pop.	2.6	secondary[a]	58
Improved-water source access,		tertiary[a]	15
% of pop.	82		

Society

No. of households	16.4m	Colour TVs per 100 households	67.4
Av. no. per household	4.1	Telephone lines per 100 pop.	28.1
Marriages per 1,000 pop.	8.3	Mobile telephone subscribers	
Divorces per 1,000 pop.	0.6	per 100 pop.	34.8
Cost of living, Dec. 2003		Computers per 100 pop.	4.5
New York = 100	81	Internet hosts per 1,000 pop.	5.0

a 2000

UKRAINE

Area	603,700 sq km	Capital	Kiev
Arable as % of total land	56	Currency	Hryvnya (UAH)

People

Population	48.7m	Life expectancy: men	64.7 yrs
Pop. per sq km	80.7	women	74.7 yrs
Av. ann. growth		Adult literacy	99.6%
in pop. 2000–05	-0.78%	Fertility rate (per woman)	1.2
Pop. under 15	17.8%	Urban population	68.0%
Pop. over 60	20.6%		per 1,000 pop.
No. of men per 100 women	87	Crude birth rate	8.4
Human Development Index	76.6	Crude death rate	14.2

The economy

GDP	UAH221bn	GDP per head	$850
GDP	$41.5bn	GDP per head in purchasing	
Av. ann. growth in real		power parity (USA=100)	13.3
GDP 1992–2002	-5.0%	Economic freedom index	3.49

Origins of GDP

	% of total
Agriculture	15.3
Industry, of which:	38.2
manufacturing	23.2
Services	46.5

Components of GDP

	% of total
Private consumption	68.3
Public consumption	8.1
Investment	19.1
Exports	56.3
Imports	-51.8

Structure of employment

	% of total		% of labour force
Agriculture	20	Unemployed 2002	10.2
Industry	31	Av. ann. rate 1995–2002	9.8
Services	49		

Energy

	m TOE		
Total output	83.4	Net energy imports as %	
Total consumption	141.6	of energy use	41
Consumption per head,			
kg oil equivalent	2,884		

Inflation and finance

Consumer price		av. ann. increase 1997–2002	
inflation 2003	5.2%	Narrow money (M1)	34.8%
Av. ann. inflation 1998–2003	13.3%	Broad money	38.7%
Money market rate, 2003	7.90%		

Exchange rates

	end 2003		December 2003
UAH per $	5.33	Effective rates	1995 = 100
UAH per SDR	7.92	– nominal	118.2
UAH per €	6.72	– real	96.7

Trade

Principal exports		Principal imports	
	$bn fob		*$bn cif*
Metals	6.9	Fuels, mineral products	6.6
Machinery & equipment	2.5	Machinery & equipment	3.6
Food & agricultural produce	2.3	Chemicals	2.1
Fuels & mineral products	2.0	Food & agricultural produce	1.1
Chemicals	1.7		
Total incl. others	**18.0**	Total incl. others	**17.0**

Main export destinations		Main origins of imports	
	% of total		*% of total*
Russia	17.1	Russia	35.2
Italy	6.6	Turkmenistan	10.5
Turkey	4.4	Germany	9.2
Germany	4.0	Poland	3.0
China	2.8	United States	2.6

Balance of payments, reserves and debt, $bn

Visible exports fob	18.7	Overall balance	1.2
Visible imports fob	-18.0	Change in reserves	1.3
Trade balance	0.7	Level of reserves	
Invisibles inflows	4.8	end Dec.	4.4
Invisibles outflows	-4.3	No. months of import cover	2.4
Net transfers	1.9	Foreign debt	13.6
Current account balance	3.2	– as % of GDP	37
– as % of GDP	7.7	– as % of total exports	63
Capital balance	-1.0	Debt service ratio	15

Health and education

Health spending, % of GDP	4.3	Education spending, % of GDP	4.2
Doctors per 1,000 pop.	3.0	Enrolment, %: primary	78
Hospital beds per 1,000 pop.	8.7	secondary	105
Improved-water source access,		tertiary	43
% of pop.	98		

Society

No. of households	18.5m	Colour TVs per 100 households	75.7
Av. no. per household	2.6	Telephone lines per 100 pop.	21.6
Marriages per 1,000 pop.	5.9	Mobile telephone subscribers	
Divorces per 1,000 pop.	3.3	per 100 pop.	8.4
Cost of living, Dec. 2003		Computers per 100 pop.	1.9
New York = 100	64	Internet hosts per 1,000 pop.	2.0

UNITED ARAB EMIRATES

Area	83,600 sq km	Capital	Abu Dhabi
Arable as % of total land	1	Currency	Dirham (AED)

People

Population	2.7m	Life expectancy: men	73.7 yrs
Pop. per sq km	32.3	women	77.4 yrs
Av. ann. growth		Adult literacy	77.3%
in pop. 2000–05	1.9%	Fertility rate (per woman)	2.3
Pop. under 15	26.9%	Urban population	87.0%
Pop. over 60	2.2%		per 1,000 pop.
No. of men per 100 women	190	Crude birth rate	16.7
Human Development Index	81.6	Crude death rate	2.4

The economy

GDP	AED261bn	GDP per head	$26,280
GDP	$71.0bn	GDP per head in purchasing	
Av. ann. growth in real		power parity (USA=100)	66.5
GDP 1992–2002	4.2%	Economic freedom index	2.60

Origins of GDP[a]

	% of total	Components of GDP	% of total
Agriculture	2	Private consumption	47.7
Industry, of which:	57	Public consumption	17.0
manufacturing	8	Investment	24.2
Services	40	Exports	73.5
		Imports	-62.5

Structure of employment

	% of total		% of labour force
Agriculture	8	Unemployed 2001	2.3
Industry	33	Av. ann. rate 1995–2001	2.1
Services	59		

Energy

	m TOE		
Total output	144.6	Net energy imports as %	
Total consumption	32.6	of energy use	-343
Consumption per head,			
kg oil equivalent	10,860		

Inflation and finance

Consumer price		av. ann. increase 1997–2002	
inflation 2003	3.2%	Narrow money (M1)	13.2%
Av. ann. inflation 1998–2003	2.4%	Broad money	12.9%

Exchange rates

	end 2003		December 2003
AED per $	3.67	Effective rates	1995 = 100
AED per SDR	5.46	– nominal	111.1
AED per €	4.62	– real	...

Trade

Principal exports		Principal imports[b]	
	$bn fob		*$bn cif*
Crude oil	16.9	Consumer goods	15.2
Re-exports	14.6	Capital goods	12.6
		Intermediate goods	5.3
Total incl. others	**49.6**	Total incl. others	**38.1**

Main export destinations		Main origins of imports	
	% of total		*% of total*
Japan	27.9	United States	8.0
South Korea	10.1	Germany	7.7
India	3.8	Japan	6.6
Oman	3.8	France	6.3

Balance of payments, reserves and debt, $bn

Visible exports fob	49.6	Overall balance[c]	0.5
Visible imports fob	-35.2	Change in reserves	1.1
Trade balance	14.4	Level of reserves	
Invisibles inflows	8.0	end Dec.	15.4
Invisibles outflows	-9.5	No. months of import cover	4.1
Net transfers	-4.4	Foreign debt	19.7
Current account balance	8.4	– as % of GDP	28
– as % of GDP	11.9	– as % of total exports	38
Capital balance[c]	-9.5	Debt service ratio	2

Health and education

Health spending, % of GDP	3.5	Education spending, % of GDP	1.9
Doctors per 1,000 pop.	...	Enrolment, %: primary	99
Hospital beds per 1,000 pop.	...	secondary	75
Improved-water source access,		tertiary	12
% of pop.	...		

Society

No. of households	0.5m	Colour TVs per 100 households	96.1
Av. no. per household	6.7	Telephone lines per 100 pop.	31.4
Marriages per 1,000 pop.	3.3	Mobile telephone subscribers	
Divorces per 1,000 pop.	1.1	per 100 pop.	69.6
Cost of living, Dec. 2003		Computers per 100 pop.	12.0
New York = 100	73	Internet hosts per 1,000 pop.	...

a 1993
b 2000
c 1999

UNITED KINGDOM

Area	242,534 sq km	Capital	London
Arable as % of total land	24	Currency	Pound (£)

People

Population	59.7m	Life expectancy: men	75.7 yrs
Pop. per sq km	246.1	women	80.7 yrs
Av. ann. growth		Adult literacy	99.0%
in pop. 2000–05	0.31%	Fertility rate (per woman)	1.6
Pop. under 15	19.1%	Urban population	89.5%
Pop. over 60	20.7%		per 1,000 pop.
No. of men per 100 women	95	Crude birth rate	11.0
Human Development Index	93.0	Crude death rate	10.4

The economy

GDP	£1,043bn	GDP per head	$26,240
GDP	$1,566bn	GDP per head in purchasing	
Av. ann. growth in real		power parity (USA=100)	73.6
GDP 1992–2002	2.8%	Economic freedom index	1.79

Origins of GDP

	% of total
Agriculture	1.0
Industry, of which:	27.3
manufacturing	16.6
Services	71.8

Components of GDP

	% of total
Private consumption	66.4
Public consumption	20.0
Investment	15.9
Exports	26.1
Imports	-29.1

Structure of employment

	% of total		% of labour force
Agriculture	1	Unemployed 2002	5.1
Industry	25	Av. ann. rate 1995–2002	6.4
Services	74		

Energy

	m TOE		
Total output	261.9	Net energy imports as %	
Total consumption	235.2	of energy use	-11
Consumption per head,			
kg oil equivalent	3,982		

Inflation and finance

Consumer price		av. ann. increase 1997–2002
inflation 2003	2.9%	Narrow money (M0) 7.3%
Av. ann. inflation 1998–2003	2.2%	Broad money 6.9%
Money market rate, 2003	3.59%	Household saving rate, 2002 5.3%

Exchange rates

	end 2003		December 2003
£ per $	0.56	Effective rates	1995 = 100
£ per SDR	0.83	– nominal	118.3
£ per €	0.71	– real	138.7

Trade

Principal exports		Principal imports	
	$bn fob		*$bn fob*
Finished manufactured		Finished manufactured	
products	159.2	products	197.1
Semi-manufactured products	74.9	Semi-manufactured products	78.5
Fuels	23.7	Food, beverages & tobacco	28.7
Food, beverages & tobacco	14.9	Fuels	14.7
Basic materials	4.0	Basic materials	8.1
Total incl. others	**278.6**	Total incl. others	**330.2**

Main export destinations		Main origins of imports	
	% of total		*% of total*
United States	15.2	United States	13.7
Germany	11.8	Germany	11.3
France	10.0	France	8.5
Ireland	8.2	Netherlands	6.8
Netherlands	7.5		
EU15	58.7	EU15	53.7

Balance of payments, reserves and aid, $bn

Visible exports fob	280.0	Capital balance	10.5
Visible imports fob	-350.0	Overall balance	-0.6
Trade balance	-70.2	Change in reserves	2.4
Invisibles inflows	320.1	Level of reserves	
Invisibles outflows	-263.7	end Dec.	42.9
Net transfers	-13.0	No. months of import cover	0.8
Current account balance	-26.7	Aid given	4.58
– as % of GDP	-1.7	– as % of GDP	0.31

Health and education

Health spending, % of GDP	7.6	Education spending, % of GDP	4.5
Doctors per 1,000 pop.	2.0	Enrolment, %: primary	99
Hospital beds per 1,000 pop.	4.1	secondary	156
Improved-water source access,		tertiary	60
% of pop.	100		

Society

No. of households	24.5m	Colour TVs per 100 households	98.6
Av. no. per household	2.4	Telephone lines per 100 pop.	59.1
Marriages per 1,000 pop.	5.2	Mobile telephone subscribers	
Divorces per 1,000 pop.	3.1	per 100 pop.	84.1
Cost of living, Dec. 2003		Computers per 100 pop.	40.6
New York = 100	109	Internet hosts per 1,000 pop.	62.2

UNITED STATES

Area	9,372,610 sq km	Capital	Washington DC
Arable as % of total land	19	Currency	US dollar ($)

People

Population	288.5m	Life expectancy: men	74.3 yrs
Pop. per sq km	30.8	women	79.9 yrs
Av. ann. growth		Adult literacy	99.0%
in pop. 2000–05	1.03%	Fertility rate (per woman)	2.1
Pop. under 15	21.8%	Urban population	77.4%
Pop. over 60	16.1%		per 1,000 pop.
No. of men per 100 women	97	Crude birth rate	14.5
Human Development Index	93.7	Crude death rate	8.3

The economy

GDP	$10,383bn	GDP per head	$35,990
Av. ann. growth in real		GDP per head in purchasing	
GDP 1992–2002	3.3%	power parity (USA=100)	100
		Economic freedom index	1.85

Origins of GDP[a]

Components of GDP

	% of total		% of total
Agriculture	1.4	Private consumption	69.9
Industry, of which:	20.3	Public consumption	18.9
manufacturing	14.1	Investment	15.2
Services[b]	78.3	Exports	9.7
		Imports	-13.7

Structure of employment

	% of total		% of labour force
Agriculture	2	Unemployed 2002	5.8
Industry	23	Av. ann. rate 1995–2002	4.9
Services	75		

Energy

	m TOE		
Total output	1,711.8	Net energy imports as %	
Total consumption	2,281.4	of energy use	25
Consumption per head,			
kg oil equivalent	7,996		

Inflation and finance

Consumer price		av. ann. increase 1997–2002	
inflation 2003	2.3%	Narrow money (M1)	2.5%
Av. ann. inflation 1998–2003	2.5%	Broad money	9.5%
Treasury bill rate, 2003	1.01%	Household saving rate, 2002	3.7%

Exchange rates

	end 2003		December 2003
$ per SDR	1.49	Effective rates	1995 = 100
$ per €	1.26	– nominal	104.8
		– real	110.9

Trade

Principal exports

	$bn fob
Capital goods, excl. vehicles	290.5
Industrial supplies	156.8
Consumer goods, excl. vehicles	84.4
Vehicles & products	78.9
Food & beverages	49.6
Total incl. others	**693.9**

Principal imports

	$bn fob
Consumer goods, excl. vehicles	307.9
Industrial supplies	283.9
Capital goods, excl. vehicles	267.7
Vehicles & products	203.7
Food & beverages	49.7
Total incl. others	**1,164.7**

Main export destinations

	% of total
Canada	23.2
Mexico	14.1
Japan	7.4
United Kingdom	4.8
Germany	3.8
EU15	20.7

Main origins of imports

	% of total
Canada	18.0
Mexico	11.6
China	10.8
Japan	10.5
Germany	5.4
EU15	19.4

Balance of payments, reserves and aid, $bn

Visible exports fob	685.4	Capital balance	533.0
Visible imports fob	-1,164.8	Overall balance	3.7
Trade balance	-479.4	Change in reserves	27.7
Invisibles inflows	544.3	Level of reserves	
Invisibles outflows	-486.9	end Dec.	157.8
Net transfers	-58.9	No. months of import cover	1.1
Current account balance	-480.9	Aid given	13.14
– as % of GDP	-4.6	– as % of GDP	0.13

Health and education

Health spending, % of GDP	13.9	Education spending, % of GDP	5.6
Doctors per 1,000 pop.	2.7	Enrolment, %: primary	101
Hospital beds per 1,000 pop.	3.6	secondary	95
Improved-water source access,		tertiary	73
% of pop.	100		

Society

No. of households	106.5m	Colour TVs per 100 households	99.5
Av. no. per household	2.6	Telephone lines per 100 pop.	64.6
Marriages per 1,000 pop.	8.4	Mobile telephone subscribers	
Divorces per 1,000 pop.	4.7	per 100 pop.	48.8
Cost of living, Dec. 2003		Computers per 100 pop.	66.0
New York = 100	100	Internet hosts per 1,000 pop.c	533.6

a 2001
b Including utilities.
c Includes all hosts ending ".com", ".net" and ".org" which exaggerates the numbers.

VENEZUELA

Area	912,050 sq km	Capital	Caracas
Arable as % of total land	3	Currency	Bolivar (Bs)

People

Population	25.1m	Life expectancy: men		70.9 yrs
Pop. per sq km	27.6	women		76.7 yrs
Av. ann. growth		Adult literacy		93.1%
in pop. 2000–05	1.86%	Fertility rate (per woman)		2.7
Pop. under 15	34.0%	Urban population		87.2%
Pop. over 60	6.6%			per 1,000 pop.
No. of men per 100 women	101	Crude birth rate		22.8
Human Development Index	77.5	Crude death rate		4.6

The economy

GDP	Bs109,524bn	GDP per head	$3,760
GDP	$94.3bn	GDP per head in purchasing	
Av. ann. growth in real		power parity (USA=100)	14.5
GDP 1992–2002	-0.2%	Economic freedom index	4.18

Origins of GDP

	% of total
Agriculture	4.9
Industry, of which:	46.3
manufacturing	14.3
Services	48.9

Components of GDP

	% of total
Private consumption	65.4
Public consumption	8.1
Investment	13.8
Exports	29.3
Imports	-16.5

Structure of employment[b]

	% of total		% of labour force
Agriculture	10	Unemployed 2002	15.8
Industry	22	Av. ann. rate 1995–2002	12.8
Services	68		

Energy

	m TOE		
Total output	216.0	Net energy imports as %	
Total consumption	54.9	of energy use	-294
Consumption per head,			
kg oil equivalent	2,227		

Inflation and finance

Consumer price		*av. ann. increase 1997–2002*	
inflation 2003	31.1%	Narrow money (M1)	17.4%
Av. ann. inflation 1998–2003	21.0%	Broad money	18.0%
Money market rate, 2003	13.23%		

Exchange rates

	end 2003		December 2003
Bs per $	1,598	Effective rates	1995 = 100
Bs per SDR	2,375	– nominal	12.2
Bs per €	2,013	– real	114.6

Trade

Principal exports

	$bn fob
Oil	21.5
Non-oil	2.9
Total incl. others	**24.4**

Principal imports

	$bn cif
Intermediate goods	7.8
Consumer goods	2.4
Capital goods	2.1
Total incl. others	**11.8**

Main export destinations

	% of total
United States	58.9
Colombia	3.2
Brazil	3.1
Germany	1.0

Main origins of imports

	% of total
United States	41.3
Japan	10.4
Italy	8.6
Germany	6.6

Balance of payments, reserves and debt, $bn

Visible exports fob	26.7	Overall balance	-4.4
Visible imports fob	-13.6	Change in reserves	-0.2
Trade balance	13.0	Level of reserves	
Invisibles inflows	2.6	end Dec.	12.1
Invisibles outflows	-8.1	No. months of import cover	5.0
Net transfers	-0.2	Foreign debt	32.6
Current account balance	7.4	– as % of GDP	29
– as % of GDP	7.9	– as % of total exports	101
Capital balance	-9.4	Debt service ratio	23

Health and education

Health spending, % of GDP	6.0	Education spending, % of GDP	5.2
Doctors per 1,000 pop.	...	Enrolment, %: primary	102
Hospital beds per 1,000 pop.	...	secondary	59
Improved-water source access,		tertiary	29
% of pop.	83		

Society

No. of households	5.4m	Colour TVs per 100 households	92.8
Av. no. per household	4.8	Telephone lines per 100 pop.	11.3
Marriages per 1,000 pop.	4.0	Mobile telephone subscribers	
Divorces per 1,000 pop.	0.9	per 100 pop.	25.6
Cost of living, Dec. 2003		Computers per 100 pop.	6.1
New York = 100	61	Internet hosts per 1,000 pop.	1.4

VIETNAM

Area	331,114 sq km	Capital	Hanoi
Arable as % of total land	20	Currency	Dong (D)

People

Population	80.2m	Life expectancy: men	66.9 yrs
Pop. per sq km	242.2	women	71.6 yrs
Av. ann. growth		Adult literacy[a]	92.5%
in pop. 2000–05	1.35%	Fertility rate (per woman)	2.3
Pop. under 15	33.4%	Urban population	24.5%
Pop. over 60	7.5%		per 1,000 pop.
No. of men per 100 women	99	Crude birth rate	20.2
Human Development Index	68.8	Crude death rate	6.4

The economy

GDP	D536trn	GDP per head	$440
GDP	$35.1bn	GDP per head in purchasing	
Av. ann. growth in real		power parity (USA=100)	6.4
GDP 1992–2002	7.5%	Economic freedom index	3.93

Origins of GDP

	% of total
Agriculture	23.0
Industry, of which:	38.5
manufacturing	20.6
Services	38.5

Components of GDP

	% of total
Private consumption	64.9
Public consumption	6.2
Investment	32.1
Exports	55.5
Imports	-59.5

Structure of employment

	% of total		% of labour force
Agriculture	69	Unemployed 2002	...
Industry	14	Av. ann. rate 1995–2002	...
Services	17		

Energy

	m TOE		
Total output	50.3	Net energy imports as %	
Total consumption	39.4	of energy use	-28
Consumption per head,			
kg oil equivalent	495		

Inflation and finance

Consumer price			av. ann. increase 1997–2002
inflation 2003	3.1%	Narrow money (M1)	25.7
Av. ann. inflation 1998–2003	1.8%	Broad money	32.0
Treasury bill rate, mid-2003	6.25%		

Exchange rates

	end 2003		December 2003
D per $	15,646	Effective rates	1995 = 100
D per SDR	23,249	– nominal	...
D per €	19,713	– real	...

Trade

Principal exports		Principal imports	
	$bn fob		*$bn cif*
Crude oil	3.2	Machinery & spare parts	3.7
Textiles & garments	2.7	Petroleum products	2.0
Fisheries products	2.0	Textiles	1.8
Footwear	1.8	Steel	1.3
Rice	0.7	Cloth	1.0
Total incl. others	**16.5**	Electronic goods	0.6
		Total incl. others	**19.0**

Main export destinations		Main origins of imports	
	% of total		*% of total*
United States	15.0	South Korea	13.0
Japan	14.9	China	12.3
Australia	7.6	Japan	12.3
China	6.6	Singapore	11.9
Germany	6.5	Thailand	5.4
Singapore	5.5	Hong Kong	4.1
United Kingdom	4.3	Malaysia	3.7

Balance of payments, reserves and debt, $bn

Visible exports fob	16.7	Overall balance	0.4
Visible imports fob	-17.8	Change in reserves	0.5
Trade balance	-1.1	Level of reserves	
Invisibles inflows	3.1	end Dec.	4.2
Invisibles outflows	-4.6	No. months of import cover	2.3
Net transfers	1.9	Foreign debt	13.3
Current account balance	-0.6	– as % of GDP	41
– as % of GDP	-1.7	– as % of total exports	72
Capital balance	2.1	Debt service ratio	6

Health and education

Health spending, % of GDP	5.1	Education spending, % of GDP	...
Doctors per 1,000 pop.	0.5	Enrolment, %: primary	106
Hospital beds per 1,000 pop.	...	secondary	67
Improved-water source access,		tertiary	10
% of pop.	77		

Society

No. of households	16.1m	Colour TVs per 100 households	38.6
Av. no. per household	5.1	Telephone lines per 100 pop.	4.8
Marriages per 1,000 pop.	...	Mobile telephone subscribers	
Divorces per 1,000 pop.	...	per 100 pop.	2.3
Cost of living, Dec. 2003		Computers per 100 pop.	1.0
New York = 100	63	Internet hosts per 1,000 pop.	...

a 2000 estimate.

ZIMBABWE

Area	390,759 sq km	Capital	Harare
Arable as % of total land	8	Currency	Zimbabwe dollar (Z$)

People

Population	13.1m	Life expectancy: men	33.7 yrs
Pop. per sq km	33.6	women	32.6 yrs
Av. ann. growth		Adult literacy	90%
in pop. 2000–05	0.49%	Fertility rate (per woman)	3.9
Pop. under 15	43.9%	Urban population	36.0%
Pop. over 60	4.9%		per 1,000 pop.
No. of men per 100 women	99	Crude birth rate	32.1
Human Development Index	49.6	Crude death rate	27.0

The economy

GDP	Z$977bn	GDP per head	$630
GDP	$8.3bn	GDP per head in purchasing	
Av. ann. growth in real		power parity (USA=100)	6.0
GDP 1992–2002	0.5%	Economic freedom index	4.54

Origins of GDP

Components of GDP[a]

	% of total		% of total
Agriculture	17.4	Private consumption	71.7
Industry, of which:	23.8	Public consumption	15.4
manufacturing	13.0	Investment	13.5
Services	58.8	Net exports	-0.6

Structure of employment

	% of total		% of labour force
Agriculture	...	Unemployed 1999	6
Industry	...	Av. ann. rate 1995–99	6.5
Services	...		

Energy

	m TOE		
Total output	8.5	Net energy imports as %	
Total consumption	9.9	of energy use	14
Consumption per head,			
kg oil equivalent	769		

Inflation and finance

Consumer price			av. ann. increase 1997–2002
inflation 2002	140.1%	Narrow money (M1)	75.7%
Av. ann. inflation 1998–2002	79.9%	Broad money	76.3%
Money market rate, 2003	110.1%		

Exchange rates

	end 2003		December 2003
Z$ per $	826	Effective rates	1995 = 100
Z$ per SDR	1,227	– nominal	...
Z$ per €	1,041	– real	...

Trade

Principal exports[a]		Principal imports[a]	
	$m fob		$m cif
Tobacco	609	Machinery & transport	
Food	265	equipment	544
Textiles & cotton	245	Manufactured products	312
Iron & steel	175	Chemicals	310
Nickel	108	Petroleum products &	
		electricity	207
Total incl. others	**1,925**	Total incl. others	**1,869**

Main export destinations		Main origins of imports	
	% of total		% of total
China	5.8	South Africa	47.7
Germany	5.6	Dem Rep of Congo	5.7
South Africa	5.6	Mozambique	5.3
United Kingdom	4.8	United Kingdom	3.1
Japan	4.6	United States	3.0

Balance of payments[b], reserves and debt, $bn

Visible exports fob	1.6	Overall balance	-0.4
Visible imports fob	-1.8	Change in reserves	0.0
Trade balance	-0.2	Level of reserves	
Net invisibles outflows	-0.4	end Dec.	0.1
Net transfers	0.3	No. months of import cover	0.6
Current account balance	-0.3	Foreign debt	4.1
– as % of GDP	-3.8	– as % of GDP	35
Capital balance	-0.4	– as % of total exports	197
		Debt service ratio	3

Health and education

Health spending, % of GDP	6.2	Education spending, % of GDP	10.4
Doctors per 1,000 pop.	0.1	Enrolment, %: primary	95
Hospital beds per 1,000 pop.	...	secondary	44
Improved-water source access,		tertiary	4
% of pop.	83		

Society

No. of households	3.3m	Colour TVs per 100 households	2.1
Av. no. per household	3.8	Telephone lines per 100 pop.	2.5
Marriages per 1,000 pop.	...	Mobile telephone subscribers	
Divorces per 1,000 pop.	...	per 100 pop.	3.0
Cost of living, Dec. 2003		Computers per 100 pop.	5.2
New York = 100	...	Internet hosts per 1,000 pop.	0.3

a 2000
b 2001 estimates.

EURO AREA[a]

Area	2,497,000 sq km	Capital	–
Arable as % of total land	25.7	Currency	Euro (€)

People

Population	303.5m	Life expectancy: men	75.3 yrs
Pop. per sq km	128.3	women	81.8 yrs
Av. ann. growth		Adult literacy	98.3%
in pop. 2000–05	0.4%	Fertility rate (per woman)	1.5
Pop. under 15	16.2%	Urban population	77.4%
Pop. over 60	21.9%		per 1,000 pop.
No. of men per 100 women	95.9	Crude birth rate	9.9
Human Development Index	92.1	Crude death rate[b]	10.0

The economy

GDP	€7,064bn	GDP per head	$22,870
GDP	$6,648bn	GDP per head in purchasing	
Av. ann. growth in real		power parity (USA=100)	71.2
GDP 1992–2002	1.9%	Economic freedom index	2.27

Origins of GDP		Components of GDP	
	% of total		% of total
Agriculture	2	Private consumption	57.1
Industry, of which:	28	Public consumption	20.3
manufacturing	21	Investment	20.2
Services	70	Exports	36.4
		Imports	-33.9

Structure of employment

	% of total		% of labour force
Agriculture	4.5	Unemployed 2002	8.5
Industry	29.6	Av. ann. rate 1995–2002	9.4
Services	65.9		

Energy

	m TOE		
Total output	466.1	Net energy imports as %	
Total consumption	1,189.0	of energy use	56
Consumption per head,			
kg oil equivalent	3,904		

Inflation and finance

Consumer price		av. ann. increase 1997–2002	
inflation 2003	2.1%	Narrow money (M1)	9.0%
Av. ann. inflation 1998–2003	2.0%	Broad money	6.4%
Interbank rate, 2002	2.34%	Household saving rate, 2002	11.6%

Exchange rates

	end 2003		December 2003
€ per $	0.79	Effective rates	1995 = 100
€ per SDR	1.18	– nominal	93.5
		– real	84.8

Trade[b]

Principal exports[b]

	$bn fob
Machinery & transport equip.	424
Manufactures	252
Chemicals	144
Food, drink & tobacco	49
Energy	25
Raw materials	19
Total incl. others	**935**

Principal imports[b]

	$bn cif
Machinery & transport equip.	335
Manufactures	261
Energy	129
Chemicals	76
Food, drink & tobacco	55
Raw materials	43
Total incl. others	**929**

Main export destinations[c]

	% of total
United States	24.0
Switzerland	7.1
Japan	4.2
Poland	3.7
China	3.4
Russia	3.0

Main origins of imports[c]

	% of total
United States	17.6
China	7.5
Japan	7.0
Switzerland	5.9
Russia	4.6
Norway	4.2

Balance of payments, reserves and aid, $bn

Visible exports fob	1,000.9	Capital balance	-84.4
Visible imports fob	-876.9	Overall balance	2.6
Trade balance	124.0	Change in reserves	37.7
Invisibles inflows	551.6	Level of reserves	
Invisibles outflows	-566.7	end Dec.	383.3
Net transfers	-44.6	No. months of import cover	3.2
Current account balance	64.4	Aid given	19.85
– as % of GDP	1.0	– as % of GDP	0.30

Health and education

Health spending, % of GDP	9.3	Education spending, % of GDP	4.81
Doctors per 1,000 pop.	3.5	Enrolment, %: primary	104
Hospital beds per 1,000 pop.	8.0	secondary	106
Improved-water source access,		tertiary	54
% of pop.	...		

Society

No. of households	122.4m	Colour TVs per 100 households	96.6
Av. no. per household	2.48	Telephone lines per 100 pop.	55.4
Marriages per 1,000 pop.	4.8	Mobile telephone subscribers	
Divorces per 1,000 pop.	1.6	per 100 pop.	78.2
Cost of living, Dec. 2003		Computers per 100 pop.	31.9
New York = 100	...	Internet hosts per 1,000 pop.	56.4

---

a Data refer to the 12 EU members that have adopted the euro.
b EU15 data.
c Extra-EU15 data.

WORLD

Area	148,698,382 sq km	Capital	...
Arable as % of total land	10.8	Currency	...

People

Population	6,211.1m	Life expectancy: men		63.3 yrs
Pop. per sq km	41.8	women		67.6 yrs
Av. ann. growth		Adult literacy		79.0%
in pop. 2000–05	1.22%	Fertility rate (per woman)		2.69
Pop. under 15	30.1%	Urban population		48.0%
Pop. over 60	10.0%		per 1,000 pop.	
No. of men per 100 women	101	Crude birth rate		21.3
Human Development Index	72.2	Crude death rate		9.1

The economy

GDP	$32.3trn	GDP per head	$5,200
Av. ann. growth in real		GDP per head in purchasing	
GDP 1992–2002	2.8%	power parity (USA=100)	21.5
		Economic freedom index	3.20

Origins of GDP

	% of total
Agriculture	4
Industry, of which:	29
manufacturing	19
Services	68

Components of GDP

	% of total
Private consumption	63
Public consumption	17
Investment	20
Exports	24
Imports	-23

Structure of employment[a]

	% of total		% of labour force
Agriculture	4		
Industry	26	Unemployed 2002	7.0
Services	70	Av. ann. rate 1995–2002	6.9

Energy

	m TOE		
Total output	10,140.7	Net energy imports as %	
Total consumption	10,009.6	of energy use	0
Consumption per head,			
kg oil equivalent	1,686		

Inflation and finance[a]

Consumer price		av. ann. increase 1997–2002	
inflation 2003	3.6%	Narrow money (M0)	9.9%
Av. ann. inflation 1998–2003	4.1%	Broad money	9.9%
LIBOR rate, 3-month, 2003	1.22%	Household saving rate, 2002	6.4%

Trade
World exports

	$bn fob		$bn fob
Manufactures	5,035	Agricultural raw materials	129
Food	452	Ores & metals	129
Fuels	452	Total incl. others	**6,455**

Main export destinations

	% of total
United States	17.6
Germany	7.6
United Kingdom	5.4
France	5.0
Japan	4.8

Main origins of imports

	% of total
United States	11.3
Germany	9.1
China	7.3
Japan	6.9
France	4.6

Balance of payments, reserves and aid, $bn

Visible exports fob	6,369	Capital balance	101
Visible imports fob	-6,325	Overall balance	0
Trade balance	44	Change in reserves	430
Invisibles inflows	2,886	Level of reserves	
Invisibles outflows	-2,986	end Dec.	2,833
Net transfers	-20	No. months of import cover	4
Current account balance	-76	Aid given[b]	59.3
– as % of GDP	-0.2	– as % of GDP[b]	0.18

Health and education

Health spending, % of GDP	9.8	Education spending, % of GDP	4.5
Doctors per 1,000 pop.	…	Enrolment, %: primary	103
Hospital beds per 1,000 pop.	…	secondary	70
Improved-water source access,		tertiary	24
% of pop.	81		

Society

No. of households	…	TVs per 100 households	…
Av. no. per household	…	Telephone lines per 100 pop.	12.9
Marriages per 1,000 pop.	…	Mobile telephone subscribers	
Divorces per 1,000 pop.	…	per 100 pop.	19.1
Cost of living, Dec. 2003		Computers per 100 pop.	9.9
New York = 100	…	Internet hosts per 1,000 pop.	37.5

a OECD countries.
b OECD and Middle East countries.

Glossary

Balance of payments The record of a country's transactions with the rest of the world. The **current account** of the balance of payments consists of: visible trade (goods); "invisible" trade (services and income); private transfer payments (eg, remittances from those working abroad); official transfers (eg, payments to international organisations, famine relief). Visible imports and exports are normally compiled on rather different definitions to those used in the trade statistics (shown in principal imports and exports) and therefore the statistics do not match. The **capital account** consists of long- and short-term transactions relating to a country's assets and liabilities (eg, loans and borrowings). The current account and the capital account, plus an errors and omissions item, make up the **overall balance**. In the country pages of this book this item is included in the overall balance. **Changes in reserves** include gold at market prices and are shown without the practice often followed in balance of payments presentations of reversing the sign.

Body-mass index A measure for assessing obesity – weight in kilograms divided by height in metres squared. An index of 30 or more is regarded as an indicator of obesity; 25 to 29.9 as over-weight. Guidelines vary for men and for women and may be adjusted for age.

CFA Communauté Financière Africaine. Its members, most of the francophone African nations, share a common currency, the CFA franc, which used to be pegged to the French franc but is now pegged to the euro.

Cif/fob Measures of the value of merchandise trade. Imports include the cost of "carriage, insurance and freight" (cif) from the exporting country to the importing. The value of exports does not include these elements and is recorded "free on board" (fob). Balance of payments statistics are generally adjusted so that both exports and imports are shown fob; the cif elements are included in invisibles.

Commonwealth of Independent States All former Soviet Union Republics, excluding Estonia, Latvia and Lithuania. It was established January 1 1992; Azerbaijan joined in September 1993 and Georgia in December 1993.

Crude birth rate The number of live births in a year per 1,000 population. The crude rate will automatically be relatively high if a large proportion of the population is of childbearing age.

Crude death rate The number of deaths in a year per 1,000 population. Also affected by the population's age structure.

Debt, foreign Financial obligations owed by a country to the rest of the world and repayable in foreign currency. **The debt service ratio** is debt service (principal repayments plus interest payments) expressed as a percentage of the country's earnings from exports of goods and services.

EU European Union. Members are: Austria, Belgium, Denmark, Finland, France, Germany, Greece, Ireland, Italy, Luxembourg, Netherlands, Portugal, Spain, Sweden and the United Kingdom and, as of May 1 2004, Cyprus, Czech Republic, Estonia, Hungary, Latvia, Lithuania, Malta, Poland, Slovakia and Slovenia.

Effective exchange rate The nominal index measures a currency's depreciation (figures below 100) or appreciation (figures over 100) from a base date against a trade-weighted basket of the currencies of the country's main trading partners. The real effective exchange rate reflects adjustments for relative movements in prices or costs.

Euro area The 12 euro area members of the EU are Austria, Belgium, Finland, France, Germany, Greece, Ireland, Italy,

Luxembourg, Netherlands, Portugal and Sweden. Their common currency is the euro, which came into circulation on January 1 2002.

Fertility rate The average number of children born to a woman who completes her childbearing years.

GDP Gross domestic product. The sum of all output produced by economic activity within a country. GNP (gross national product) and GNI (gross national income) include net income from abroad eg, rent, profits.

Household saving rate Household savings as % of disposable household income.

Import cover The number of months of imports covered by reserves, ie reserves ÷ $\frac{1}{12}$ annual imports (visibles and invisibles).

Inflation The annual rate at which prices are increasing. The most common measure and the one shown here is the increase in the consumer price index.

Internet hosts Websites and other computers that sit permanently on the internet.

Life expectancy The average length of time a baby born today can expect to live.

Literacy is defined by UNESCO as the ability to read and write a simple sentence, but definitions can vary from country to country.

Median age Divides the age distribution into two halves. Half of the population is above and half below the median age.

Money supply A measure of the "money" available to buy goods and services. Various definitions exist. The measures shown here are based on definitions used by the IMF and may differ from measures used nationally. Narrow money (M1)

consists of cash in circulation and demand deposits (bank deposits that can be withdrawn on demand). "Quasi-money" (time, savings and foreign currency deposits) is added to this to create broad money.

OECD Organisation for Economic Co-operation and Development. The "rich countries" club was established in 1961 to promote economic growth and the expansion of world trade. It is based in Paris and now has 30 members.

Opec Organisation of Petroleum Exporting Countries. Set up in 1960 and based in Vienna, Opec is mainly concerned with oil pricing and production issues. Members are; Algeria, Indonesia, Iran, Iraq, Kuwait, Libya, Nigeria, Qatar, Saudi Arabia, United Arab Emirates and Venezuela.

PPP Purchasing power parity. PPP statistics adjust for cost of living differences by replacing normal exchange rates with rates designed to equalise the prices of a standard "basket"of goods and services. These are used to obtain PPP estimates of GDP per head. PPP estimates are shown on an index, taking the United States as 100.

Real terms Figures adjusted to exclude the effect of inflation.

Reserves The stock of gold and foreign currency held by a country to finance any calls that may be made for the settlement of foreign debt.

SDR Special drawing right. The reserve currency, introduced by the IMF in 1970, was intended to replace gold and national currencies in settling international transactions. The IMF uses SDRs for book-keeping purposes and issues them to member countries. Their value is based on a basket of the US dollar (with a weight of 45%), the euro (29%), the Japanese yen (15%) and the pound sterling (11%).

List of countries

Whenever data is available, the world rankings consider 177 countries: all those which had (in 2002) or have recently had a population of at least 1m or a GDP of at least $1bn. Here is a list of them.

	Population	GDP	GDP per head	Area	Median age
	m	$bn	$PPP	'000 sq km	years
Afghanistan	23.3	19.0[ac]	820[ac]	652	18.1
Albania	3.2	4.8	4,960	29	26.7
Algeria	31.4	55.9	5,530	2,382	21.7
Andorra	0.1	1.3[ac]	19,000[ac]	0.4	37.0
Angola	13.9	11.2	1,840	1,247	16.3
Argentina	37.9	102.0	10,190	2,767	27.9
Armenia	3.8	2.4	3,230	30	30.7
Aruba	0.1	1.9	28,000[ac]	0.2	34.0
Australia	19.5	409.4	27,440	7,682	35.2
Austria	8.1	204.1	28,910	84	38.3
Azerbaijan	8.1	6.1	3,010	87	25.6
Bahamas	0.3	4.8[c]	16,080[c]	14	26.1
Bahrain	0.7	7.7	16,190	1	26.9
Bangladesh	143.4	47.6	1,770	144	20.0
Barbados	0.3	2.5	14,660	0.4	32.6
Belarus	10.1	14.3	5,500	208	36.5
Belgium	10.3	245.4	28,130	31	39.1
Benin	6.6	2.7	1,060	113	16.6
Bermuda	0.1	2.3[a]	35,200[a]	1	36.0
Bhutan	2.2	0.6	1,300[a]	47	18.3
Bolivia	8.7	7.8	2,390	1,099	20.1
Bosnia	4.1	5.6	1,900[a]	51	35.1
Botswana	1.6	5.3	7,740	581	19.1
Brazil	174.7	452.4	7,450	8,512	25.4
Brunei	0.3	6.5[a]	18,600[a]	6	25.0
Bulgaria	7.8	15.5	7,030	111	39.1
Burkina Faso	12.2	3.1	1,090	274	15.5
Burundi	6.7	0.7	630	28	15.8
Cambodia	13.8	4.0	1,970	181	17.5
Cameroon	15.5	9.1	1,910	475	18.1
Canada	31.3	714.3	28,930	9,971	36.9
Cayman Islands	0.0[d]	1.3[a]	35,000[a]	0.3	34.0
Central African Rep	3.8	1.0	1,170	622	18.3
Chad	8.4	2.0	1,010	1,284	16.7
Channel Islands	0.1	3.5[c]	23,300[ac]	0.2	38.6
Chile	15.6	64.2	9,420	757	28.3
China	1,294.4	1,266.1	4,520	9,561	30.0
Colombia	43.5	80.9	6,150	1,142	24.0
Congo-Kinshasa	54.3	5.7	630	2,345	16.5
Congo-Brazzaville	3.2	3.0	710	342	16.7

	Population	GDP	GDP per head	Area	Median age
	m	$bn	$PPP	'000 sq km	years
Costa Rica	4.2	16.8	8,560	51	24.5
Côte d'Ivoire	16.7	11.7	1,450	322	18.1
Croatia	4.7	22.4	10,000	57	38.9
Cuba	11.3	30.7[a]	2,700[a]	111	33.0
Cyprus	0.8	10.1	18,560	9	33.4
Czech Republic	10.3	69.5	14,920	79	37.6
Denmark	5.3	172.9	30,600	43	38.7
Dominican Republic	8.6	21.7	6,270	48	23.1
Ecuador	13.1	24.3	3,340	272	22.7
Egypt	70.3	89.9	3,810	1,000	21.3
El Salvador	6.5	14.3	4,790	21	21.8
Equatorial Guinea	0.5	2.1	9,110	28	18.2
Eritrea	4.0	0.6	1,040	117	16.9
Estonia	1.4	6.5	11,630	45	37.9
Ethiopia	66.0	6.1	780	1,134	16.9
Faroe Islands	0.0[d]	1.0[c]	22,000[ac]	1	34.0
Fiji	0.8	1.9	5,330	18	23.1
Finland	5.2	131.5	26,160	338	39.4
France	59.7	1,431.3[a]	27,040	544	37.6
French Polynesia	0.2	3.4[c]	28,020[c]	3	25.1
Gabon	1.3	5.0	5,530	268	18.9
Gambia, The	1.4	0.4	1,660	11	19.4
Georgia	5.2	3.4	2,270	70	34.8
Germany	82.0	1,984.1	26,980	358	39.9
Ghana	20.2	6.2	2,080	239	18.8
Greece	10.6	132.8	18,770	132	39.1
Greenland	0.1	1.1[ac]	20,000[ac]	2,176	31.0
Guadeloupe	0.4	5.3[c]	12,000[c]	2	31.8
Guam	0.2	3.2[ac]	21,000[ac]	1	27.4
Guatemala	12.0	23.3	4,030	109	17.8
Guinea	8.4	3.2	2,060	246	17.6
Guinea-Bissau	1.3	0.2	680	36	16.6
Haiti	8.4	3.4	1,610	28	18.9
Honduras	6.7	6.6	2,540	112	18.7
Hong Kong	7.0	161.5	27,490	1	36.1
Hungary	9.9	65.8	13,070	93	38.1
Iceland	0.3	8.4	29,240	103	32.9
India	1,041.1	510.2	2,650	3,287	23.4
Indonesia	217.5	172.9	3,070	1,904	24.6
Iran	72.4	108.2	6,690	1,648	20.6
Iraq	24.2	26.8[a]	2,400[a]	438	18.7

	Population	GDP	GDP per head	Area	Median age
	m	$bn	$PPP	'000 sq km	years
Ireland	3.9	121.4	29,570	70	31.9
Israel	6.3	103.7	19,000	21	27.9
Italy	57.4	1,184.3	26,170	301	40.2
Jamaica	2.6	7.9	3,680	11	24.1
Japan	127.5	3,993.4	27,380	378	41.3
Jordan	5.2	9.3	4,180	89	20.1
Kazakhstan	16.0	24.6	5,630	2,717	27.9
Kenya	31.9	12.3	1,010	583	17.7
Kirgizstan	5.0	1.6	1,560	583	23.2
Kuwait	2.0	35.4	17,780	18	28.6
Laos	5.5	1.7	1,660	237	18.5
Latvia	2.4	8.4	9,190	64	37.8
Lebanon	3.6	17.3	4,600	10	25.2
Lesotho	2.1	0.7	2,970	30	18.8
Liberia	3.3	0.6	1,000[a]	111	16.6
Libya	5.5	19.1	6,200[a]	1,760	21.8
Lithuania	3.7	13.8	10,190	65	36.0
Luxembourg	0.4	21.0	53,290	3	37.0
Macau	0.4	6.8	21,910	0.02	33.5
Macedonia	2.1	3.8	6,420	26	32.3
Madagascar	16.9	4.4	730	587	17.5
Malawi	11.8	1.9	570	118	17.1
Malaysia	23.0	94.9	8,500	333	23.6
Mali	12.0	3.4	860	1,240	15.4
Malta	0.4	3.9	17,710	0.3	36.5
Martinique	0.4	5.5[c]	14,030[c]	1	33.8
Mauritania	2.8	1.0	1,790	1,031	18.2
Mauritius	1.2	4.5	10,820	2	28.9
Mexico	101.8	637.2	8,800	1,973	22.9
Moldova	4.3	1.6	1,600	34	31.7
Mongolia	2.6	1.1	1,710	1,565	21.8
Morocco	31.0	36.1	3,730	447	23.0
Mozambique	19.0	3.6	990	799	17.8
Myanmar	49.0	5.7[c]	1,700[a]	677	23.4
Namibia	1.8	2.9	6,880	824	18.4
Nepal	24.2	5.5	1,370	147	19.5
Netherlands	16.0	417.9	28,350	42	37.6
Netherlands Antilles	0.2	2.4[a]	11,400[a]	1	32.0
New Caledonia	0.2	2.7[c]	14,000[a]	19	26.9
New Zealand	3.8	58.6	20,550	271	34.5
Nicaragua	5.3	4.0	2,350	130	18.1
Niger	11.6	2.2	800	1,267	15.1

	Population	GDP	GDP per head	Area	Median age
	m	$bn	$PPP	'000 sq km	years
Nigeria	120.0	43.5	800	924	17.3
North Korea	22.6	22.3[a]	1,000[a]	121	29.4
Norway	4.5	190.5	36,690	324	37.2
Oman	2.7	20.3	13,000	310	21.2
Pakistan	148.7	59.1	1,960	804	18.8
Panama	2.9	12.3	6,060	77	24.8
Papua New Guinea	5.0	2.8	2,180	463	19.1
Paraguay	5.8	5.5	4,590	407	19.7
Peru	26.5	56.5	4,880	1,285	22.7
Philippines	78.6	78.0	4,450	300	20.9
Poland	38.5	189.0	10,450	313	35.2
Portugal	10.0	121.6	17,820	89	37.0
Puerto Rico	4.0	67.9	16,250[c]	9	31.8
Qatar	0.1	17.5	20,100[a]	11	31.0
Réunion	0.7	7.8[c]	10,500[c]	3	28.3
Romania	22.3	45.7	6,490	238	34.7
Russia	143.8	346.5	8,080	17,075	36.8
Rwanda	8.1	1.7	1,260	26	17.0
Saudi Arabia	21.7	188.5	12,660	2,200	20.6
Senegal	9.9	5.0	1,540	197	17.6
Serbia & Montenegro	10.5	15.7	2,200[a]	102	35.4
Sierra Leone	4.8	0.8	500	72	17.9
Singapore	4.2	87.0	23,730	1	34.5
Slovakia	5.4	23.7	12,590	49	34.0
Slovenia	2.0	22.0	18,480	20	38.1
Somalia	9.6	4.3[ac]	600[a]	638	16.0
South Africa	44.2	104.2	9,810	1,226	22.6
South Korea	47.4	476.7	16,960	99	31.8
Spain	39.9	653.1	21,210	505	37.4
Sri Lanka	19.3	16.6	3,510	66	28.1
Sudan	32.6	13.5	1,740	2,506	19.7
Suriname	0.4	1.0	3,400[a]	164	23.5
Swaziland	0.9	1.2	4,730	17	17.4
Sweden	8.8	240.3	25,820	450	39.6
Switzerland	7.2	267.4	31,840	41	40.2
Syria	17.0	20.8	3,470	185	19.0
Taiwan	22.5	281.6	18,000[a]	36	31.0
Tajikistan	6.2	1.2	930	143	19.9
Tanzania	36.8	9.4	580	945	16.8
Thailand	64.3	126.9	6,890	513	27.5
Togo	4.8	1.4	1,450	57	17.7

	Population	GDP	GDP per head	Area	Median age
	m	*$bn*	*$PPP*	*'000 sq km*	*years*
Trinidad & Tobago	1.3	9.6	9,000	5	27.6
Tunisia	9.7	21.0	6,440	164	24.4
Turkey	68.6	183.7	6,300	779	24.2
Turkmenistan	4.2	7.7	4,780	488	21.6
Uganda	24.8	5.8	1,360	241	15.1
Ukraine	48.7	41.5	4,800	604	37.3
United Arab Emirates	2.7	71.0	24,030	84	29.6
United Kingdom	59.7	1,566.3	26,580	243	37.7
United States	288.5	10,383.1	36,110	9,373	35.2
Uruguay	3.4	12.1	7,710	176	31.4
Uzbekistan	25.6	7.9	1,640	447	21.5
Venezuela	25.1	94.3	5,220	912	23.1
Vietnam	80.2	35.1	2,300	331	23.1
Virgin Islands	0.1	2.4[ac]	19,000[ac]	0.4	31.4
West Bank and Gaza	3.4	3.4	800[a]	6	16.8
Yemen	19.9	10.0	800	528	15.4
Zambia	10.9	3.7	800	753	16.7
Zimbabwe	13.1	8.3	2,180	391	17.5
Euro area (12)	303.5	6,648.5	25,700	2,497	38.7
World	6,211.1	32,300.0	7,770	148,698	26.4

a Estimate.   b Including French Guiana, Guadeloupe, Martinique and Réunion.
c Latest available year.
d Populations less than 50,000.

Sources

Airports Council International, *Worldwide Airport Traffic Report*

BP, *Statistical Review of World Energy*

British Mountaineering Council

CB Richard Ellis, *Global Market Rents*

Central Intelligence Agency, *The World Factbook*

Centre for International Earth Science Information Network, Columbia University

Commission for Distilled Spirits, *World Drink Trends*

Confederation of Swedish Enterprise

Corporate Resources Group, *Quality of Living Report*

Council of Europe

Economist Intelligence Unit, *Cost of Living Survey*; *Country Forecasts*; *Country Reports*; *Global Outlook – Business Environment Rankings*

ERC Statistics International, *World Cigarette Report*

Euromonitor, *International Marketing Data and Statistics*; *European Marketing Data and Statistics*

Europa Publications, *The Europa World Yearbook*

Eurostat, *Statistics in Focus*

FAO, *FAOSTAT database*; *State of the World's Forests*

Financial Times Business Information, *The Banker*

The Heritage Foundation, *The 2001 Index of Economic Freedom*

IMD, *World Competitiveness Yearbook*

IMF, *Direction of Trade*; *International Financial Statistics*; *World Economic Outlook*

International Cocoa Organisation, *Quarterly Bulletin of Cocoa Statistics*

International Coffee Organisation

International Cotton Advisory Committee, *Bulletin*

International Criminal Police Organisation (Interpol), *International Crime Statistics*

International Road Federation, *World Road Statistics*

International Rubber Study Group, *Rubber Statistical Bulletin*

International Federation of the Phonographic Industry

International Grains Council, *The Grain Market Report*

International Sugar Organisation, *Sugar Yearbook*

International Tea Committee, *Annual Bulletin of Statistics*

International Telecommunication Union, *ITU Indicators*

International Wool Textile Organisation

ISTA Mielke, *Oil World*

Johnson Matthey

Lloyd's Register, *World Fleet Statistics*

Mercer Human Resource
  Consulting

National statistics offices
Network Wizards
Nobel Foundation

OECD, *Development Assistance
  Committee Report;
  Environmental Data; Main
  Economic Indicators*

Space.com
Standard & Poor's *Emerging
  Stock Markets Factbook*
Swiss Re, *sigma*

Taiwan Statistical Data Book
The Times, *Atlas of the World*
Time Inc Magazines, *Fortune
  International*
Transparency International

UN, *Demographic Yearbook;
  Global Refugee Trends; State
  of World Population Report;
  Statistical Chart on World
  Families; World Contraceptive
  Use; World Population; World
  Population Prospects; World
  Urbanisation Prospects*
UN Development Programme,
  Human Development Report
UNESCO, website: unescostat.
  unesco.org
Union Internationale des
  Chemins de Fer, *Statistiques
  Internationales des Chemins
  de Fer*

US Census Bureau
US Department of Agriculture,
  Rice Report
University of Michigan,
  Windows to the Universe
  website

WHO, *Health Behaviour in
  School-aged Children;
  Mortality Database; Weekly
  Epidemiological Record;
  World Health Statistics
  Annual; World Report on
  Violence and Health*
World Bank, *Global
  Development Finance; World
  Development Indicators;
  World Development Report*
World Bureau of Metal
  Statistics, *World Metal
  Statistics*
World Economic
  Forum/Harvard University,
  *Global Competitiveness
  Yearbook*
World Resources Institute,
  World Resources
World Tourist Organisation,
  Yearbook of Tourism Statistics
World Trade Organisation,
  Annual Report
World Water Council
World Wide Fund for Nature